William Allison

Breeding racehorses by the figure system

William Allison

Breeding racehorses by the figure system

ISBN/EAN: 9783337145590

Printed in Europe, USA, Canada, Australia, Japan

Cover: Foto ©Andreas Hilbeck / pixelio.de

More available books at **www.hansebooks.com**

BREEDING RACEHORSES

BY THE

FIGURE SYSTEM.

COMPILED BY

The Late C. BRUCE LOWE.

EDITED BY

WILLIAM ALLISON

(The Special Commissioner, London "Sportsman," Hon. Sec. Sporting League, and Manager of the International Horse Agency and Exchange).

WITH NUMEROUS ILLUSTRATIONS OF CELEBRATED HORSES.
(From Photographs by Clarence Hailey, Newmarket.)

NEW YORK:

WILLIAM R. JENKINS,

Veterinary Publisher,

851 & 853 SIXTH AVENUE (Cor. 48th St.).

1898.

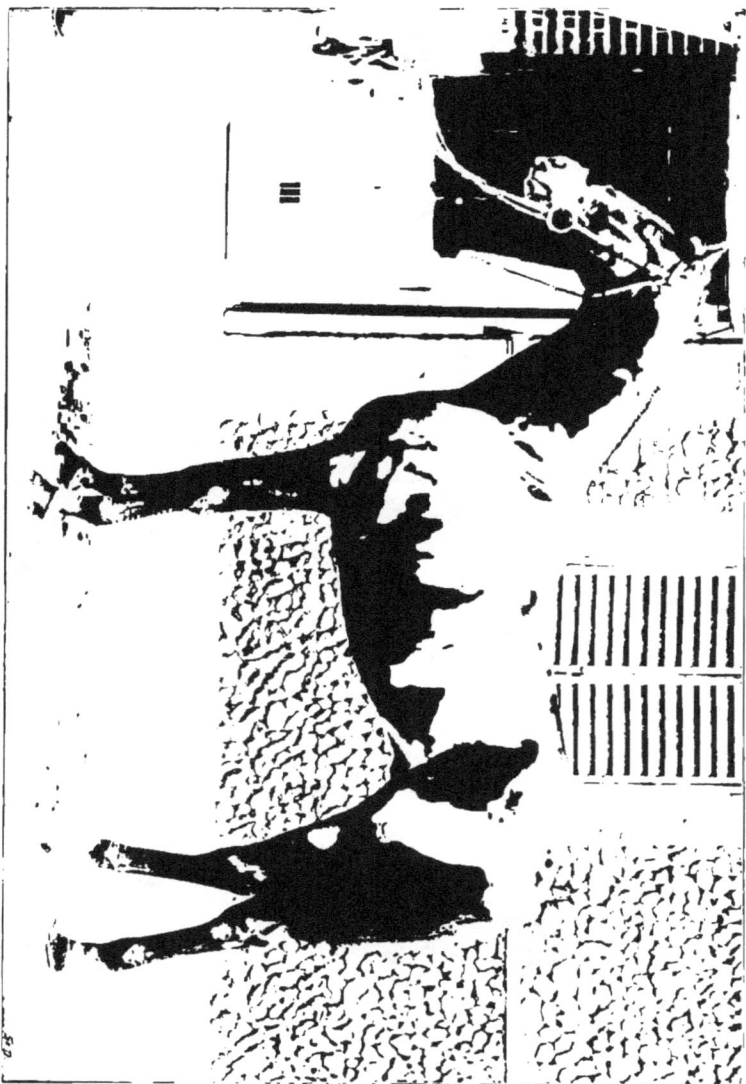

No. 3. RUNNING AND SIRE FAMILY.

ISINGLASS

By Isonomy (49) out of Deadlock (3).   (Winner of the 2000 Guineas, Derby, and St. Leger.)

MORION

No. 3. RUNNING FAMILY

ST. SERF

By St. Simon (H) out of Feronia (S). (Winner of the Rous Memorial Stakes, Ascot.)

No. 8. SIRE FAMILY.

No. 11. SIRE FAMILY.

PRINCE RUDOLPH

No. 14. SIRE FAMILY

SARABAND

PREFACE.

IN presenting the late Mr. Bruce Lowe's book to the public, I am much afraid that I have by no means done him justice. The difficulty of checking an immense mass of pedigrees—English, Australian, and American—is in itself a very serious one to any but an idle man; but the further and more important trouble has been that Mr. Bruce Lowe left a very large portion of his work unrevised, and inaccuracies here and there which he no doubt would have detected, had he lived, could not be corrected without also some attempt to assume how far such correction would have altered the tenor of his argument.

The most important of these inaccuracies I have thought it best to leave standing. This occurs in the pedigree of Ormonde, for it seems better that the reader should know what was in Mr. Bruce Lowe's mind when he wrote about the breeding of that horse.

Taken as a whole, the book will be found full of interest, sound reasoning, and novel ideas; the Figure System in itself being a model of convenience and simplicity, serviceable to all breeders alike, whether they agree with the author's deductions from it or not. Personally, I think his views on the " Sire Families " and " Running Families " are sound, as also his theory of Saturation. Indeed, curiously enough, though by different (and slower) methods, I had arrived at similar conclusions to Mr. Bruce Lowe's long before I ever saw him. This is evidenced by the fact that he specially selected for his friend, Mr. White, at the Cobham sale of 1894, the yearling filly by Prince Rudolph out of The Lady by Charibert, her dam Select, by Thunderbolt out of Pandore, by Newminster out of Caller Ou. I did not at this time know Mr. Lowe, and he afterwards told me that as the filly was according to his system one of the very best bred ones possible, he and Mr. White had been thinking they had taken an unfair advantage over the seller, who probably did not know what a gem of a pedigree it was. To his surprise I was able to inform him that this was the very filly which was bred as the result of one of our "mating competitions" in the *Sportsman*, and that I myself had selected the prize cross of Prince Rudolph for the mare, The Lady, my view being exactly in accord with his own as to the suitability of the blood.

I had many conversations with him after this, and later on he wrote for me a brief but lucid explanation of his figure system, which I cannot do better than introduce here.

LONDON, W., *October* 1, 1894.

MY DEAR MR. ALLISON,

Without the preliminary matter (which my book will contain) leading up to a certain point, it is somewhat difficult to give in a few words a sketch of the system of breeding racehorses by the Figure System.

Put as briefly as possible, the figures are derived from a statistical compilation of the winners of the three great English classic races, Derby, Oaks, and Leger. The family with largest number of wins is No. 1, the next No. 2, and so on to No. 34, though the figures actually run up to 43, and include families whose descendants have never won a classic race. By placing the figures on to any ordinary tabulated pedigree, the studmaster can tell at a glance what families have been brought into the combination, and whether they happen to be the high class running families, 1, 2, **3**, 4, and 5, or outside ones, such as

10, 14, 15, 18, 33 and so on ; also how much *sire* blood (*i.e.*, members of the five great sire families, **3**, **8**, **11**, **12**, and **14** is present. It does not follow, because a stallion's pedigree is rich in the running strains, 1, 2, 4, and 5, that he is going to be a success at the stud. On the contrary, paradoxical though it seems, he is likely to prove a failure ; except when mated with mares from the sire families, **3**, **8**, **11**, **12**, and **14**. All the great sires of the world, from Eclipse to the present day, either descend *directly* from these five families or are inbred to them —and horses not in these families (or inbred strongly to them) are, so to speak, *powerless* to sire winners, unless the sire element is strong in their mates. As an ounce of illustration is better than a ton of assertion, I give you the pedigrees of those great contemporaries, Eclipse and Herod, for comparison.

ECLIPSE.

HEROD.

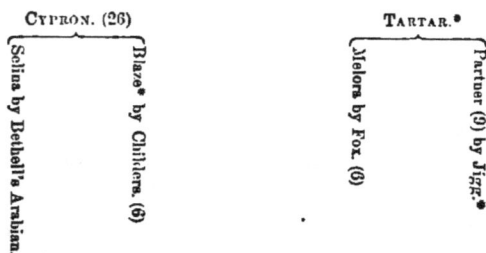

The heavy type denotes sire figures. Eclipse not only comes from the **12** family through Spiletta, but his sire Marske is from the **8** line, and his grandsire Squirt from the

---

* Family has never won a classic race.

11 line; also his maternal grandsire Regulus is from the latter line. Eclipse was so remarkably inbred to sire figures that it is no wonder he has distanced Herod and Matchem in the struggle for male supremacy. Neither of the two last named horses possessed a *single* strain of the original females forming the tap roots of the five sire families, **3, 8, 11, 12,** and **14,** and Herod's successes came mostly from the **3** line (two Oaks winners), while Bridget (Oaks) was from the **8** family. The dams of Phenomenon (Leger) and Whiskey came from the **2** family, and Woodpecker from the **1** line, and again Cœlia (Oaks) was out of Eclipse's sister. Eclipse, on the other hand, being so rich in sire blood did not require it in his mates, and all his celebrated sons and daughters were from dams with *no sire blood* in their veins. I also give the pedigrees of the best Australian bred sire, Chester, and the best English contemporary sire, Isonomy. It will be seen that they were both strongly inbred to sire figures.

CHESTER.

LADY CHESTER. (8)		YATTENDON. (17)	
Dr. of Harkaway. (2)	Stockwell. (3)	Dr. of Tros (imp.) (12)	Sir Hercules. (3)

ISONOMY.

ISOLA BELLE. (19)		STERLING. (12)	
Dr. of Ethelbert. (12)	Stockwell. (3)	Dr. of Flatcatcher. (3)	Oxford. (12)

The admitted best horse—bar, perhaps, Ormonde—that ever started in an English race was Gladiateur. In Australia it is a disputed matter whether The Barb was as good a racehorse as Carbine. They certainly were the two most phenomenal ever bred at the Antipodes. When put to stud work both Gladiateur and The Barb were pronounced failures. Compare their pedigrees with those just given, and the reasons why are obvious. Neither are in (or inbred to) sire families.

GLADIATEUR.

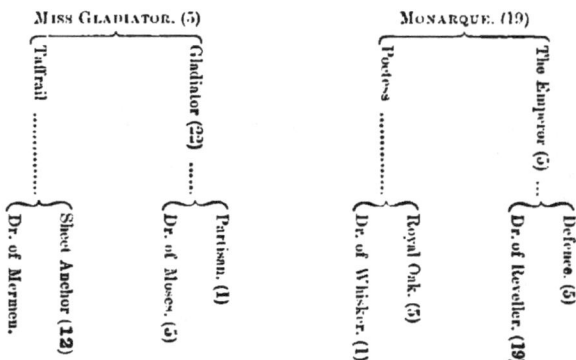

THE BARB.

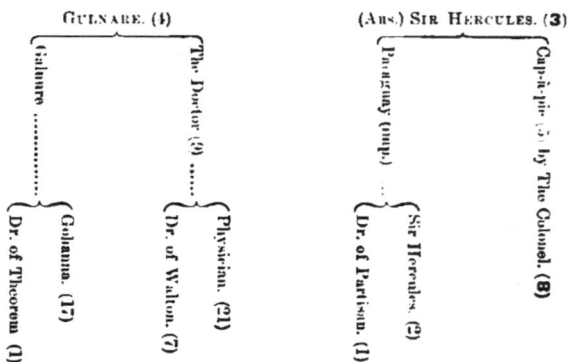

As you will, no doubt, be better able to appreciate the above figures in connection with Prince Rudolph, the handsome stallion I saw one day at Cobham, I have run him out by the figure test, and find that he is bred like some of the best sires of past and present days. The pedigree is, in respect to figures, very like that of America's greatest racehorse, Salvator, who gives early promise of becoming one of the best sires in the States.

PRINCE RUDOLPH.

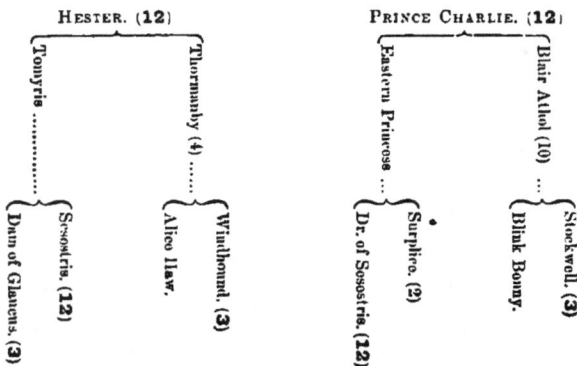

HESTER. (12)

Tomyris ....

Thormanby (4) ......

Sesostris. (12)

Dam of Glaucus. (3)

Alice Haw.

Windhound. (3)

PRINCE CHARLIE. (12)

Eastern Princess ...

Blair Athol (10) ...

Surplice. (2)

Dr. of Sesostris. (12)

Blink Bonny.

Stockwell. (3)

SALVATOR.

SELINA. (12)

PRINCE CHARLIE (above). (12)

Lightsome.

Lexington. (12)

Gloucoo. (1)

Lovily.

Alice Carneal.

Boston. (10)

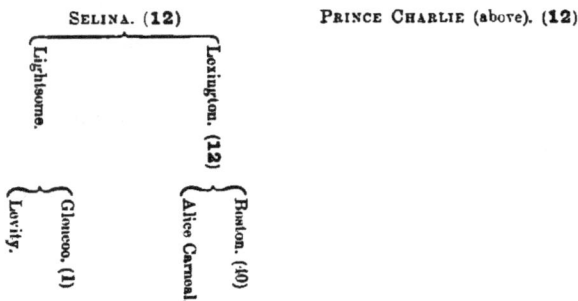

The last two examples are the results of inbreeding a male and female of same family (12), and being a sire one it intensifies this element. In this fashion Weatherbit and Sterling were bred, and as they both descend from the 12 family it points to the advantage of crossing this line upon itself. Springfield's dam is bred in the same manner. I should mate Prince Rudolph with mares from the 1, 2, 3, or 4 families (the latter for preference as it is Thormanby's family), having in their veins strong infusions of Stockwell and Blacklock.

I hope the above sketch will give you some idea of the main principles of the system, which has been very successfully worked by my friend, Mr. Frank Reynolds, in his big stud of thoroughbreds in Australia for the last twenty years. He is the only man I gave the figures to up to three years ago, when I explained the system to Mr. Henry White, of Havilah, a very successful all-round breeder, who now makes no move in either mating or buying racehorses until he has submitted their pedigrees to the Figure Key. It is needless to tell you, who have given so much time to the study of pedigrees, that there are many other important conditions to be observed in mating thoroughbreds, which space will not permit me to touch upon here, but which are dealt with in my treatise on the breeding of racehorses, now in the publisher's hands.

I may add that after twenty years' close criticism of the Figure System by Mr. Frank Reynolds and myself, we are every day more convinced of its great value as a test, or key, to pedigree.

To a student like you, the system will open up new and most interesting phases of breeding, otherwise not available. In other words, though it immensely extends the field of operations, it reduces the chances of failure to a minimum, because it is based upon the sound principles of "judgment by results." Indeed, I venture to predict that it will to a great extent revolutionise the present methods of mating thoroughbreds.

Many thanks for your statistical table of respective winnings of the three great male lines up to date. With your permission I will include it in my book.

Yours very truly,

C. BRUCE LOWE.

He was also good enough to furnish me with a synopsis of the families arranged according to their figures (which means according to the number of classic winners they have produced), and against each ancestress of a family he set two or more of her principal descendants to serve as a useful mnemonic. It will, I am sure, be especially useful to students of his book if I give them this synopsis for purposes of ready reference. Here it is exactly as he wrote it :

THE ALLOTMENT OF FIGURES.

No. 1.—Tregonwell's Natural Barb mare............ Whalebone, Minting.
No. 2.—Burton's Barb mare .... Voltigeur, Blacklock.
No. 3.—The dam of Two True Blues .... Stockwell, Sir Peter.
No. 4.—Layton Barb mare .... Matchem, Thormanby.
No. 5.—Dr. of Massy's Black Barb .... Gladiateur, Hermit.
No. 6.—Old Bald Peg .... Priam, Diomed.
No. 7.—Darcy's Black Legged Royal mare......... West Australian, Donovan.

No. **8.**—Bustler mare (dam of Byerly Turk mare). Marske, Newminster, Sultan.
No. 9.—Old Vintner mare .... Mercury, Bendigo, Peter.
No. 10.—Dr. of Gower's stallion .... Blair Athol, Hampton.
No. **11.**—Sedbury Royal mare .... Regulus, Birdcatcher, St. Simon.
No. **12.**—A Royal mare (Montagu mare).............. Eclipse, Sterling, Prince Rudolph
No. 13.—A Royal mare (dam of Turk mare) .... Highflyer, Orlando.
No. **14.**—The Oldfield mare .... Touchstone, Macaroni.
No. 15.—Royal mare (dam of Old Whynot) .... Soothsayer, Jerry, Foxhall.
No. 16.—Sister to Stripling by Hutton's Spot ...... Ormonde and Agnes family.
No. 17.—Byerly Turk mare .... Pantaloon, Yattendon.
No. 18.—Old Woodcock mare (dam of Old Spot mare) Waxy, Trenton (Aus.).
No. 19.—Dr. of Davill's Old Woodcock .... Isonomy, Sir Hugo.
No. 20.—Dr. of Gascoigne's Foreign horse .... Citadel, Traducer (N.Z.), Ghuznee.
No. 21.—Moonah Barb mare.......................... Sweetmeat, Lonely.
No. 22.—Belgrade Turk mare .... Gladiator, St. Blaise.
No. 23.—Piping Peg .... Ossian, Barcaldine.
No. 24.—Helmsley Turk mare .... Camel, The Baron, Hindoo (Am.).
No. 25.—Brimmer mare............................... Y. Melbourne, Comus, Sefton.
No. 26.—Merlin mare................................ Herod, Promised Land.
No. 27.—Spanker mare .... Saunterer, Pero Gomez.
No. 28.—Dr. of Place's White Turk .... Emilius, Dalesman.
No. 29.—Natural Barb mare (dam of Basset Arab Landscape, Ashton.
      mare)
No. 30.—Dr. of Duc de Chartres' Hawker .... Paris, Delpini, Stamford.
No. 31.—Dick Burton's Barb mare .... Ruler, Fazzoletto.
No. 32.—Barb mare (Dodsworth's dam).............. Nike, Fitz-Gladiator.
No. 33.—Sister to Honeycomb Punch .... Sergeant, Dungannon.
No. 34.—Hautboy mare .... Antonio, Birmingham.
No. 35.—Dr. of Bustler .... Haphazard, Bustard (Castrel).
No. 36.—Dr. of Curwen's Bay Barb .... Economist, Old Engineer.
No. 37.—Sister to Old Merlin .... Dr. Syntax, Little Red Rover.
No. 38.—Thwaits' Dun mare .... Pot-8-os.
No. 39.—Bonny Black .... Dagworth (Aus.).
No. 40.—Royal mare (dam of Brimmer).............. Boston (Am.).
No. 41.—Grasshopper mare .... Bagot, Portrait.
No. 42.—Spanker mare .... Oiseau, Cestus.
No. 43.—Natural Barb mare (Emperor of Morocco's Balfe, Underhand.
      gift)

I can conceive that among the many people interested in blood-stock there will be a large proportion unable readily to hit off the line of any given animal back to its family figure, but a glance through

the list of classic winners, which are arranged by Mr. Lowe under
their respective families, will generally throw a light on this, and the
revised first volume of the Stud Book also serves as a tolerably easy
guide. For absolutely convenient study, however, especially where
a pedigree is of no great distinction on the maternal side for a few
generations back, Mr. Hermann Goos' Tables, which are published
by F. W. Rademacher, Hamburg, will be found invaluable, and
though Mr. Bruce Lowe had not seen them before he came to
England on his last visit, he most fully recognised their use.

I little thought when he honoured me by asking me to finish his
book if anything happened to him, that I should actually be called
on to do so, but so it was. The poor fellow left a properly attested
document, which ran as follows :

> "30, Bury Street, St. James's,
> "*October* 23rd, 1894.
>
> "I, C. Bruce Lowe, hereby express my definite wish that my book on 'Breeding by
> the Figure System' should be carried to completion and published by Mr. W. Allison, of
> 46A, Pall Mall, S.W."

I did not hesitate to undertake the task, but much corre-
spondence with Australia was necessary before technical and legal
details could be settled. Since then I have made the best progress I
could amid immense pressure of other business, culminating with the
general election, prior to and throughout which I had to control the
organisation and working of the Sporting League.

A good friend, whose contributions on horse-breeding to the
literature of the day stand, in my opinion, the highest of any, has
kindly assisted me by reading the proofs. When I say that his
nom de plume is " Oxonian," I have given a voucher for the truth of
my description of his merits.

I can only hope that the work, though by no means what its author would have made it had he lived, will be found worthy to occupy a place in the library of every man who is interested in thoroughbred horses, and that any trifling demerits or inaccuracies will be leniently considered under all the circumstances.

I am sure the readers will not forget that the book is the embodiment of at least twenty years' study on the part of Mr. Bruce Lowe, while my editing of it has necessarily been hurried and imperfect.

W. ALLISON.

CONTENTS.

LIST OF PLATES.

(From Photographs by Clarence Hailey, Newmarket.)

BREEDING RACEHORSES

BY THE

FIGURE SYSTEM.

———:•••:———

CHAPTER I.

INTRODUCTORY.

It would serve no practical purpose in a treatise of this kind to enter into an exhaustive history of the origin of the English thoroughbred horse. The work has already been accomplished by such world-wide authorities as Youatt, "Stonehenge" (to whom I am greatly indebted for my early lessons in pedigree), Sir Francis Hastings Doyle, Col. Upton, Col. Bruce (of America), and many others, including Mr. Joseph Osborne, whose very valuable Handbook to Breeders has saved much reference to that splendid fountain of pedigree lore, the English General Stud Book. The United research of the above-mentioned writers, which has thrown so much light on this interesting subject, is always available to students ; and it is with no intention of attempting to rival their labours in the history of the racehorse that this book is written, but rather to take up the subject where they have dropped it, and to show by means of a series of Figures and tables which are the strains that have *persistently* succeeded in the past, and *must* in the nature

B

of things continue to do so. One of the many truths gleaned from these authorities is contained in the fact that out of about one hundred imported Eastern stallions, including Arabs, Barbs, and Turks, only three are represented to-day in male descent, viz., the Darley Arabian, Byerly Turk, and Godolphin Barb; and the theory of the "survival of the fittest" would *seem* to point to these three horses being superior for racing purposes to all the rest of the Eastern sires. It is, however, quite possible that they were more favoured in the class of mares bred to them. Take the instance of the Godolphin Barb. But for the chance of being mated with Roxana (the rejected of Hobgoblin) and producing Lath, a high-class racehorse, the Godolphin would undoubtedly have (so say the records) died in obscurity. But nothing succeeds like success, and the stud masters of old days were cast in a very similar mould to those of the present, for after this happy accident our hero got his choice of the best mares, and right valuable his blood has proved to be.

Mr. Joseph Osborne contends that the merit of Eclipse was quite as much (if not considerably more) due to the *five* strains of the Lister Turk than to the single strain of Darley Arabian, but by the same reasoning the admirers of D'Arcy's White Turk might put forward stronger claims for that horse, seeing that his name occurs no less than *nine* times in the pedigree table of Eclipse. But this line of reasoning would open up no end of argument, and at this distance from the efforts of early stud breeders the discussion could lead to no practical results. We must, perforce, accept the plain fact that none of the many Eastern horses are *tangibly* represented at the present day except the trinity already mentioned, and, willy-nilly they must be credited with being superior to the balance. My own impression is that even these three great progenitors owe their survival and fame mostly to the *female lines* they were mated with. The Figure system is based mainly upon identifying and tracing the origin of these *female* lines. While admitting the important part a sire plays in the creation of a racehorse, it will be conceded generally that the dam exercises a greater influence upon his constitution and temper; and I hope to prove to the satisfaction of my readers later on, that a successful sire derives his excellence principally from the combination of certain *female* lines in his pedigree table.

Until the last four or five years, or about the time Messrs. Weatherby issued the revised edition of No. 1. vol. English Stud Book, few writers outside of America (none that I am aware of *) had taken up the position that it was equally necessary to trace the female lines to their "tap roots"; but since the advent of the volume referred to above, we find this phase of breeding is beginning to attract the attention of students. True it is, that in English pedigree tables there have been certain mares selected by reason of their great excellence, to wit Beeswing, Alice Hawthorn, Pocahontas, Queen Mary, Martha Lynn, &c., &c., and these have served the purpose of milestones along the path of students; but they have in most instances stopped short at these, not deeming it necessary to identify the family tap roots, as in the case of male descent. Every day, however, it is becoming more apparent that the importance of the female descent cannot be overrated, and, as a result of this new departure in breeding, I feel that I am speaking to a more sympathetic audience than could have been hoped for in 1882, when I first contemplated publishing the Figure system.

* See Preface.

CHAPTER II.

THE ORIGIN OF THE VITALITY OF THE ENGLISH RACEHORSE.

THE question *Why is one horse so superior to his racing contemporaries?* intrudes itself with the advent of every unusually good performer. That there is a larger accumulation of vital force in the veins of one animal as compared with another is evidenced at every race meeting. This superiority of racing power does not necessarily lie in his more perfect symmetry or better condition; because we frequently see the inferior-looking and smaller horse vanquish his bigger, better looking, and equally conditioned opponents. It undoubtedly consists of a greater concentration of *vitality* or *nervous force* in the animal. A close study of the pedigrees of great racehorses should always reveal excellent reasons why they are so, and where that vitality comes from. The main difficulty for students has been to decide amid such a variety of strains which are the most potent. Some writers build their theories upon the amount of Eclipse blood in the pedigree, others incline to Herod or Matchem. One will tell you that the mare furnishes all the racing qualities, and another says, " given a good sire, I will breed racehorses out of all sorts and conditions of mares." There is much truth in all these statements, but they are only theories after all, and very few are based upon more than a few selected cases to prove certain contentions, while as many examples might be cited to prove the contrary. To be of real value a theory must be based upon the bed rock of *results*—unmistakable and undeniable, such as the fact that the

Eclipse line is the dominant one of the three great male lines. This, indeed, is about the only *proved* theory on horse breeding. The truth is so apparent that we may not hazard a doubt to the contrary. It is, in fact, no longer a theory, for it has been reduced to a simple statistical fact! In like manner I can claim that the Figure system is derived from the statistical results of the three great English classic events of Derby, Oaks, and Leger, since their inauguration in 1777, 1779, and 1780, and consequently it is also based upon the sound principle of judgment by results.

When the English Stud Book was first compiled it contained not more than about one hundred original mares or tap roots. Of these nearly fifty are represented in the last volume of the Stud Book, and of this number less than twenty play any prominent part in the pedigrees of modern horses; while, again, only about nine appear to be *indispensable* in the pedigree of any first-class horse of the present day. Every racehorse of to-day, as a fact, contains in his table the whole of the nine, either direct or through collateral branches some distance back. But my contention is that some of the branches of these choice families must be represented within the *three top removes*, and in proportion to the amount of inbreeding to these few choice families will be the measure of vitality contained in the individual other conditions of course being equal. What those conditions are will be explained later on. I have divided these nine families into two classes, *running* and *sire*, or, in other words, *feminine* and *masculine*. These two qualities permeate all nature, and without both there could of course be no reproduction, either in animal or vegetable life. It does not, however, follow that because a mare is a mare she must necessarily be feminine in her temperament. Breeders will understand what is meant by my saying that we often find the real stoutness and inbreeding to Eclipse (a decidedly masculine strain) on the *dam's side* of the pedigree, and on the sire's side of the table the soft, flashy, effeminate strains of Bay Middleton, Orlando, &c., of the Herod line. It is very clear to me that the effeminacy is derived from the Barb origin, as against the " Royal," or old English blood, for while the families descended from three *imported Barb mares* have proved far away most prolific in winners of classic events, the *great sires* of the English stud mostly trace their descent to Royal and English *native bred* mares. The Arab and Barb breeds are undoubtedly the purest known form of what are called thorough-bred horses. All other varieties have been formed from these, and the wide differences seen at present in the shape and size of the various breeds of draught, coaching, pony, &c., are merely the results of evolution, due to the effects of climate, occupation, and pasture. The Barb and Arab are practically identical in race and surroundings, and may be classed under the same heading, and, without doubt, represent, pure and undefiled up to the present day, the great fountain heads or sources from which sprang our present English racing stock.

In the matter, therefore, of pure lineage, our much boasted thoroughbred racehorse cannot compare with a true specimen of Nedgean or Anazeh Arab or the steeds of Abd-el-Kader. It is true that a first-class English racehorse would distance the best of any of the desert breeds in a race of one or ten miles, but, all the same, he owes that very superiority to the infusions of Eastern blood which were crossed upon the " royal " and native bred horses of England. And while this desert blood played such an important part in making the racehorse of to-day what he is, it has only in three instances been able to assert itself, as already shown, in the *male* line through the Darley Arabian, Byerly Turk, and Godolphin Barb, and of these three the former is slowly but surely pushing out of existence the representatives of the two latter, and we shall see the very evident reason later on.

Let us now consider the claims to recognition of the Eastern mares introduced to England in early days. It is possible that some of the so-called " royal mares " were of pure Eastern descent, but in the absence of any certain records proving this, it has not hitherto been deemed advisable to include them as such, and very properly so In the revised edition of Vol. I. (issued in 1891) English Stud Book, it is stated that Charles I. had three Morocco mares at Tutbury in 1643, but we find nothing tracing to them. The only authentic ones are the " Natural Barb mare of Mr. Tregonwell," Burton's Barb mare, Layton's Barb mare, a Barb mare (dam of Old Bald Peg, see Flying Childers), a Barb mare the dam of Dodsworth, also two other so-called Natural Barb mares. The descendants of the last three have almost died out. While there are seven Barb mares, we find no records of any Arab mares ; at least, none are, as far as I can find, represented in Vol. XVII. of the English Stud Book. This may be accounted for because of the difficulty of obtaining pure Arabians, *especially mares*, in the seventeenth century, and it would appear as if the horse breeders of the deserts were fully aware of the risk of parting with good females if they desired to retain the supremacy of the equine world.

It is a recognised axiom with both physiologists and practical breeders of all kinds of stock, that the value of any family is mainly in proportion to the *purity of its origin*. In the case of thoroughbred horses this fundamental law of Nature has been amply sustained by the interesting fact that the descendants of Tregonwell's Natural Barb mare, Burton's Barb mare, and Layton's Barb mare have won nearly one-third of the English classic races (Derby, Oaks, Leger) since these contests were first established. I think this will be conceded as an extraordinary showing, when we reflect that they had to compete against at least one hundred rival families. In the revised edition of No. 1. vol. before referred to, there is an attempt to prove that the Byerly Turk mare, dam of the Two True Blues (Stockwell's family in female line), is descended from Burton's Barb mare. There is not sufficient evidence to support this statement, and the family must be treated as a separate one until proved to the contrary. If, however, it is to be judged by its success as a classic winner, it may fairly claim to be of pure descent, seeing that no less than forty-two of the three great classic races (Derby, Oaks, and Leger) have fallen to its descendants, and students of pedigree will, I am sure, be interested to know that these three magnificent running lines, having as tap roots respectively Tregonwell's Natural Barb mare, Burton's Barb mare, and the dam of the Two True Blues, have practically run a *dead heat* for supremacy in this great classic contest, commencing in 1776, continuing up to and including 1894, winning something over one-third of the total of all the other families combined.   This is not so startling when we pursue the inquiry further and find that, like their great male contemporaries in this struggle for turf honours, they have succeeded by sheer merit and superior fruitfulness in pushing most competitors aside.   These characteristics were no doubt large factors in their favour, but, be that as it may, the fact remains that they now greatly outnumber the other families, except that of the Layton Barb mare, which is treading closely upon the heels of the other three, and the four combined include considerably more than one-third of the mares in the last volume of the English Stud Book.   There is a valuable lesson to be derived from these facts.   Just as we now go to the Eclipse line for sires in preference to the lines of Herod and Matchem, because it is *the dominant* line. so we should in like manner select mares from the most successful running (and sire) lines if we would court success in breeding racehorses.

    To show how this works out in practice, take the experiences of the four most successful breeders ever seen in England, the Duke o Grafton, Lords Jersey, Egremont. and Falmouth.   These noble lords in their own particular epochs, held almost a monopoly of the One and Two Thousand, Derby, Oaks, and Leger.   It is apparent that they were fully cognizant of the value of the mares descended from the three top lines of Tregonwell's Natural Barb mare, Burton's Barb mare, and dam of Two True Blues, as the majority of their winners came from these three lines.   Lord Jersey bred mostly from the former family, through the descendants of Prunella, and his principal wins were accomplished by the following animals tracing to Tregonwell's Natural Barb mare: Riddlesworth (Two Thousand Guineas, 1831), Glencoe (Two Thousand Guineas, 1834), Ibrahim, Bay Middleton, and Achmet in 1835-36-37; Cobweb and Charlotte West, the One Thousand Guineas; Middleton and Bay Middleton, the Derby; and Cobweb, Oaks. The Duke of Grafton was even more successful with this family, for he won the Two Thousand Guineas five times with Pindarrie, Reginald, Pastille, Dervise, and Turcoman; the One Thousand Guineas four times, with Rowena, Whizgig, Tontine, and Problem; the Derby three times, with Pope, Whalebone, and Whisker. No less than six Oaks fell to his share by the aid of Pelisse, Morel, Music, Minuet, Pastille, and Turquoise. Lord Grosvenor won the Oaks with Ceres, the Derby with Rhadamanthus and Dædalus. Lord Egremont won no classic races with descendants of this family, but from that of the dam of Two True Blues he pulled off three Derbies and one Oaks. It may not be generally known that the Duke of Grafton performed the unprecedented feat of winning five successive One Thousand Guineas, missed a year, and then won three more successive victories in the same classic stake.

Lord Falmouth was, in every sense of the word, a clever breeder. Not only did he confine himself (in the main) to these three top lines, but it is also quite evident that he mated his mares on scientific principles, and his success was amply demonstrated by the following formidable roll of classic and other celebrities: Queen Bertha (Oaks), Spinaway (One Thousand and Oaks), Wheel of Fortune (One Thousand and Oaks), Jannette (Oaks and Leger), Busybody (One Thousand and Oaks), Charibert (Two Thousand), Silvio (Derby, Leger), also Queen's Messenger, Blanchefleur, Gertrude (a high class mare), Paladin, Fame, Silverhair, Chevisaunce. The above and many other winners trace to Tregonwell's Natural Barb mare.

The descendants of Burton's Barb mare produced for him

Cantinière and her flying filly Bal Gal, also Dutch Oven (Leger). The dam of the Two True Blues is responsible for Hurricane (One Thousand Guineas), and Atlantic (Two Thousand Guineas), King Ban (sent to America, where he proved a great sire), and others too numerous to particularise. The above examples of the wisdom of following winning female lines may well point a moral to stud masters to go and do likewise.

So far as my judgment and research permit me to give an opinion, it appears that the vitality of any racehorse (up to a certain point) is in proportion to the amount of blood of these four great *running* lines contained in his veins. I would not have the stud master infer from this that they should be bred to alone and to the exclusion of the other families, even if such a course were possible, because it is essential that the less successful running lines, five of which I shall distinguish as *sire* lines, should be judiciously mated with them to produce great racehorses. This is only following up the natural law known to physiologists as the " mating of opposites " (a subject which has been admirably treated by Starkweather in his " Law of Sex "); and just as it would be productive of bad results to mate two tall, angular human beings of same temperament, so would it be disastrous in horses to mate a large-boned 16-hands horse of the Melbourne type and strains to a mare built upon the same lines. Rather should we choose him a mate inbred to blood of quality like Sweetmeat, Kingston, Macaroni, &c., and, by so doing, each individual will supply to the other those elements which were lacking when separate.

CHAPTER III.

IDENTIFICATION OF FEMALE LINES BY FIGURES.

HAVING in the previous chapter touched upon the Eastern origin of a few of the many female lines in the Stud Book, and shown that these few lines are responsible for a large proportion of the classic winners, I now propose to identify the original mares or tap roots of all the surviving families in the last volume of the English Stud Book. Before doing so it will greatly simplify matters if I explain again how I arrived at the figures which distinguish this system from any previous methods of testing pedigree. As before stated, the three *top* winning lines are now almost level, but as one must take precedence of the others, I named the Natural Barb mare (Tregonwell's) No. 1.* Burton's Barb mare comes next as No. 2 ; the dam of the Two True Blues No. 3 ; and so on to No. 34. There will occasionally be some slight alteration in the position of these three leading lines, but for practical purposes it matters very little so long as the figure identifies the family and shows at the same time its approximate position as a producer of classic winners of Derby, Oaks, and Leger.

The advantages to be gained by the adoption of the figures can hardly be overrated. In the first place, they identify the family without any tedious repetition of the names of the tap roots, if indeed, it were possible to include these in a tabulated pedigree. Secondly, they show the position the family has attained in the three great classic races, thus, No. 1, 2, 3, 4, 5, and so on up to 34; the

---

* If the One and Two Thousand are included it places No. 1 considerably ahead.

larger the figure the less successful have been the descendants of that family. Thirdly, when a figure is placed against the name of each male in a tabulated pedigree it shows at a glance the family (or tap root he descends from), and informs the student what *main families* have been brought into combination. Where is the sense of carefully mating your mare so that a nick of Stockwell appears at three and four removes in the pedigree table if you neglect to acquaint yourself with the *winning* status of those families *upon which Stockwell has been grafted ?*

Is it not clear to my readers, even at this early stage, that if there is a preponderance of *large* figures or *non-winning* families the potency of Stockwell will be powerless against such a bad combination, and the result almost certain failure, even though the yearling shows superior shape and symmetry, larger size, and better bone than his rivals at the sale ring, and by reason of these very advantages runs into bigger figures? But all these essential points are of little service to the colt when he comes to be raced if there is a lack of the blood of the Nos. 1, 2, 3, 4, and 5 families (to give the necessary *vitality*) grafted upon the *sire* families Nos. 3, 8, 11, 12, 14. While fully appreciating the good effects the royal mares and native English blood have had upon the racehorse of to-day, we cannot disguise from ourselves the fact that their descent is in some cases very questionable. If this supposition is correct, whenever these lines are bred to one another without a preponderance of running blood as a check, there should be a tendency (according to all good authorities) "to revert to the parent stock." This is a recognised truism amongst breeders, and no doubt accounts for the extra size and coarseness so frequently seen in young stock coming from parents which do not themselves lack quality, though descended from obscure origin, and the advantage of the figure key is that it reveals to the stud master in a simple and concise form which of the original families he is bringing together in any given mating.

After nearly twenty years trial of it upon the past and present pedigrees of English, American, and Australian racehorses, Mr. Reynolds (and more recently Mr. H. C. White) and myself are thoroughly convinced that it is indispensable in the breeding of high-class racehorses with any prospect of *certainty, i.e.*, so far as the term may be applied to such an uncertain science as physiology, and in connection with its most uncertain branch, the breeding of racehorses. This is necessarily so because of the curious diversity of strains of blood which have been brought together in the pedigree of every English racehorse of the present day, making it almost imperative that breeders should possess a picture gallery of past celebrities to show somewhat more clearly what ancestor the colt has taken after.

In fixing the standard of racing excellence, I was guided by the fact that to be of any real value it must be *high*, and it will be generally admitted by racing men that the three great classic races of Derby, Oaks, and Leger, with their high scale of weights and honourable competition, are very rarely won by other than the best horses of the year. The Derby is an exceptionally severe race, taking into consideration the heavy impost of 9 stone (for colts), time of year, and the gradients of the course. This classic test would not be of great value over a short term, but in the course of considerably over 100 years every family must surely have a reasonable chance of coming to the front. It is true that cases occur, like Isonomy, where the best colt of the year is not engaged, but, taking one year with another, the classic winners are the best colts and fillies of that year. The object of breeders, I take it, is to produce an animal that will win the important stake races at two and three years, nor can we suppose that any man ever set to work deliberately to breed a high-class *handicap* horse, whose powers would not be developed until four or five years old; nor are such horses desirable, in view of the heavy and expensive engagements of two and three year olds. For this reason I have not considered handicap or cup winners in the calculation, nor have I included the

One and Two Thousand, which partake more of the nature of feeders for the later and more valuable classic events

The reasons for deciding upon the *sire* families will more fully develop themselves as we take up the different threads of the history and performances of turf and stud celebrities. After I had given the figures to my friend Mr. Frank Reynolds, back in the early seventies, we went carefully through this question of sires, and traced the stud performances of all the prominent sires in the Stud Book, up to Eclipse, the king of sires, with the result that not more than half a dozen of any importance were found *outside* of these five families of 3, 8, 11, 12, 14, (or not much inbred to them), and these few (Blacklock, to wit) never scored a marked success, except with mares coming either *directly* from these five sire families or else *inbred* to them closely. Nor have I been able to discover any horse of note bred within the past 100 years whose pedigree table does not disclose some of the sire and *running* figures in the first three removes. In other words, every great racehorse and sire of this century will be found to have in his *three top removes* one or more of the following figures, 1, 2, 3, 4, 5, 8, 11, 12, 14.

I now propose to give a short sketch of the specialities and peculiarities of some of the families now existing, showing the tap roots and classic winners descended from them, so as to more clearly impress the identity of each family in the minds of readers. It would occupy too much space to deal with all in the same manner that I have done in the case of No. 1, nor would it serve any practical purpose. No. 1 is given somewhat more in detail to show the sequence of descent of the most prominent living representative of the line (Minting in this case) through the main branch of Penelope, while on the same page I have inserted the winners of the One Thousand Guineas, Two Thousand Guineas, Derby, Oaks, and Leger, also Australian and some American classic winners when present. That each family has retained the main characteristics of its earliest known progenitors is very plainly to be observed, and by the doctrine of heredity this should be so, because not only is a main line often directly inbred to itself by meeting with a branch of the same family, as in Minting's case; but in addition to this nearly every family in the Stud Book contains in his or her veins more or less of the blood of the first fifteen or twenty winning families through repeated crossings. In some of the families, no matter how inbred they may be to sire figures, no record of a stallion of the *first class* can be found in the present century, though scores of high class racehorses have from time to time emanated from these very same families. The four top families, for instance, are prolific in female classic winners, while in many other families the proportion of good males over females is just as marked.

We will consider the Natural Barb mare (No. 1) and her descendants first, taking the others in the order of their figures.

No. 1.—This is essentially a *running*, as distinguished from a *sire*, line. It is very prominent as a winner of the three classic events (forty-two)—(fourteen Derbies, sixteen Oaks, twelve Legers). It has figured more largely than any line as a winner of One Thousand and Two Thousand Guineas, and the fillies have proved themselves high class, prolific brood mares. The earliest horses of note in the family were Old Snap, and his son Goldfinder, never beaten. Very few great sires have sprung from this line in proportion to its winners. The best are Partisan, Melbourne, Bay Middleton, Glencoe, Whalebone, and Whisker. Minting is from this line, also his sire Lord Lyon, Silvio, Craig Millar, Trumpator. The above, except Whalebone and Whisker, (both good all-round horses), are mostly esteemed through their female progeny. The members of the family possess great quality, brilliancy, and good looks as a rule. In Australia it is well represented by Wellington (V. R. C. Derby), Gibralta (A. J. C. Derby and Leger), Titan (sold as a two-year-old gelding for 1600 guineas), Tempe, Algerian, &c. In America by imp. Glencoe, (imp.) Eclipse, Sir Excess (and his brother Connoisseur) by Sir Modred, &c.

I have selected Minting as the best living exponent of this line, both by performances and the fact that he is the result of the line being bred into itself. This should make his fillies very valuable to race, and good dams when put to stud work.

No. 1.

TREGONWELL'S NATURAL BARB MARE.

Achievement (1000, L).	Dr. of Place's White Turk.	Mustard (1000).
Achmet (2000).		Nemesis (1000).
Bay Middleton (2000, D).	Dr. of Taffolet Barb.	Oxygen (O).
Bend Or (D).	Dr. of Byerly Turk.	Pastille (2000, O).
Blue Gown (D).		Pelisse (O).
Busybody (1000, O).	Dr. of Darley Arabian.	Pilgrimage (1000, 2000).
Ceres (O).		Pindarrie (2000).
Charibert (2000).	Bonny Lass by Bay Bolton.	Pope (D).
Charlotte West (1000).	Dr. of Partner.	Preserve (1000).
Clementina (1000).		Princess (O).
Cobweb (1000, O).	Spectator's dam by Crab.	Problem (1000).
Conyngham (2000).	Julia by Blank.	Pussy (O).
Cossack (D).		Queen Bertha (O).
Craig Millar (L).	Promise by Snap.	Reginald (2000).
Dædalus (D).		Rhadamanthus (D).
Dervise (2000).	Prunella by Highflyer.	Riddlesworth (2000).
Fitz Roland (2000).	Penelope by Trumpator.	Robert the Devil (L).
Gibraltar (Aus. D, L).		Rockingham (L).
Glencoe (2000).	Waltz by Election.	Rowena (1000).
Hambletonian (L).	Morisca by Morisco.	Scot Free (2000).
Hawthornden (L).		Silvio (D. L).
Ibrahim (2000).	Zillah by Reveller.	Spinaway (1000, O).
Jannette (O, L).		Sunbeam (L).
Ladas (2000, D).	Prairie Bird by Touchstone.	Tiresias (D).
Lambkin, The (L).		Tontine (1000).
Lord Lyon (2000, D, L).	England's Beauty by Birdcatcher.	Turcoman (2000).
Mango (L).	Rose of Kent by Kingston.	Turquoise (O).
Middleton (D).		Wellington (Aus. D).
Minthe (1000).	Syree by Marsyas.	Whalebone (D.)
Minnet (O).		Wheel of Fortune (1000, O).
Morel (O).	Mint Sauce by Y. Melbourne.	Whisker (D).
Music (O).	**MINTING** by Lord Lyon.	Whizgig (1000).

N.B.—D Derby; O, Oaks; L Leger; 1000, One Thousand Guineas; 2000, Two Thousand Guineas; Aus., Australian importations, or bred there; Am., American importations, or bred there.

No. 2.

BURTON'S BARB MARE.

Burton's Barb mare family, like its rival line, is a very valuable dam strain, and has furnished a large contingent of Oaks winners. Forty-four classic events have fallen to its share, (nine Derbies, sixteen Oaks, nineteen Legers). In Leger winners it nearly doubles No. 1, which would point to its being better staying blood, though it is somewhat behind No. 1 as a Derby winner. As a sire line it is distinctly ahead of its great rival, and though not in the front rank by a long way, many celebrities may be counted among its members. Prominent are Whiskey, Blacklock, Sir Hercules, Selim, and Castral, Voltigeur, Harkaway, Surplice, St. Albans, Lord Clifden, Ithuriel, &c., in England. It was never strongly represented in America in early days, except through Yorkshire (imp.) and Hurrah (imp.), but of recent years frequent importations of the family have filled up this gap. In Australia its fame has been worthily upheld by Carbine, son of Musket (imp.) from The Mersey (imp.), by Knowsley. Carbine covered himself with glory by winning the Melbourne Cup (two miles) against thirty-nine competitors, carrying 10st. 5lb. in 3 min. 2⁸½sec., thus beating all previous records. Also in this family are the meritorious (Australian) racehorses Admiral, Malvolio, Sandal, and Jeweller. It will be seen later on that while several successful sires sprang from this family, they were either got by horses which were in sire families, or else won their successes by being mated with dams from the sire families, thus showing their dependence on sire blood. This was very marked in the case of Blacklock and Sir Hercules, as may be seen later on.

The two best living representatives of this No. 2 family to-day are probably Carbine (Australia) and Petronel (England), but I give below, a list of its classic winners, to enable the stud master to judge for himself as to its wonderful running and, in a lesser degree, sire qualities.

Amato (D).	Cwrw (2000).	Industry (O).	Placida (O).
Ambidexter (L).	Cymba (O).	Lady Evelyn (O).	Prince Leopold (D).
Amiable (1000, O).	Destiny (1000).	Lilias (O).	Queen of Trumps
Angler (Aus. L).	Didelot (D).	Lord Clifden (L).	(O. L).
Briseis (O).	Don John (L).	Lounger (L).	St. Albans (L).
Bronze (O).	Dutch Oven (L).	Marchioness (O).	Sainfoin (D).
Butterfly (O).	Enguerrande (O).	Margrave (L).	Siberia (1000).
Camballo (2000).	Fishook (Aus. L).	Marquis (L, 2000).	Spread Eagle (D).
Carbine (Aus. L).	Florence (Aus. D, O).	Meteor (2000).	Surplice (D, L).
Cecilia (1000).	Gang Forward (2000)	Omphale (L).	Tartar (L).
Cockfighter (L).	Grey Momus (2000).	Paragon (L).	Teddington (D).
Corinne (1000, O).	Hamlet (Aus. L).	Parasote (O).	Theodore (L).
Cremorne (D).	Hermione (O).	Petronel (2000).	Vauban (2000).
Crucifix (1000, 2000,	Imperatrix (L).	Phenomenon (L).	Voltigeur (D, L).
O).	Impérieuse (1000, L).		

No. 3.

DAM OF TWO TRUE BLUES.

This is perhaps the most valuable family in the Stud Book, because it possesses the *dual* qualities of both a running and sire line. Its descendants have won forty-two of the three great classic races (fifteen Derbies, fourteen Oaks, thirteen Legers). It has produced more Derby winners than its two great rivals, and nearly as many winners of the Oaks, and the fillies are both prolific and successful as dams. As a sire line it stands nearly, if not quite, at the top of the tree, and mates well with all the other families, being very *pliable* in its nature, and improving every other strain of blood it is crossed with. It is only necessary to mention the following names to show how prolific of winners its sons have invariably been when put to stud work :—Sir Peter Teazle, Buzzard (by Woodpecker), Tramp, Master Henry, Velocipede, The Saddler, Lancercost, Flatcatcher, Pyrrhus I., Van Tromp, The Flying Dutchman, Stockwell, Sir Hercules (Aus.), Musket, Favonius Galopin, King Tom, Maribyrnong (Aus.), Tim Whiffler (imp. to (Aus.), Mr. Pickwick (imp. to Am.), American bred Eclipse, Rayon

d'Or, Wellingtonia, and many others. The following are the classic
winners claiming descent from this splendid family :—

Abercorn (Aus. D. L).
Ambrosio (L).
Assassin (D).
Atlantic (2000).
Bellissima (O).
Bosworth (Aus. L).
Bothwell (2000).
Bridget (O).
Cara (1000).
Chamant (2000).
Champion (D, L).
Charlotte (Orville). (1000).
Dreadnought (Aus. (D, L).
Ephemera (O).

Faith (O).
Favonius (D).
Flying Dutchman (D, L).
Galantina (1000).
Galata (1000, O).
Galopin (D).
General Peel (2000).
Hannah (O, L).
Hannibal (D).
Hephestion (2000).
Hurricane (1000).
Idas (2000).
Isinglass (2000). D, L).
Kettledrum (D).

La Flèche O, L, (1000).
Lapdog D).
Maid of the Oaks (O).
Maid of Orleans (O).
Mameluke (D).
Mayonaise (1000).
Melos (Aus. D).
Memoir (O, L).
Mincemeat (O).
Mincepie (O).
Moslem (2000).
Ninety Three (L).
Pic-Nic (1000).
Pyrrhus I. (D).

Rayon d'Or L).
Richmond Aus. D. L).
Sagitta 1000).
Sapphire (Aus. O).
Sir Peter D).
Skyscraper (D).
Spadille (L).
Spaniel D .
Stockwell 2000, L).
Tomato 1000).
Trifle O .
Tyrant (D .
Van Tromp (L).
Violante O
Young Flora (L).

No. 4.

THE LAYTON BARB MARE.

This family is prolific both in numbers and classic winners,
twenty-eight having fallen to its share, seven Derbies, eleven Oaks,
and ten Legers. It comes from a pure Barb source, and is
distinctly feminine in character. No great all-round sires have
sprung from this family, though many of them have been highly
valued through their fillies, to wit, Matchem, Thormanby, Kisber,
Iroquois, Emigrant, (Aus.), imported by the late Admiral Rous, and
notably Wenlock, whose daughters are veritable gold mines. The
following is a list of the classic winners :—

Apology (1000, O, L).
Azor (D).
Blucher (D).
Bonavista (2000).
Brigantine (O).
Chorister (L).
Common (2000, D, L).
Corsair (2000).
Duchess, The (L).
Flea, The (1000).

Gamos (O).
Gulnare (O).
Hauteur (1000).
Iroquois (D, L).
Kate (1000).
Kisber (D).
Lord of the Isles (2000).
Macgregor (2000).
Manganese (1000).

Medora (O).
Miss Jummy (1000, O).
Nightshade (O).
Our Nell (O).
Reve d'Or (1000, O).
St. Marguerite (1000).
St. Patrick (L).
Schahriar (2000).

Sea Breeze (O. L).
Sir Harry (D).
Staveley (L).
Thebais (1000, O).
Thormanby (D).
Throstle (L).
Ugly Buck 2000
Virago (1000).
Wenlock (L).

c 2

No 5.

DAUGHTER OF MASSY'S BLACK BARB.

Twenty-four classic events have been credited to No. 5, in the proportion of nine Derbies, nine Oaks, and six Legers. The horses of this family which stand out conspicuously are Gladiateur, Hermit and Doncaster. As a running line it is most valuable, and from its pliability mates with most strains, preferring sire blood. Great sires in the family are few and far between, *i.e.*, as compared with some of the sire lines. Appended are its classic winners :—

Barefoot (L).	Fille de l'Air (O).	Matilda (L).	Portia (O).
Dangerous (D).	Frederick (D).	Merry Monarch (D).	Pretender (D).
Deception (O).	Gladiateur (D. L).	Miami (O).	Quiz (L).
Doncaster (D).	Hermit, The (D).	Moses (D).	Refraction (O).
Election (D).	Jack Spigot (L).	Neva (O, 1000).	Reine (O).
Elizabeth (1000).	Marie Stuart (O, L).	Platina (O).	

No. 6.

OLD BALD PEG.

This family played a conspicuous part in the early and middle ages of classic racing. To Diomed, one of its members, was accorded the honour of winning the first Derby, run for in 1780. Diomed was imported to America, where his blood was highly esteemed, seeing that his stock (through Lexington principally) were dominant for many years on the American turf. That the blood is only valuable as dam blood is now generally recognized by American breeders. The Diomed male line was successful across the water in early days because there was little or no good Eclipse male blood from sire families to contend against. No. 6 has always been a poor sire family. The best horse it ever produced was Priam, and his failure in America was mainly owing to being bred back to his *own family descendants from Diomed*. No less than twelve Derbies have fallen to the share of No. 6, also three Oaks and two Legers. The paucity of Oaks winners indicates the decadence of the line. No line had better chances, as it attracted attention in early racing days through Flying Childers, Young Giantess, Eleanor, Julia, and Priam. Musjid was its last classic winner in the Derby of 1859.

Antar (2000).	Fidget Colt (D).	Plenipotentiary (D).	Sorella (1000).
Carnetacus (D).	Musjid (D).	Priam (D).	Tarrare (L).
Cœlia (O).	Nicolo (2000).	Sailor (D).	William (L).
Diomed (D).	Phantom (D).	Sam (D).	Y. Eclipse (D).
Eleanor (O. D).	Phosphorus (D).	Shoveller (O).	

No. 7.*

BLACK-LEGGED ROYAL MARE.

Nine Derbies, two Oaks, and three Legers.

This line is familiar to pedigree men through West Australian, its best representative. Like No. 6 there is a preponderance of Derby over Oaks (and Leger winners) which would seem to point to its fillies being, as a general thing, wanting in feminine character, and not over good producers. The classic winners are given below :—

Annette (O).	Extempore (1000).	Pan (D).	Semolina (1000).
Beningbrough (L).	Feu de Joie (O).	Saltram (D).	West Australian
Cotherstone (D)	Gustavus (D).	Scottish Queen	(2000, D. L).
Ditto (D).	Mundig (D).	(1000).	Wild Dayrell (D).
Donovan (D, L).			

No. 8.

BUSTLER MARE (Dam of Byerly Turk M).

I cannot help regarding this line as being one of the most valuable sire families in the Stud Book, not excepting No. 3. Not only have many great sires come directly from the line, such as Marske, Orville, Sultan, Newminster, Cain, Humphrey Clinker,

---

* Mr Bruce Lowe would probably have raised his estimate of this family somewhat if he had not allowed that very great sire, Wisdom (7), to slip his memory.—W.A.

Chester (Aus.), &c., but there is a marked tendency to leave equally great sons (and sires) behind them. Marske begot Eclipse, a greater sire than himself; Orville was inferior as a racehorse and sire to Emilius his son; Bay Middleton was more esteemed than his sire Sultan, as was Melbourne than his sire Humphrey Clinker; while few will be found to dispute the fact that, great as Newminster proved to be at turf and stud, he was outclassed by both Lord Clifden and Hermit in these respects. Chester (Aus.) proved himself to be a racehorse and sire of the highest class, but it remains to be proved whether his sons can rival him at the stud. The No. 8 line claims thirteen classic winners, as given below :—

Andover (D).	Governess (1000, O).	Orville (L).	Sir Tatton Sykes
Ayrshire (2000, D).	Melton (D, L).	Paulina (L).	(2000,L).
Camelia (1000).	Mrs. Butterwick (O).	Pewett (L).	Trenchant (Aus. D).
Chester (Aus. D, L).	Newminster (L).	Rhedycina (O).	Y. Mouse (2000).
Colonel, The (L).	Nunnykirk (2000).	Siffleuse (1000).	

No. 9.

THE OLD VINTNER MARE.

If any proof were wanting to show that families retain their *original* characteristics, even though they carry much contemporary blood in their veins, the history of this family affords strong evidence of the fact. Though not so high on the roll of winners as many of its rivals, it makes a goodly show with five Derbies, two Oaks, and six Legers, and the names of such remarkable racehorses as Mercury, Dick Andrews, Barefoot, Peter, Bendigo, and in Australia Navigator (D, L), Trident (D, L), Camoola (D, L). Despite this, it would be a difficult task for the warmest believer in the family to point to one really high class sire in its ranks. This is the more remarkable because of the proportion of Leger winners over Derby and Oaks, showing how really stout its sons have been,

as witness Peter and Bendigo. The three Australian horses
mentioned above were noted for their staying powers; also
Commotion (by Panic), winner of Leger (and two champion races.
three miles, under 5min. 27sec.), yet a pronounced stud failure
Appended is a list of its classic winners :—

Bloomsbury (D).	Hollandaise (L).	Nutwith (L).	Trident (Aus. D. L.
Camoola (Aus. D. L).	Kilwarlin (L).	Peregrine (2000).	Trophonius 2000)
Cedric (D).	Lady Oxford (1000).	Remembrancer (L).	Warlock L.
Commotion (Aus. L).	Navigator (Aus. D,	St. Giles (D).	Wizard, The (2000,
DanielO'Rourke (D,.	L).	Serina (L).	Variation O).
Habena (1000).	Noble (D).	Tag (O).	

No. 10.

DR. OF GOWER STALLION (Dam of Childers' Mare).

Five Derbies, three Oaks, and three Legers, as follows :—

Aimwell (D).	Caller Ou (L).	Manfred (2000).	Sir Bevis (D.
Blair Athol (D, L).	Fireworks (Aus. D,	Petrarch (2000. L).	Tormentor (O).
Blink Bonny (O, D).	L).	Pretender (2000. D).	Vesta (O).

This line came to the front early in its career by winning the
sixth Derby with Aimwell, a son of Mare Antony. After this
winners were returned at rare intervals, and the family never
assumed any importance until Blink Bonny appeared upon the
scene and accomplished Eleanor's hitherto unrivalled performance of
winning the double of Oaks and Derby. The line cannot be included
amongst the high class running lines. As a sire line it has been
successful when backed up with plenty of sire and running blood.
as witness Blair Athol, Petrarch, Hampton, and Fireworks Aus.
As we proceed in these investigations in pedigree it will be found
that many of the outside (obscure origin) families have suddenly
blazoned into notoriety after years of silence, and this has been
brought about in nearly all cases by striking combinations of the
running lines 1, 2, 3, 4, and 5, which have been grafted on to
the parent stems of the outside lines. Take the case under consideration, and look back into Queen Mary's pedigree for a few

generations. Her second dam, Myrrha, was by Whalebone, the best representative of No. 1 family in the Stud Book. Queen Mary's first dam was by Plenipotentiary (No. 6), inbred to the 2 and 3 families through Whiskey (2), Selim (2), Phenomenon (2), Sir Peter (3) twice, and Buzzard (3). This was a grand building up of a hitherto rather obscure line, but still more running blood was yet to come in through Queen Mary's sire Gladiator of the 22 line, himself a singular instance of the same process of inbreeding to 1, 2, and 3. His sire Partisan (1), was cousin to Whalebone, his dam Pauline by Moses (5)—generally accredited to Whalebone (1); (and if by Seymour, 4), and Gladiator's second dam was by Selim (a combination of 2, 3, and 1), his third dam by Whiskey (2). Such cases as this, and scores of others which I shall adduce in support of this view, warrant me in the presumption that the racing power of the English horse is derived from the five great running families 1, 2, 3, 4, and 5.

No. 11.

THE SEDBURY ROYAL MARE.

Four Derbies, two Oaks, and three Legers have fallen to the descendants of this family, which includes many illustrious names that have helped to make the English stud famous. The first prominent horses of the family were Squirt and Regulus, and more recently Birdcatcher and Faugh a Ballagh kept up its *prestige*. St. Simon, at the present moment the premier sire of England, hails from its ranks. In America the name of "Australian" (imp.) will long be treasured; while at the Antipodes, Marvellous (imp.) claims the honour of siring Marvel, probably the fastest mile horse ever saddled in Australia, and the conqueror of Carbine over that distance of ground. These are only a few of its great sons, and pages might be devoted to the career of old Fisherman, who ended his days in

Australia, leaving a long roll of classic winners to keep his memory green. The winners of English classic races are given in detail :—

Altisidora (L).	Enamel (2000).	Kingcraft (D).	Memnon (L).
Bellina (O).	Faugh-a-Ballagh (L).	Little Wonder (D).	Ralph (2000).
CardinalBeaufort(D)	John Bull (D).	Mamuella (O).	Zoe (1000).

There seems to have been a doubt in the minds of the compilers of the revised Vol. I. of English Stud Book as to whether Grey Royal (page 10) comes from the same origin as Grey Wilkes (some times Old Wilkes), page 11, and "The Pet Mare," page 15. To my mind it is probable that Grey Royal, Grey Wilkes, and Grey Robinson, as well as "The Pet Mare," all descend from the same Sedbury Royal Mare. The fact of their being grey is of itself strong collateral evidence, if better were not forthcoming in the similarity of names and ownership by Lord Darcy's daughter, Mr. Robinson, of Easby, and Mr. Wilkes. The grey hairs seen in Venison (11), Birdcatcher (11), and Sir Hercules (from a mare by Wanderer, 11), are probably the results of transmission from the original mare.

No. 12.

ROYAL MARE (Dam of Brimmer Mare).

This family claims one Derby, six Oaks, and two Legers, a total of nine, as given below :—

Archibald (2000).	Hermit (Bay Mid).	Miss Letty (O).	Scotia (O).
Brown Duchess (O).	(2000)	Poison (O).	Sorcery (O).
Cadland (D):	Hester (1000).	Prince Charlie	Tigris (2000).
Catgut (1000).	Mimi (1000, O).	(2000).	Y. Traveller (L).
Filho da Puta (L).			

This line affords an instance of one of the anomalies of breeding, for whereas the Oaks winners (six) are out of all proportion to the solitary and fluky Derby winner Cadland (and two Leger winners), and would thereby lead one to the conclusion that it is effeminate in its nature, experience shows it to be the stoutest and most masculine line in the Stud Book all the way up from Eclipse It is generally conceded that this latter horse was far and away the best sire of early days, and when I take up the subject of sires later on I hope to be able to show very clearly whence he derived this remarkable sire potency. To the name of Eclipse we can add a larger number of good sires from this family than from any line now existing except No. 3. Some of the best known names are Conductor, Voltaire, Sheet Anchor, Weatherbit, Edmund, Oxford, Sterling, Scottish Chief, Marsyas, Prince Charlie (and his son Salvator, Am.), Ethelbert, Restitution, Adventurer, Kingston, Springfield, Lexington (Am.), and some of the males of the Levity family. In Australia Tros and Glorious imported. It is also a line which stands *inbreeding to itself.* This is more noticeable in America, where there has been a great deal of inbreeding to the Levity family, and with good results. The champion racehorse (a few years back) of that country, Salvator, was the result of a cross of Prince Charlie (12) on to Selina of the same family; and, what is more remarkable, Prince Charlie is himself inbred to 12, and Selina is by Lexington of same line. In England we have Weatherbit from Miss Letty (12), and his sire, Sheet Anchor, is also 12. Again, Sterling's dam is 12, and his sire Oxford 12. Also that brilliant racehorse and successful sire Springfield comes from this family, and so does his dam's sire Marsyas. Prince Rudolph (now at Cobham Stud) is similarly bred to the above renowned stallions, as both his sire and dam come from the 12 family. It will, however, be found that in all these cases of inbreeding the 12 line to itself with *success*, it was accompanied by a strong return to the *running* families as well, (through collateral branches) to ensure the requisite amount of racing vitality to the offspring.

No. 13.

ROYAL MARE (Dam of Mare by Darcy's White Turk).

Four Derbies, two Oaks, and two Legers, as detailed :—

Beadsman (D).	Elis (L).	George Frederick(D)	Orlando (D).
Belphœbe (1000).	Fyldener (L).	Mendicant (O, 1000).	Shotover (2000, D).
Chapeau d'Espagne (1000).	Galliard (2000).	Olive (2000).	Stella (O).

The first horse to give any prominence to this line was the unbeaten Highflyer, the property of the founder of the present firm of Mr. Edmund Tattersall and Sons, in whose possession the original oil painting of this famous racehorse remains, and shows him to have been a horse of much symmetry and racing power. Stella (Oaks), in 1784, was the first classic winner, then Fyldener won the Leger in 1806, and we find nothing classical again till Elis won the Leger in 1836. Then appeared the sensational Orlando (D), and after this winners cropped up every now and then. If, as I have suggested before when dealing with No. 11, Grey Wilkes, Grey Robinson, and Grey Royal claim a common origin from the "Sedbury Royal Mare," then also would No. 13. This I think probable, but consider it the best plan to treat as separate. If we were to judge this family by its Australian records, and add classic wins there to its credit, it would rank very high. In 1860 Mr. C. B. Fisher, of Victoria, did the colonies a signal service by importing Juliet (No. 13) by Touchstone, in foal to Stockwell, and from this family have sprung some of the most illustrious horses in Australia, to wit, Goldsborough (L), Robinson Crusoe (D and L), Robin Hood (D and L), Charon (D and L), Benvolio (D), Sylvia (O) the latter three horses direct from Juliet Nordenfeldt (D) Martini Henry (D and L), and many others of note. The late Mr. James White purchased in 1882, and imported two daughters of Princess of Wales (dam of George Frederick), La Princess (by Cathedral), dam of the V.R.C.

Newmarket winner Cranbrook (by Chester), a slashing weight
carrier up to a mile. The other mare. Princess Maud by Adventurer,
produced the well-performed Acme; so that the No. 13 family may
be said to have done excellent service for Australia.

No. 14.

THE OLDFIELD MARE.

As a classic winner this family does not take high rank, only one
Derby (through the aid of Macaroni), two Oaks, and three Legers.

Geheimniss (O).	Lancelot (L).	Satirist (L).
Hippia (O).	Macaroni (2000, D).	Touchstone (L).

Taking into consideration the inferior figure it cuts as a classic
winner, one would hardly look to its ranks for great sires if one
followed the orthodox plan of "using only running families." This
case especially strengthens my position in assuming that *sire* and
running qualities are not necessarily akin. On the one side we
require stout, masculine breeding, combined with strong individuality,
symmetry, and ability to race, if possible, and on the other soundness
of constitution with an accumulation of vitality only to be acquired
by close inbreeding to Nos. 1, 2, 3, 4, and 5. But of this more
anon. The first sire of any note in the 14 line was Trumpator (of
the God. Barb branch). Then came Touchstone, a horse that has
made himself a great name for all time; The Libel, Macaroni,
Touchet, Buccaneer, Saraband, Carnival, and Saccharometer. Also
Leamington, imported to America, destined to sire Iroquois and
make the hearts of all American sportsmen thrill with pleasure
when the news flashed across the ocean that this great horse had
won the "Blue Ribbon" of the English turf. The 14 line has done
still further service in the States, for has it not given them that
greatest of all winning horses Tammany (from Tullahoma, 14)?
Two of the best sires ever imported to Australia, Panic and
Grandmaster, hail from the 14 line, and a possibly better than

either, Middlesex, died during his first season at Gordon Brook, New South Wales. But I think the foregoing list is sufficient to place it beyond doubt that this family ranks high as a sire line.

No. 15.

ROYAL MARE (Dam of Old Whynot).

The classic winners are nine :—

Attila (D).	Jerry (L).	Symmetry (L).
Eager (D).	Petronius (L).	Theophania (O).
Harvester (D).	Soothsayer (L).	Tommy (L).

It is very evident that the members of this family do not come early, or else are not partial to short courses, for I cannot find a winner of either 1000 or 2000 Guineas, and this is corroborated by the fact that its Leger winners are out of proportion to the Oaks and Derby. This paucity of good females would indicate its gradual extinction, and such appears to be the case, though it has come again with a spurt in the shape of Foxall and Harvester. As a sire family it has always been a pronounced failure.

No. 16.

SISTER TO STRIPLING BY HUTTON'S SPOT.

Two Derbies, two Oaks, and one Leger through the following horses is all the line has been able to accomplish so far.

Bonny Jean (O).	L'Abbesse de Jouarre (O).	St. Gatien (D).
Farewell (1000).	Ormonde (2000, D, L).	

Up to the time St. Gatien (1884) ran a dead heat for the Derby with Harvester, the line had been absolutely silent as regards classic winners, though many fair racehorses (and sires) came from its ranks, notably Tibthorpe, Brown Bread, &c. The line is better known to the breeding and sporting world as " the Agnes family." The gradual building up of the Agnes family is one of the most interesting problems in the annals of breeding, because it demonstrates clearly that if so much could be accomplished by what must have been to a large extent " accidental selection," what untold probabilities lie in the paths of young breeders in the future, if they will only study earnestly by the lamplight of experience.

It will not be out of place to show again how useful the figures are as a guide or key to determine the value of any given combinations of blood.   Later on I will deal with Ormonde's pedigree under the heading of " How to Breed Phenomenal Racehorses," but while the family is under discussion a cursory glance at the bottom of that wonderful horse's pedigree, by the aid of the figures, will be of interest to students.   If they will turn over a few pages and look at the tabulated pedigree, it will be seen that Ormonde's fifth dam was by Don John of the 2 family, he again by Waverley (2) of same family, who in his turn was by Whalebone (1) from a mare by Sir Peter (3).   The fourth dam of Ormonde (Annette) was by that sire of good fillies Priam (6), *inbred* to Whiskey (2).   Then we get some outside blood through Clarion of the Godolphin line, the sire of third dam Agnes.   This mare was put to Birdcatcher (11) by Sir Hercules (2), by Whalebone (1).   The outcome of this union, Miss Agnes, was bred to The Cure (6) by Physician (21), by Blacklock (2), by Whitelock (2), by Hambletonian (1).   Further, Blacklock's dam was by Coriander (4), and Whitelock's dam by Phenomenon (2).   The Cure's *third* dam Cressida (by Whiskey, 2) was also the *first* dam of Priam (above), which gives us a further inbreeding to that overproof blood Whiskey.   The Cure was out of Morsel by Mulatto (5), by Catton (2), and his second dam, Linda, was by Waterloo (1), a half-brother to Whalebone.   All this repeated inbreeding to the best running strains (1, 2, 3, 4, and 5) would of itself have warranted the stud master in looking for

NOTE.—Mr. Bruce Lowe has here made a somewhat unaccountable slip, which I think best to leave as it stands, for it is important that the readers of his book should understand what was in his mind when formulating his theory.   Ormonde's fifth dam was not by Don John but by *Don Juan*, who was of No. 9 family.   Then, again, Clarion, sire of Agnes, was not of the Godolphin line, but was himself of No. 6 family, by Sultan (**8**), dam by Filho da Puta (**12**).—W. A.

splendid results. But we find that the edifice was not crowned until Polly Agnes (by the Cure) was bred to Macaroni (14) by Sweetmeat (21), whose dam Lollipop was incestuously bred to Blacklock (above), and we have already seen in Queen Mary's case how in-bred Gladiator, the sire of Sweetmeat, was to 1, 2, and 3. Is it any wonder then that, given the right mate, Lily Agnes was capable of producing the "horse of the century" that Ormonde proved himself. There is no pedigree in the Stud Book with so much concentrated vital force as this of Lily Agnes.

No. 17.

BYERLY TURK MARE (Dam of Mare by Carlisle Turk).

This line has not won a Derby, but two Oaks and three Legers have fallen to its descendants in England, as follows :—

Betrayer (N. Zealand D).	Meteora (O).	Sancho (L).
Cowslip (L).	Nectar (2000).	Saucebox (L).
Interpreter (2000).	Regalia (O).	Sir Modred (N. Zealand D).

The family is best known in England through Pantaloon, in Australia by Yattendon, and America by Sir Modred and Cheviot, his brother, sire of this year's American Derby winner, Rey el Santa Anita. Pantaloon's blood has always been esteemed highly, and should be more bred to than it is, considering how well it blends with Touchstone, Blacklock, Stockwell, and Melbourne. The 17 line, though not a prolific one, has turned out a few really high-class sires, and one would infer that the line readily assimilates with other families. The late Mr. E. K. Cox's valuable colonial bred sire Yattendon of this line, was the best all-round sire in Australia, for not only did he leave two great sons (and sires) behind him in Chester and Grand Flaneur, but his fillies have also proved to be the best of brood mares. Sir Modred is the best all-round sire in America, and there is no question that good individuals of this family are valuable acquisitions to any stud and in any country.

No. 18.

DR. OF OLD WOODCOCK (Dam of Dr. of Old Spot).

Though a slightly larger classic winner than three of the preceding lines, Nos. 14, 16, and 17, I have placed it behind them in order of merit, as it appears to be on the decline. Most of its victories were won in the early and middle days by the aid of the following individuals :—

Ellington (D).	Sir Thomas (D).	Summerside (O).
Formosa (1000, O, L).	Smolensko (2000).	Waxy (D).
Oriana (O).		

Admirers of Waxy may take exception to my sentiments respecting that much eulogised horse, but since working by the Figure system I have been convinced that, except for the lucky mating with Penelope of No. 1, we should have seen Waxy's name in very few pedigrees of note. That he hit with Penelope is beyond question, but Penelope made Waxy famous, for we cannot find the great excellence claimed for him by his numerous admirers developed through any other channel.

No. 19.

DR. OF DAVILL'S OLD WOODCOCK.

The descendants of this line have been singularly unfortunate as regards the higher classic races, considering the number of *phenomenal* horses the family has produced. Only one Derby and three Legers can be placed to its credit. Sir Hugo in 1892, was the first Derby winner, but Isonomy would undoubtedly have won Sefton's Derby in 1878 had he been nominated. No. 19 has produced no Oaks winners, and, indeed, very few mares of high class racing form (if we except Plaisanterie and one or two others), though they develop into good dams. The Leger winners are Ebor,

in 1817; Reveller, in 1818; and Gamester, 1859. In spite of its
want of success in classic events, a glance at some of the celebrated
horses descended from its ranks shows how valuable the blood is:
Isonomy, Vespasian, Monarque, Vedette (2000), Plaisanterie, Alarm,
Sabinus, Clearwell (2000), Surefoot (2000). The sons have not only
been great racehorses, but good sires, as a rule.

No. 20.

DR. OF GASCOIGNE'S FOREIGN HORSE.

Four Oaks and Leger winners come from this family. Blue
Bonnet (L), Ghuznee (O), Jenny Howlet (O), and Otterington (L).
Also Lady Augusta and Repulse, winners of the One Thousand
Guineas. The line is an effeminate but improving one, and more
largely represented to-day in last vol. of the Stud Book than Nos. 15,
16, 17, 18, and 19. Traducer (20) (imp. to New Zealand) proved
to be a high-class sire. Winslow, Strauss, and Citadel were about
the most prominent males in England of this family of late years,
until we come to Heaume, Hawkeye, and Chitabob.

No. 21.

THE MOONAH BARB MARE OF QUEEN ANNE.

A family well known to pedigree students through that excellent
horse, Sweetmeat. Like the 20 line, it has not produced a Derby
winner yet, and runs mostly to good fillies. The Oaks winners
are Hyppolita, 1790; Iris 1851; and Lonely, 1885. Charles XII.
placed a Leger to its credit in 1839. The members of the family
are evidently not early beginners or sprinters, as none of the
shorter classic races have fallen to their share. In America
the line is well and favourably known through imported Tranby
by Blacklock), whose name occurs in so many good pedigrees
across the water, where he undoubtedly helped to lay the
foundation of Levity's greatness. William Tell, by Touchstone

D

from Miss Bowe, by Catton from Tranby's dam, was imported
to Australia, and sired Archer, a double winner of the Melbourne
Cup under very big weights.   Boiardo by Orlando from Miss
Bowe (above), was sent to Australia, and sired Florence, one of
the best mares ever raced out there.   She won the A. J. C. Derby,
V. R. C. Oaks, and V. R. C. Derby.   It is worth noting that the
triumphs of this family have been mainly owing to its association
with the No. 2 line.   Tranby, a great racehorse, was by Blacklock
(2) by Whitelock (2).   William Tell and Boiardo were from Miss
Bowe (by Catton, 2), from Tranby's dam by Orville (8).   Sweetmeat's dam is intensely inbred to Blacklock, and Lonely is from
Anonyma by Stockwell (3) (inbred to 2 and Blacklock), from Miss
Sarah by Don John (2), by Waverley (2).   From this I would
infer that the fillies of this family should be put to sires closely
inbred to Blacklock through the 2 and 3 lines to give their
progeny the necessary running qualities.

This crossing of males in (or inbred closely to) the best running
lines on to females coming from the outside lines cannot be too
strongly impressed upon the student.   To inbreed 21 to itself or to
14, 15, 16, 17, 18, 19, and so on, is only excusable where there is
some *intense inbreeding* to Nos. 1, 2, 3, and 4 on *both* sides, and
in the first two or three removes, as I will show later on in the
cases of Barcaldine and Domino.   When these conditions do not
exist it is clearly a step *backward* in breeding, and yet for lack of
some clearly defined guide these mistakes are being unknowingly
perpetrated and perpetuated for all time by stud masters.   The
fact of a mare being in an outside line is not an objection by
any means, if such a course as I have sketched above has been
pursued in her back breeding.   We have seen in the case of the
Agnes family that the hitherto unfruitful parent stem (16) readily
accepted the numerous grafts of choice blood (2), and finally ended
in producing not only the greatest racehorse of modern days, but
also the most commanding and symmetrical individual it has ever

been my lot to see. After looking at the horse one day at Mr. Macdonough's ranch in California, I asked a very excellent judge of bloodstock whether he could improve upon his shape? "If I could alter him the space of my thumb I would not do so," was his answer. And those were very much my sentiments, bar his jowl and throat, which are not quite as one would wish them, though the rest of his head is very good, and he certainly possesses the most royal pair of eyes I have ever seen in a horse's head.

No. 22.

BELGRADE TURK MARE (Dam of Bay Bolton Mare).

Gladiator has made this family famous for all time, and evidence is forthcoming that the family is by no means dead (despite the poor figure it has cut in the Derby, Oaks, and Leger), as St. Blaise and Merry Hampton testify. Up to the time of St. Blaise's win in 1883 the line had not been fortunate enough to win a Derby. Its classic winners are St. Blaise (D) and Merry Hampton D., Catherine Hayes (O), Tarantella (1000), Barcarolle (1000), and Rhoda (1000).

It is no exception to the rest of the outside families in requiring the aid of the running lines, as I have shown through Gladiator, in Queen Mary's case. It is decidedly feminine in its character, as shown by a goodly roll of females, Fuzee, Venus (by Sir Hercules), Mrs. Quickly by Longbow, &c. Fuzee was a high class mare, her dam Vesuvienne was a daughter of Gladiator, from Venus by Sir Hercules (2), by Whalebone (1).

No. 23.*

PIPING PEG (Dam of the Hobby Mare).

One Derby, three Oaks, and one Leger, through the aid of Octavius (D), Caroline (O), Cyprian (O), Songstress O), and Ossian L).

* Other well-known stallions of this family deserve mention, such as Hagioscope, Pepper and Salt, and Miguel, being prominent at the present day.

D 2

The other prominent horses of the family are Solon and his son Barcaldine. In America, Duncombe (imp.), and all the "Gallopade" family. In Australia, Splendor (imp.), a very promising sire, whom I remember well seeing stripped for the Middle Park Plate in 1882. He is now in Mr. Frank Reynold's stud. He sired a very good racehorse, Jeweller, from a mare in the No. 2 family, and I take it will always prefer mares inbred to the running lines. Nothing could have justified Solon being bred back to his own family in Barcaldine's case save the intense and close inbreeding to Blacklock (2) and Birdcatcher, by Sir Hercules (2), and I take it the issue would have been a failure but for this counteracting influence to an *otherwise* pernicious breeding back to such an outside family as 23. The family is, however, a valuable one, and the above example shows how easily it assimilates with the best running blood.

No. 24.

HELMSLEY TURK MARE (Dam of Rockwood Mare).

If this line were to be judged by classic wins it stands very low, only a solitary Leger by The Baron. Yet some of the males of the family have been such excellent sires that it almost deserves the rank of a sire line, and, indeed, at one time Mr. Reynolds and I took it to be a branch of No. 8. Both lines in "Stonehenge's" tabulated pedigrees, and also in old Vol. I. Stud Book, ended in "daughters of Bustler," and for some years we considered that the mares were identical. I lean to that opinion still, seeing that the original mares were almost contemporary and bred in the same locality apparently. If the Lowther records are correct (page 15, Rev. Vol. I.), the change from Dr. of Bustler to Dr. of Helmsley Turk was not very great, because Bustler was a son of the H. Turk. The Rockwood mare (above) was the dam of Old Lady, owned by the Duke of Bolton. And if we turn to the tap root of the 8 family, Dr. of Bustler, and run her female produce down five generations, we find a mare by Foxcub) bred to Bay Bolton. Also if we turn to Vol. I., page 33, we find a Bay Bolton mare, owned by the Duke of Bolton, going back to a Dr. of Bustler, and the presumption is admissible that the tap root of all three families is identical. Anyhow, the sons of this 24 line have, in two cases (Camel and The Baron), earned imperishable fame as the sires respectively of Touchstone and Stockwell. Other good horses in this family were Old Starling, Pumpkin, Gohanna, Mountain Deer, Claret, Camerino, Y. Gladiator, and Chippendale. In America, a high class racehorse and sire, Hindoo; and in Australia, imported New Warrior, an excellent sire; also Welcome Jack (N.Z.), a brilliant racehorse.

No. 25.

A BRIMMER MARE (Dam of Old Scarborough Mare)-

Though low in scale of winners (three), the honours are equally divided between the three classic events, viz., Sefton (D), Bourbon (L), and Zinc (O). This filly won the One Thousand Guineas, as did also Zeal and Arab from this family. Other notable horses are Y. Melbourne and Slane.

No. 26.

DR. OF MERLIN (Dam of Mare by Darley Arabian).

There is no plea (save its unfitness) for this family being so low on the list of classic winners (one Derby, one Oaks, and one Leger), because few lines got such an excellent send off consequent upon King Herod's success as a racehorse and sire. In 1841 Coronation won the Derby. Previous to this (1821) Augusta won the Oaks and Two Thousand Guineas, and in 1854 Knight of St. George (by Birdcatcher) the Leger. In 1859 Promised Land won the Two Thousand Guineas.

The family will always have an interest for students, because it produced Herod. Why Herod's *male* line has, to a great extent, died out will be explained later on when treating of sires.

No. 27.

A SPANKER MARE (Dam of a Byerly Turk Mare).

One Derby and one Leger, viz., Pero Gomez (D) and Phosphorus (L); while Firebrand and May Day won the One Thousand Guineas in 1842 and 1834. Enthusiast (by Sterling) and Saunterer come also from this family, which has not singled itself out by any speciality, and, like all the outside lines, is wholly dependent upon the more favoured ones.

No. 28.

DR. OF PLACE'S WHITE TURK (Dam of Coppin Mare).

Emilius (D) has made this family famous, but nothing else of note has sprung from its ranks except Wings (O, 1825), Imperator Actæon, Dalesman, Barbillon, &c. Emilius is the only high class sire in the line, which is evidently going to the wall, and is poorly represented in last vol. of Stud Book.

No. 29.

A NATURAL BARB MARE (Dam of a Basset Arabian Mare).

One Oaks (Landscape) and two Legers (Ashton and Rowton). This family is dying out apparently. In Australia it is known as the Lady Emily family; Reprieve, Pardon, and Queen's Head (by Yattendon) brought the line into some prominence a few years back.

No. 30.

DR. OF DUC DE CHARTRES' HAWKER.

Two Derbies, by Archduke and Paris, full brothers (by Sir Peter). Stamford and Delpini are the best known horses of a line which is poorly represented to-day. Stamford was a full brother to Archduke and Paris, the three being from Horatia by Eclipse, and she was bred for ten years consecutively to Sir Peter. There was an interval of five years between the two Derby winners, Paris being the tenth foal to Sir Peter.

No. 31.

DICK BURTON'S MARE (sometimes called a Barb Mare).

If this line really had a pure origin, it has failed to fulfil expectation. The only classic winners are Ruler (L) in 1780 and Fazzoletto (2000) in 1856. It will be recognised of late years by Cape Flyaway, and that good mare Canezou, by Melbourne (1), dam by Velocipede (3), he by Blacklock (2).

No. 32.

BARB MARE (Dam of Dodsworth).

It is very evident (as in case of 31) that the pure origin availed nothing in this case, for we find only one Oaks winner. Niké (1797, by Alexander. The line will be better identified by horses of a later date—Caster, Barbarian, Fitz-Gladiator, and Arthur Wellesley.

It is quite probable that Nos. 29, 31, and 32 were not of pure Eastern descent at bottom. It has been a loose fashion from all time to designate a filly of first cross by an Arab stallion as "an Arab" amongst men who do not breed to race and attach no value to pedigree, and in early days the mistake might easily have crept into records unwittingly.

No. 33.

SISTER TO HONEYCOMB PUNCH.

This line can only claim a solitary Derby winner, Sergeant in 1784. Dungannon is from this line, which has almost died out

No. 34.

DR. OF HAUTBOY (Dam of Coneyskin's Mare, progenitor of Hutton's Daphne).

Antonio in 1819 and Birmingham in 1830 placed two Legers to the credit of this family, not otherwise distinguished.

The foregoing numbers include all the classic winners of the Derby, Oaks, and Leger, excepting the first (?) Leger winner, Allabaculia, whose pedigree is not given in the Stud Book. There are a few well known English, American, and Australian horses from families that have never produced a classic winner in England, though they trace to English Stud Book, and for this latter reason I have included them in a non-classic list to follow, so that the horses of the line may also be identified by a figure.

No. 35.

DR. OF BUSTLER (the Dam and Grandam of Byerly Turk and Bay Bolton Mares).

It is quite possible this Bustler mare is identical with the "Dr. of Bustler, dam of Dr. of Byerly Turk," forming tap root of the No. 8 line, but in the absence of actual proof they must be classed as separate families. The prominent horses from this family are Haphazard, Bustard (by Castrel); Newcourt, Consul, Battledore, Le Marechal.

No. 36.

DR. OF CURWIN'S BAY BARB.

From this mare Economist descends. Economist is the only horse of note in the family. He was a son of Whisker (1) from Floranthe, by Octavian (8), the latter by Stripling (2), and he by Phenomenon (2), showing once more that the outside lines *must* be crossed with Nos. 1, 2, 3, and 4 to ensure success.

No. 37.

SISTER TO OLD MERLIN.

Dr. Syntax and Little Red Rover trace to this mare, but the family is gradually getting extinct.

No 38.

THWAITS' DUN MARE.

I can find no horses of any note, save Pot-8-os, in this line, which speaks volumes for the potency of Eclipse as a sire. Few better horses than Pot-8-os ever carried a saddle. Thwaits' Dun Mare was evidently not a thoroughbred, judging by her colour.

No. 39.

BONNY BLACK (from a Dr. of Persian Stallion.

Splendora, imported to Australia, and her descendants, including a high class horse, Dagworth, by Yattendon. I know of nothing attaining any prominence in England from this family during this century.

No. 40.

A ROYAL MARE (Dam of Brimmer Mare).

Boston, sire of Lexington (Am.), traces to this mare.

No. 41.

A GRASSHOPPER MARE (Dam of Dr. of Hartley's Blind Horse).

From this mare come Bagot and Portrait.

No. 42.

A SPANKER MARE (Dam of Mare by Pulleine's Arabian).

Oiscan, Cestus, and Theobald are from this line.

No. 43.

NATURAL BARB MARE (presented by Emperor of Morocco).

Balfe and Underhand come under this family.

CHAPTER IV.

A CLASSIFICATION OF THE FAMILIES.

Having now dealt with the several families in detail, and touched upon their specialities and peculiarities, and identified each by a figure, I propose to class them under three general headings of *running*, *sire*, and *outside* lines. The running lines Nos. 1, 2, 3, 4, and 5, are entitled to this distinction by reason of their commanding position as classic winners. As before shown, 1, 2, and 3 have won respectively forty-two, forty-four, and forty-two each of the three great classic events. No. 4 comes next with twenty-eight wins, and No. 5 follows with twenty-four wins. The nearest approach to these are Nos. 6 and 7. The former has seventeen wins, the latter fourteen. No. 6's winnings were gained in the early days by Diomed, Eleanor, Priam, &c., but the last fifty years it has been, with the exception of Musjid (winner of the Derby in 1859), unfruitful as regards classic wins, and is not worthy to be included as a *running* line. No. 7 has also been barren of winners (bar Donovan, Derby and Leger) since West Australian's year, 1853. The sire lines **3, 8, 11, 12, 14,** have well earned this distinction, seeing that nearly all the successful sires of the world since, and including Eclipse, have come direct from mares in these families, or, where not actually in these lines, their *sires* or *dams' sires* were from one of these five families. Where there is any exception to the above the stallion so bred has only been successful when mated with mares from sire families, or having a strong inbreeding in their top removes to sire figures, showing very plainly that great sires cannot be bred without their aid. In order to better show the amount of sire blood and its position in a pedigree, I have thought it better to mark the sire figures in heavy type. The *outside* figures include all the numbers outside of the five running and five sire figures. Because they occupy this position it must not be supposed that they play no part in pedigrees. Many of the phenomenal racehorses of turf history trace back to these outside families in female line. It will be shown, however, that in all such cases there has been an unusually strong inbreeding to the *running* families and sire also. Nor can I discover a single instance in this century of any great racehorse inbred to outside lines alone in the three top removes, and without the aid of the running and sire families close up. Judged by the laws of heredity this is easy of explanation. From the obscurity of their origin it is to be presumed there must have been numerous crosses of coarse strains somewhere prior to their first being recorded in the Stud Book, consequently, when bred, even at the present day *too closely* to themselves, the tendency is to reproduce the original parent stock of the family, be it of pony, Flemish, or coaching origin, &c.

The same natural law would apply to the pure running lines of Nos. 1, 2, and 4. Though admirable as winning lines, their descendants are decided failures as sires if *inbred to themselves* (without strong infusions of **3, 8, 11, 12, 14**), because this inbreeding would tend also to reproduce the characteristics of their *pure* Eastern origin ; and, just as no stud master to-day would put an Arab stallion to his mares, hoping to get as *immediate* results high class racers, so in like manner should he avoid, as a sire, any race-horse *very closely inbred* to these three pure lines, 1, 2, 4, in his main top branches. Pursuing the same line of reasoning to its logical conclusion, whatever excellent qualities are possessed by the sire families, which make them so valuable in that capacity, will certainly be strengthened and invigorated by inbreeding closely to one another ; and, indeed, as we shall see, most of the notably good sires in the Stud Book have been bred in this fashion. It will be readily understood by students of pedigree that in the early stages of gathering together all the present elements of the English racehorse, individual members of the sire and running families were rarely met with in any pedigree, and scarcely ever in profusion. Nowadays it is quite common (comparatively speaking) to find in one pedigree a meeting of several members of the same family. It is necessary to draw the stud master's attention to this fact, so that he may more fully appreciate the great value of certain old names or landmarks in the Stud Book, notably Eclipse, Blacklock, Whalebone, and Sir Hercules.

This "throwing back" in shape and markings to previous ancestors is a subject that has not met with the attention it deserves at the hands of the vast majority of breeders, perhaps for the reason that so few have at their command portraits of turf and stud celebrities to make the necessary comparisons. While in England in 1882 and 1883 I visited most of the stud farms, and had very little difficulty in identifying the strains of blood or parentage of most mares by their general appearance and colour. While looking over the Burghley Paddocks stud, the owner remarked (after I had identified the parentage of several mares), " I think I can safely say you will not detect the breeding of this mare," pointing to a brown. My answer was, " She is too young to be a Wild Dayrell, but she probably is by a son of his," and in fact she turned out to be from a Wild Dayrell mare, though got by an Arab or son of a lately imported Arab, which shows how difficult it is to eradicate family traits. Many of the Wild Dayrells I had previously seen in Australia and England had the colour and characteristics of this particular mare. I had with me in California a copy of " Portraits of Celebrated Racehorses," and a friend, Mr. Simeon Reed, declared that quite a new field was opened up to him in horse study, and certainly Herring's and Hall's portraits enable one to make comparisons between the horses of to-day and those of the past, in a way that materially aids the stud master in deciding to what ancestor his colt has strained back. One point is most noticeable, viz., the general *superiority in looks* of the members of the sire families, or those in-bred strongly to them, from Eclipse downwards. To men who are familiar with these old portraits I need only mention such names as Marske (**8**), Eclipse (**12**), Sedbury (**12**) (described as " a horse of exquisite beauty, of great justness of shape and form, and the best horse of his size "), Pot-8-os (38), by Eclipse (**12**) by Marske (**8**) by Squirt (**11**; also Gohanna (24) by Eclipse, Orville (**8**), Walton (7) by Sir Peter (**3**), Whalebone and Whisker (1) from Penelope by Trumpator (**14**) by Conductor (**12**); Tramp (**3**), Filho da Puta (**12**), Sultan (**8**) (a magnificent looking horse), Emilius (29) by Orville (**8**), Lottery (**11**) by Tramp (**3**) (a beautifully proportioned horse), Memnon (**11**) (most symmetrical), Mameluke (**3**) by Partisan (1), Venison (**11**) by Partisan (very handsome), Birdcatcher (**11**) (hardly to be improved upon), Touchstone and Macaroni (both **14**), The Flying Dutchman (**3**), Velocipede (**3**), Melbourne (1) by Hy. Clinker (**8**), his Dam by Cervantes (**8**), Kingston (the beautiful) (**12**), Stockwell and Rataplan (**3**), Blair Athol (9) by Stockwell from Blink Bonny by Melbourne (above); Adventurer (**12**), Weatherbit (**12**), Newminster (**8**), St. Simon (the elegant) (**11**), Isonomy (19) by Sterling (**12**), from a Stockwell mare, Galopin (**3**), Hampton (9) from Lady Langden by Kettledrum (**3**), by Rataplan (**3**); Sterling (**12**) (by Oxford, (**2**), Favonius (**3**), Kingcraft (**11**), (a beautifully turned horse), Ayrshire (**8**), Ormonde (16) from Dr. of Macaroni (**14**), Melton (**8**), Isinglass (**3**), Springfield (**12**). In America: Leamington (**14**), Lexington (**12**), American Eclipse (**3**), Tammany (**14**), Salvator (**12**), Australian (**11**), Maxim (**12**). In Australia: Sir Hercules (**3**), Maribyrnong (**3**), Richmond (**3**), Tros (**12**), Yattendon (17) by Sir Hercules (**3**) from Tros mare, Grand Flaneur (**14**), Chester (**8**), Australian Peer by Darebin (**14**), dam by Macaroni (**14**) (a very handsome horse), (Musket (**3**), by Toxophilite (**3**). From the above list one can hardly pick an animal that did not possess either very good looks or great individuality and masculine appearance.

CHAPTER V.

SIRES.

WITH sires (as indeed with racehorses) it may be truly said that "many are called but few chosen." To-day in England, with an annual output of over 1500 yearling colts, the number of first-class sires can be counted on one's fingers. That so few succeed at stud work is partly due to the fact that very few get a fair show, as no public breeder can afford to patronise third and fourth class race-horses. The result is, that the successful dams are sent to the most fashionable horses, and outside sires are neglected, or, where used, have to be content with third, fourth, and fifth class mares. While there is no getting away from this truth, that superior performance on the racecourse, allied to undeniably good looks and soundness, are the first and most desirable requisites in a sire, it does not at all follow that a combination of these qualities will ensure his success at the stud, and in proof of this we need go no further than Gladiateur in England and The Barb in Australia, both "horses of a century," and both stud failures. Against this we find many instances of indifferent performers on the turf turning out successful at the stud. No stud master, however, with his wits about him, would, without some tangible proof of his ability, think of breeding from an indifferent performer, while access could be had to a Derby or Leger winner, combining fashionable strains with symmetry, temper, and soundness; and even then, with these advantages thrown in, half the success lies in the mating. Many scores of what are called third and fourth class horses perforce become hunting sires really for lack of a chance of being *properly mated.*

Having satisfied oneself as to looks and performance, the next step in choosing a sire is to select a horse tracing in male descent to the Darley Arabian, if we expect continuous success. That there have been scores of high-class sires bred from the other two lines of Byerly Turk and Godolphin Barb (in other words Herod and Matchem) goes without saying, yet "the long result of time" has shown that these two lines are gradually but surely going to the wall, or only exist by mating with mares *very strongly inbred* to Eclipse. Yet, as stated elsewhere, I cannot believe that this superiority of the latter line was altogether due to the Darley Arabian, and am far more disposed to think that the dominant position of the line was brought about by the extraordinary combination of *female* lines in the pedigree of Eclipse. The word extraordinary is used advisedly, because of the rarity of individuals of the *sire families*, **3**, **8**, **11**, **12**, **14**, about the time of Eclipse's birth. I cannot find any other horse of his time so favoured, and, indeed, very few at the present day. The table at end of book shows the position the three great male lines bear to one another at the present day.

This table was compiled by Mr. William Allison, of the International Horse Agency and Exchange, London, and through his kind permission I am allowed to insert it here. It shows the number of winners produced in 1893, and the number and value of stakes won respectively by the descendants of male branches of Eclipse, Herod, and Matchem, on English courses. It speaks so eloquently for itself, that comment is needless.

I will now endeavour to show by a comparison of the pedigrees of Eclipse, Herod, and Matchem, *why*, in a very great measure, this result has been brought about.

Appended are the figures of Eclipse and his two great rivals for supremacy in this struggle for sire honours. As on the turf, so it has been at the stud, a case of "Eclipse first and the rest nowhere."

ECLIPSE.

SPILETTA. (12)   **MARSKE. (8)**

MOTHER WESTERN.   REGULUS. (11)   DR. OF   SQUIRT. (11)

Bartlett's Childers (6)

Dr. of

Dr. of

Dr. of

Hutton's Blacklegs +

Bay Bolton (37)

Grey Hautboy by **Hautboy** (above).

Godolphin Barb.

Grey Robinson

Smith's son of Snake.

Dr. of

Betty Leedes

Sister to Old Country Wench.

Dr. of

Bey Turk (Hutton's).

Dr. of

Makeless.

Dr. of

Fox Cub (6)

Dr. of

Bald Galloway (15)

Sister to Old Country Wench (above).

Lister's Snake (see above).

Dr. of

Lord Darcy's Old Montague.

Dr. of

Darcy Arabian.

Old Careless

Sister to Leedes

Lister's Snake by Lister's Turk (Dr. of **Hautboy**).

Hautboy

Chuney's Sister.

Coneyskins

Dr. of

Old Club Foot by **Hautboy** (above).

Dr. of

Brimmer.

Dr. of

Chaney (11) by **Hautboy** (above).

Dr. of

Dr. of

Coneyskins (above).

Hutton's Grey Barb.

Dr. of

St. Victor's Barb.

Dr. of

Lister's Snake.

Dr. of **Hautboy** (above)

Dr. of Akaster Turk.

Dr. of Pulleine's ch. Arabian.

Brimmer

Dr. of Royal Mare.

{ **Spanker.** (6)
{ Barb Mare.

Leedes Arabian.

Dr. of { **Spanker.** (6)
{ **Spanker's** dam.

Darcy's White Turk.

Royal Mare.

Hautboy (above).

Miss Darcy's Ped Mare from Sedbury Royal Mare.

Lister's Turk.

Dr. of Jigg

{ Byerly Turk.
{ Dr. of **Spanker.**

Dimond.

Sister to Old Merlin by Bustler.

Leedes Arabian.

Spanker (6) above.

Spanker's dam.

Hutton's Royal Colt. (11)

Dr. of

Grey Whynot.

Dr. of Royal Mare.

{ Holmsley Turk.
{ Sedbury Royal Mare.

Byerly Turk.

Dr. of Bustler.

{ Darcy's Yellow Turk.
{ **Hautboy** (above).

{ Brimmer
{ Royal Mare.

E

KING HEROD.

CYPRON. (26)   TARTAR. +

SELIMA.   BLAZE. +   MELORA.   PARTNER. (9)

Jigg + ... { Byerly Turk.
           { Dr. of ...... { Dam unknown.

Sister to Mixbury ... { Curwin's Bay Barb.
                { Dr. of ....

Spanker (6) { Darcy's Yellow Turk.
          { Old Morocco Mare ...... { Morocco Barb.
                       { Old Bald Peg ... { Arab.
                                  { Barb Mare

Curwin's Old Spot.
Lowther's Barb.
Vintner Mare.

Flying Childers (6) { Darley Arabian.
          { Betty Leedes

Milkmaid ...... { Dr. of ......

Fox (6) ...... { Bay Peg

Chnuny (11) ... { Hautboy ...... { Darcy's White Turk.
               { Miss Darcy's Pet Mare from Sedbury Royal Mare
               { Leedes Arabian.
               { Royal Mare.

CY. Bald Peg ...... { Leedes Arabian.
            { **Spanker's Dam** (above)

Why Not (15) ...... { Fenwick's Barb.
           { Royal Mare.

Old Snail ...... { Wilkinson's Mare ...... { Wilkinson's Bay Arabian.
               { Natural Barb Mare.

Dr. of ...... { Shield's Galloway + (pedigree unknown).
          { Dam unknown.

Old Careless ...... { **Spanker** (6) (above).
           { Barb Mare.

Sister to Leedes (Cream Cheeks) ... { Leedes Arabian.
               { Dr. of ...... { **Spanker** (above).
                              { **Spanker's dam.**

Grey Grantham ...... { Brownlow Turk.
          { Dam unknown.

Dr. of ...... { Duke of Rutland's Black Barb.
          { Dr. of Bright's Roan.

Bethell's Arabian.

Graham's Champion ...... { Harper's Arabian

Dr. of ...... { Dr. of Old Hautboy ...... { Darcy's White Turk.
               { Royal Mare.

Dr. of ...... { Darley Arabian (above).
          { Dr. of Old Merlin by Bustler, son of Helmsley Turk.

MATCHEM.

SISTER TO MISS PARTNER. (4) CADE. (6).

BROWN FAREWELL. PARTNER. (9) ROXANA. GOD. BARB.

```
Bald Galloway (15) ...... { St. Victor Barb.
                          { Grey Why Not ... { Old Why Not ... { Fenwick's Barb.
                                                               { Royal Mare.
Sister to Chaunter ...... { Akaster Turk.
                          { Croun Cheeks      { Lawtin Arabian.
                            (Sister to second { Dr. of { Spanker ...... { Yellow Turk.
                            dam of Childers)           {               { Old Morocco Mare.
                                                       { Spanker's dam (see below).

Jigg+ ... { Byerly Turk.
          { Dr. of { Spanker ...... { Yellow Turk (Darcy's).
            { Dam unknown           { Old Morocco Mare ... { Morocco Barb.
                                                           { Old Bald Peg ... { An Arab.
                                                                              { Barb Mare.
Sister to Mixbury ...... { Curwin's Bay Barb.
                         { Dr. of { Curwin's Old Spot by Selaby Turk.
                                  { Lawther's Barb.
                                  { Dr. of { Vintner Mare.

Makeless+ ...... { Oglethorpe Arabian.
                 { Dam not known.
Dr. of ...... { Brimmer.
              { Dr. of { Yellow Turk (Darcy's).
                       { Royal Mare.
              { Trumpet's dam ... { Place's White Turk.
                                  { Dr. of { Dodsworth. (32)
                                           { Layton Barb Mare.
```

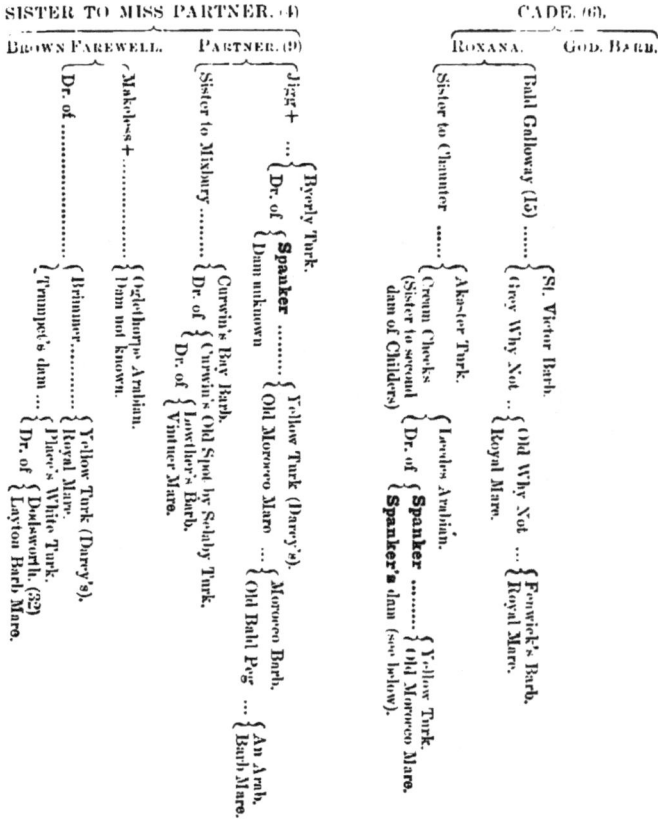

The table of Herod shows that he had no sire blood in his pedigree except Clumsey, and therefore could not sire racehorses, except from dams, either direct from the No. **3, 8, 11, 12, 14** lines, or bearing strains of these close to the surface. Failing sire lines, the

E 2

CYPRON. (26)   HEROD.   TARTAR. +

SELINA   BLAZE. +   MELIORA.   PARTNER. (9)

UNDERNEATH ARE THE PEDIGREES OF SOME OF HEROD'S BEST RACEHORSES.

Weazle.

HEROD. (26)
Dr. of .... (39)
- Eclipse. **(12 8. 11)**
- Dr. of
  - Brilliant by Crab (9) by Alcock Arabian.
  - Dr. of Shepherd's Crab (4) by Crab (9) by Alcock Arabian.

Evergreen.

Angelica **(3)**
- Snap (1) by Snip (9) by Childers.
- Dr. of
  - Regulus **(11)** by God. Barb.
  - Dr. of Bartlett's Childers. (6)

Highflyer. / Neverbeaten.

Rachel (13)
- Blank. (15)
- Dr. of Regulus. **(11)**

Highflyer's greatest son was Sir Peter Teazle, dam in the **(3)** line.

Another good son of Highflyer was Traveller, dam from the **(11)** family.

Woodpecker. / Sire of Buzzard.

Miss Ramsden (1)
- Cade (6) by God. Barb.
- Dr. of Lonsdale Bay Arab.

Woodpecker's lack of sire blood demanded a return through the dam of his greatest son Buzzard. **(3)**

Calash. / Dam of Whiskey.

Teresa (2) ...
- Matchem (4) by Cade (6) by God. Barb.
- Dr. of Regulus **(11)** by God. Barb.

Whiskey was by Saltram (7) by Eclipse. **(12, 8. 11)**

Phenomenon. / Leger, 1783.

Frenzy (2) ....
- Eclipse. **(12, 8, 11)**
- Dr. of Engineer. (36)

Bridget. / Oaks, 1776.

Jemima **(8)** ......
- Snap 1 by Snip (9) by Childers. (6)
- Dr. of
  - Matchem (4) by Cade (6) by God. Barb.
  - Dr. of Regulus. **(11)**

Maid of the Oaks. / Oaks, 1783.

Rarity **(3)** ...
- Matchem (4) by Cade (6) by God. Barb.
- Snapdragon ...
  - Snap (1) by Snip (9) by Childers.
  - Dr. of Regulus **(11)** by God. Barb.

Coelia. / Oaks, 1784.

Proserpine, sister to Eclipse. **(12, 8, 11)**

N.B.—Whenever the name of Eclipse occurs I propose to group the three figures of his dam **(12)**, his sire **(8)**, and grandsire. **(11)**

Faith. / Oaks, 1781.

Curiosity ... **(3)**
- Snap (1) by Snip (9) by Childers. (6)
- Miss Belsea
  - Regulus **(11)** by Godolphin Barb.
  - Dr. of Bartlett's Childers. (6)

Justice was full brother to Faith above.

+ Denotes a family which has never won a classic race.

alternative would be to mate him with mares in the *best* running lines to supply his deficiency in that respect also. I have in the preceding table given the dam's pedigree by itself in each case to save repeating Herod ; and from the examples of his best racehorses, readers will have an opportunity of judging for themselves whether I am right as regards his marked dependence on the Nos. 1, 2, **3**, 4, **8, 11, 12**, and **14** families.

Other good sons of Herod were Bagot (11), from a Matchem (1) mare ; Florizel (5), from Dr. of Cygnet (6), by God. Barb ; Fortitude 1), from a Snap (1) mare ; Rover (afterwards Tom Tug) (1), from Legacy, by Young Snip (1), from Snap's dam by Fox (7), &c. Turning again to the table, it will be seen that those mates which were weakest in sire blood (Teresa and Miss Ramsden) were strongest in running strains ; also that their respective produce, Calash and Woodpecker, only succeeded with mates strong in sire blood, viz., Faltram (son of Eclipse, **12**), and Misfortune (**3**) the dam of Buzzard.

Turn now to Matchem (next page), without sire strains, and it will be seen that the same rule applies. He was better off than Herod in coming direct from one of the good running lines 4, but was not inbred to them, and, like Herod, was partial to 1, 2, and 4, as well as **3, 8, 11, 12**, and **14.**

If my assumption is correct that a stallion without sire figures in his three top removes should be mated with mares from sire families, the logical inference is that a horse so rich in sire strains as Eclipse did not necessarily require the sire element in his mates, and would unite well with dams from running and outside families. The following table (p. 55) bears out this view to the letter.

This list of sons and daughters of Eclipse is selected pretty much in their order of excellence as sires and racehorses. It must not be inferred, however, that Eclipse could not sire winners from sire lines, as we find Everlasting (dam of Skyscraper and Goldfinch) was in No. **3** line from a Snap (1) mare, from Miss Belsea, by Regulus (**11**),

MATCHEM.

CADE. (6)

GOD. BARB.

DR. OF

Bald Galloway. (15)

MISS PARTNER. (4)

PARTNER. (9)

Jigg. +

Dr. of

Makeless. +

Dam of Bagot.	Marotte.	**MATCHEM.** (4)
		Dr. of (41) .... { Traveller. (25) / Dr. of Hartley's Blind Horse. (41)
Fourth Dam of Touchstone.	Mayfly.	"
		Dr. of (14) .... { Ancaster Starling. (2) / Dr. of Grasshopper (2) by Crab. (9)
Dam of Matron.	Maiden.	"
		Dr. of (24) { Squirt (11) / Dr. of .... } { Childers. (6) Mogul (15) by / God. Barb. } Maiden had several noted brothers and sisters, Xanthos, Enigma, Riddle, Purity, and Rasselas
Second Dam of Whitelock.	Atalanta.	"
		Lass of the Mill (2) { Oroonoko. (7) / Dr. of ... { Old Traveller. / Miss Makeless by son of Greyhound Barb.
In-bred to Hartley's Blind Horse.	Giantess.	"
		Dr. of ... (6) { Babraham (15) { God. Barb. / Dr. of Hartley's Blind Horse (41)* by Holderness Turk. } / Dr. of Hartley's Blind Horse (41) by Holderness Turk.
Dam of Calash.	Teresa.	"
		Brown Regulus (2).. { Regulus (11) / Sister to Starling ... { Bay Bolton. (37) / Dr. of Partner. (9)
Second dam of Bridget (Oaks).	Matchem Middleton. (3)	"
		Miss Middleton { Regulus (11) by God Barb. / Bay Camilla ... { Bay Bolton. (37) / Dr. of Bartlet's Childers. (6)
Dam of Stargazer.	Miss West.	"
		Sister to Favorite (5) { Regulus (11) by God. Barb. / Young Ebony by { Crab. (9) / Ebony by Childers. 6
His best Sons.	Conductor and Alfred.	"
		Dr. of (12) .... { Snap (1) (below). / Dr. of Cullen Arabian.
Dam of Maid of the Oaks.	Rarety.	"
		Snapdragon (3) { Snap (1) by Snip (9) by Childers. (6) / Dr. of Regulus (11) by God. Barb.

* I have stated at page 25 that it is more than probable Grey Royal, grandam of Hartley's Blind Horse, was identical with the family of (11), tracing to the Sedbury Royal Mare; and the fact of that great mare, Giantess, being in-bred to the Blind Horse, as also that the blood suited Matchem, strongly confirms that opinion.

ECLIPSE. **(12, 8, 11)**

A pedigree table with left-side vertical labels and branching lineage on the right.

Left vertical labels (bottom to top / stacked):
- MOTHER WESTERN.
- SPILLETA. **(12)**
- ECLIPSE.
- REGULUS. **(11)**
- DR. OF
- MARSKE. **(8)**
- SQUIRT. **(11)**

Name	Dam	Lineage
Laura.	Dr. of .... (2)	Locust by Crab. (9) Dr. of Cade (6) by God. Barb.
Soldier (great racehorse).	Dr. of .... (9)	Omar (10) by God. Barb. Dr. of .... { Starling. Dr. of God. Barb.
Frenzy.	Dr. of 2	Engineer (36) by Sampson + by Blaze + by Childers. (6) Dr. of Blank (15) by God. Barb.
Miss Hervey. (dam of Haphazard).	Clio (35)	Y. Cade (4) { Cade (6) by God. Barb. Dam of Matchem. (4) Dr. of Starling. (28)
King Fergus.	Polly (6)	Black and All Black (7) by Crab. (9) Fanny .... { Tartar + by Partner. (9) Dr. of Starling. 28
Don Quixote and **Alexander.**	Grecian Princess (9)	William's Forester (2) by Forester. + Dr. of Coalition colt + by God. Barb.
Volunteer, Mercury, Queen Mab.	Dr. of .... (9)	Tartar + by Partner. (9) Dr. of .... { Mogul (15) by God. Barb. Dr. of Sweepstakes.
Joe Andrews.	Amaranda (4) ..	Omnium (9) by Snap. (1) Cloudy ...... { Blank (15) by God. Barb. Dr. of Crab. (9)
Sargeant Derby 1784).	Aspasia 33 ...	Herod. (26) Doris .... { Blank (15) by God. Barb. Helen { Spectator. 1) Dr. of God. Barb.
Saltram Derby). **Annette** (Oaks).	Virago (7)	Snap (1) by Snip (15) by Childers. (6) Dr. of Regulus **(12** by God. Barb.
Y. Eclipse Derby 1781).	Juno (6)	Spectator (1) { Crab. (9) Dr. of Partner. 9 Horatia { Blank 15 by God. Barb. Dr. of Childers. 6
Pot-8-os.	Sportsmistress 38	Sportsman + by Cade (6) by God. Barb. Golden Locks { Oroonoko. (6) Dr. of Crab. (9)

but the figures Nos. 1, 2, **3**, 4, and 5, and the outside lines, are what suited him before any other blood, though he made some great hits with the 9 family.   It has been a practice amongst students to trace the three great male lines no further than Eclipse, Herod, and Matchem, because they were in a measure contemporary, and were recognised as the *principal* and most *notable* individuals of each line.   In the selection, therefore, of these three pedigrees as a test of the Figure system, it will be understood that I do not make this selection to suit the figures, but solely for the reasons given above, and students who take an interest in pedigree will do well to study closely the examples given of Eclipse's principal successes, as also those of Herod and Matchem, and note the curious regularity exhibited by each horse in mating best with the *essential* figures absent from his own pedigree, but *without which successful racehorses cannot be bred*.   In other words, a mating of opposites.   It cannot fail also to strike the reader how often the name of Snap (1) occurs in the best of the old pedigrees.   This has been already commented upon by Col. Upton in his interesting work, "Newmarket and Arabia."

Yet good as Snap was he has died out in the male line, and evidently not from lack of opportunity, for such a good horse must have been favoured with every chance.   Such also was the fate of Eclipse's great contemporary, Goldfinder, of the No. 1 line.   These two giants retired from the turf unbeaten, but unfortunately never measured strides.   Yet Goldfinder must have been largely patronised by breeders.   Like his sire Snap he was bred away from sire figures, and though he lived till a ripe old age has left no mark behind him. To return to Matchem.   It will be seen that he was fortunate from the start in being mated with Conductor's dam (**12**), and Conductor was equally favoured by meeting with the dam of Trumpator (**14**). This excellent start gave the male line of God. Barb such an impetus that its existence was assured.   This was rendered doubly so by the mating of Trumpator with Prunella of the No. 1 family.   In view of the prominent part Whalebone and his brothers and sisters play

in first-class pedigrees, it will not be out of place just here to trace
the ramifications of Whalebone's strains of blood. I have just spoken
of Snap's excellence as shown in the number of renowned mares
sired by him — such as Angelica, Curiosity, Elfrida, Hyaena, Lisette,
Papillon (dam of Sir Peter), Promise (dam of Prunella), &c. no
less than sixty odd mares were sired by him and recorded in Vol. I.

That he was a great horse goes without saying, seeing that he
hailed from such a wonderful running family on his dam's side,
while his sire Snip (9) was a son of Childers (6). Indeed, Snap, as
far as I can find, was the result of the first junction of the No. 1 line
with Darley Arabian line, nor can I find any other (with the exception of Goldfinder) notable meeting of these two great representative
female and male lines until they again coalesced in Penelope and
Prunella, though the medium of Waxy and Pot-8-os, and produced
Whalebone and Parasol. In Whalebone most of the best elements
of the Stud Book seem to have been united. His dam, Penelope,
was from the No. 1 line, and her sire, Trumpator (**14**) (by Conductor,
12), represented the very best form of Godolphin next to Regulus
(**11**), who appears as the sire of Highflyer's second dam (Highflyer
being the sire of Prunella); and Highflyer (**13**) was certainly the
best of the Byerly Turk line prior to his son, Sir Peter (**3**). In the
dam of Whalebone, therefore, we have the then two best representatives of Byerly Turk and Godolphin, viz., Highflyer and Trumpator,
with two strains of Snap (1) as well, and one Regulus (**11**). All that
was needed was a mating with the best form of Eclipse. This was
happily accomplished by crossing Penelope with Waxy, a grandson
of Eclipse (**12**), whose sire, Marske (**8**), and grandsire, Squirt (**11**)
were both in sire lines, and Spiletta, dam of Eclipse, was by
Regulus (**11**). Maria, dam of Waxy, was by Herod from Lisette
by Snap (1), which grand blood was thus *nicked* by the two strains
in Penelope, and probably as much as any other factor contributed
to the brilliant success of Whalebone and his brothers and sisters.
The figure 4 occurs twice in Whalebone, while the absence of Nos. 2

and **3** is conspicuous. The pedigree is worth reproducing here, if only to show the close inbreeding in places to the Godolphin Barb and Darley Arabian.

We have seen by the pedigree table of Eclipse that he was rich

WHALEBONE.

PENELOPE. (1)			WAXY. (18)	
PRUNELLA.	TRUMPATOR. **(14)**		MARIA.	POT-8-OS. (38).

Promise ... $\begin{cases} \textbf{Snap} \text{ (1) by Snip (9) by Childers (6) by Darley Arabian.} \\ \text{Julia ....} \begin{cases} \text{Blank (15) by Godl. Barb.-} \\ \text{Dr. of Partner (9) by Jigg + by Byerly Turk.} \end{cases} \end{cases}$

Highflyer. (13) $\begin{cases} \text{Herod (26)} \\ \text{(see above)} \\ \text{Rachel ....} \end{cases} \begin{cases} \text{Tartar+ by Partner (9) by Jigg + by Byerly Turk.} \\ \text{Cypron by Blaze+ by Childers (6) by Darley Arabian.} \\ \text{Blank (15) by Godl. Barb.-} \\ \text{Dr. of Regulus (11) by Godl. Barb.-} \end{cases}$

Brunette ... $\begin{cases} \text{Squirrel 4) by Traveller (24) by Partner (9) by Jigg + by} \\ \text{Byerly Turk.} \\ \text{Dove ....} \begin{cases} \text{Matchless+ by Godl. Barb.-} \\ \text{Dr. of Starling. (28)} \end{cases} \end{cases}$

Conductor (12) $\begin{cases} \text{Matchem (4) by Cade (6) by Godl. Barb.-} \\ \text{Dr. of } \textbf{Snap} \text{ (1) by Snip (9) by Childers (6) by Darley Arabian.} \end{cases}$

Lisette ... $\begin{cases} \textbf{Snap} \text{ (1) by Snip (9) by Childers (6) by Darley Arabian.} \\ \text{Miss Windsor by Godl. Barb.-} \end{cases}$

Herod (26) $\begin{cases} \text{Tartar+ by Partner (9) by Jigg + by Byerly Turk.} \\ \text{Cypron by Blaze+ by Childers (6) by Darley Arabian.} \end{cases}$

Dr. of Sportsman .... $\begin{cases} \text{Cade (6) by Godl. Barb.-} \\ \text{Golden Locks by Oroonoko. (7)} \end{cases}$

Eclipse (12) $\begin{cases} \text{Marske (8) by Squirt (12) by Childers (6) by Darley Arabian.} \\ \text{Spiletta by Regulus (11) by Godl. Barb.-} \end{cases}$

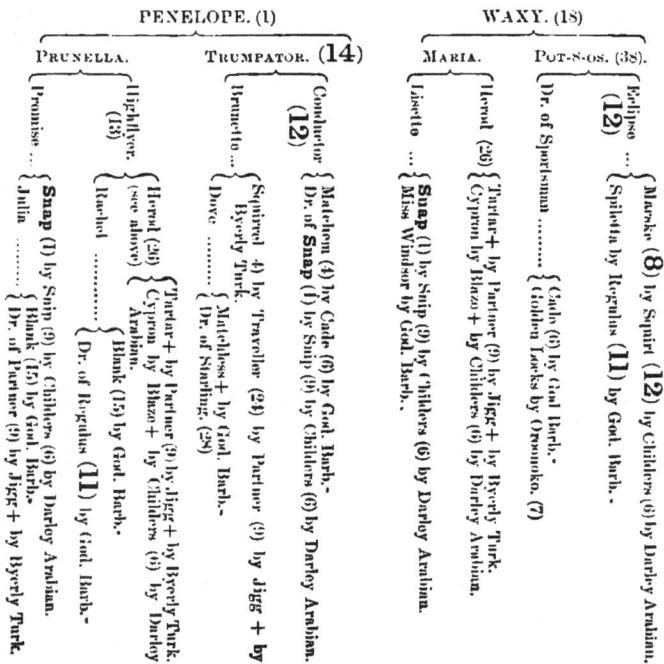

in sire figures, and proved one of the greatest successes at the stud in turf history, though as a racehorse he would probably have had to play second fiddle to the great French horse Gladiateur. Yet the latter, when relegated to stud work, turned out a rank failure. In most respects he seemed destined to have a bright career as a sire.

He was a wonderful performer at all distances, a direct descendant of Eclipse through the best source, Whalebone (presuming the Emperor to have sired Monarque), his dam was by Gladiator of the Herod line, and his inbreeding was not too close. As an individual he was open to criticism perhaps, yet a shrewd man like Mr. Blenkiron thought him good enough looking to place at the head of his stud farm. Clearly the failure emanated from his pedigree table not being orthodox in some respect. It is inserted for comparison.

GLADIATEUR.

MISS GLADIATOR. (5)		MONARQUE. (19)	
TAFFRAIL.	GLADIATOR. (23)	POETESS.	THE EMPEROR. (5)
Dr. of ... { Mermau (9) by **Whalebone.** (6) / Dr. of Arlesson. (2)	**Partisan** (1) ...... { Walton, (7) / Dr. of Pot-8os. (28)	Dr. of **Whisker** (1) { Waxy. (8) / Penelope.	Dr. of Reveller (19) ...... { Comus, (28) / Rosette.
Sheet Anchor (**12**) { **Lottery, (11)** / Dr. of Matey. (6)	Pauline .... { Moses (5) by **Whalebone.** / Dr. of Selim (2)	Royal Oak (5) ...... { Catton, (2) / Dr. of Smolensko. (19)	Defence (5) .... { **Whalebone.** (1) / Dr. of Rubens. (2)

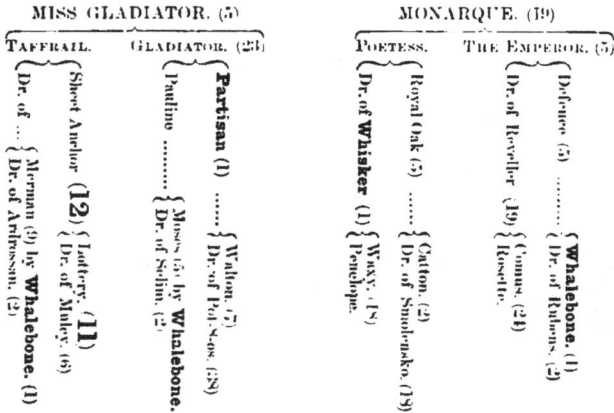

Later on, when treating of phenomenal horses, I will give this pedigree at length.

In four generations back only two sire families come into the combination, Sheet Anchor (**12**) and his sire, Lottery (**11**). There is strong inbreeding to running blood, and few outside lines, yet it would be difficult to find any such wonderful performer since the days of Herod so devoid of sire blood in his top removes. Of course, if the main lines are taken back far enough they run into Eclipse through most of the males, and that fact alone would lead

one to presuppose him a first-class sire, judged by *ordinary* methods.
But the figures prove just the contrary. All this strength of
Eclipse back in the pedigree was lost for want of *sire channels* (or
families) to *convey its influence to the surface.* And indeed the
only fashion in which this latent sire influence of Eclipse could
be so lifted up, was by mating Gladiateur with mares from (or
inbred to) those sire families (or figures) contained in his own

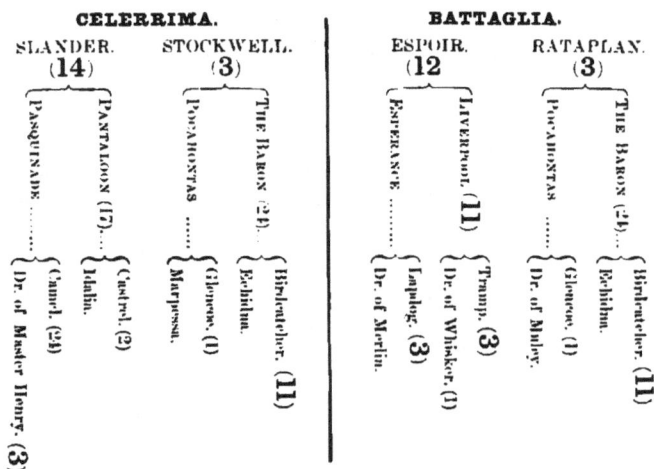

CELERRIMA.   **BATTAGLIA.**

SLANDER. (14)	STOCKWELL. (3)	ESPOIR. (12)	RATAPLAN. (3)

PASQUINADE ...... { PANTALOON (17)... { Castrel, (2) / Idalia.
{ Camel, (24) / Dr. of Master Henry. (3)

POCAHONTAS ...... { Glencoe, (1) / Marpessa.
THE BARON (29)... { Birdcatcher. (11) / Echidna.

ESPERANCE ...... { LIVERPOOL (11) { Tramp, (3) / Dr. of Whisker. (1)
{ Lapdog. (3) / Dr. of Merlin.

POCAHONTAS ...... { Glencoe, (1) / Dr. of Moisy.
THE BARON (29)... { Birdcatcher. (11) / Echidna.

pedigree some distance back. I believe I am correct in saying
that Grandmaster (Australia) and Lord Gough are the only two sons
of note he left behind him. The dams of these horses are given, and
in both cases they come *direct* from sire lines, **14** and **12.***

Celerrima, dam of Grandmaster, is (like Battaglia) rich in sire
figures. Her son has proved himself to be one of the best sires in
Australia, and his name will be handed down through more than one

* NOTE.—Highborn, by Gladiateur (5) out of Fille de l'Air (5), by Faugh-a-Ballagh (11), should be mentioned.—W. A.

son, if I mistake not. His best representative, Gibraltar (D), was dropped in the Neotsfield paddocks, near Sydney, New South Wales, and bred by the late William J. Dangar. Other good ones bred at Neotsfield by Grandmaster are Reginald, who put Commotion (a very high class horse) down three times at weight for age. Highborn, by Grandmaster, winner of Sydney Cup, two miles; Australian Cup, two and a half miles (carrying 9st. 4lb.); and subsequently won two Viceroy's Cups, Calcutta, for the Maharajah of Cooch Behar, for whom I purchased him in 1892. One of Grandmaster's sons, Ensign, a gelding, beat Carbine for the V. R. C. Derby. Paris, a 15 hands gelding, won the Metropolitan (9st. 4lb.), Caulfield Cup, and other races. Also Bungebah, a wonderful sprinter.

I have given these performances of Grandmaster's stock to show that the *racing merit* of Gladiateur only required the proper *sire* channels to bring it again into operation, and it also did good service through Lord Gough, the sire of Hasty Girl, dam of the phenomenal Bendigo. It should be noted here that Grandmaster was as conspicuous a failure on the race track as his sire was a success. Yet he far outclassed him at stud work. The case of Grandmaster also shows the wonderful pliancy of Stockwell blood, which cannot be misplaced in a pedigree, and is equally good as sire or dam blood. In this respect Australian Yattendon (a representative of Whisker line) bids fair to rival the Emperor of Stallions. He left great sires behind him in Chester (and his brothers) and Grand Flaneur (sire of Patron, V. R. C. Leger), Dainty (Oaks), and Bravo (Melbourne Cup). Yattendon's daughters can hardly be surpassed as dams. At a recent race meeting in Australia such prominent winners as Trenchant (Derby), by Trenton, Paris (Metropolitan), Lady Trenton (Sydney Cup) Brockleigh, by Goldsborough (the Epsom Stakes), Gaillardia, by Trenton, winner of many races, and others were all from Yattendon mares. I append the pedigree of Chester, his best son, a classic winner (V. R. C. Derby, A. J. C. Leger), as well as Melbourne Cup. Chester represented the Australian branch of the valuable line of Whisker, and was without doubt the best sire ever bred in Australia.

The figures demonstrate very clearly that Chester was descended from the best sire lines in the Stud Book. Sir Hercules (Aus.) is from

CHESTER.

LADY CHESTER (imp.). (8)   YATTENDON (17).

AUSTREY.   STOCKWELL. (3)   CASSANDRA.   SIR HERCULES. (3)

Zeila

Harkaway (2)

Pocahontas

The Baron (24)

Alice Grey

Tros (imp.) (12)

Paraguay (imp.)

Cap-à-pie (imp.) (5)

Emilius (28) (above) by Orville.
Apollonia by **Whisker** (1); Dr. of King Fergus. (6)

Economist (36) (above) by **Whisker.**
Dr. of Nabocklish. (?)

Marpessa

Glencoe (1)

Birdcatcher (11)

Echidna

Ross' Emigrant (4)

Priam (6)

Ally

Paradigm by Partisan. (1)

Sir Hercules (2)

The Colonel (8)

Selim (2)

Dr. of Sultan (8)

Moley (6) by Orville (8) (above).
Dr. of Marmion (28) by **Whisker.** (2)

Sultan (8) (above).
Dr. of Tramp (3)

Sir Hercules (2) (above).
Dr. of Bob Booty.

Economist (36) by **Whisker.** (1)
Dr. of Blacklock (2, 2, 1)

Pioneer (1) by **Whiskey.** (2)
Dr. of Buzzard. (3)

Emilius (28) { Orville.
Cressida by **Whisky.** (2) { Emily.

Partisan (1) (above).
Jool by Waxy. (18)

Whalebone. (1)
Dr. of Wanderer. (11)

Whisker (1) { Waxy. (18)
My Lady. { Penelope.

Selim (2) { Buzzard. (3)
      { Dr. of Alexander.

Bacchante.

Orville. (8)
Emily.

the **3** family. His sire, Cap-à-pie (5), was by The Colonel (from the **8** line), and Cap-à-pie was from a Sultan mare also (**8**). Blessed with all this sire blood, Sir Hercules was mated with Cassandra, whose sire (imp.) Tros, came from the **12** line; and, to crown matters,

Yattendon was mated with Lady Chester (imp.), by Stockwell (of **3** , she being from the **8** family herself.

This pedigree serves a double purpose, viz. to dispel the idea that it is imperative to cross the great male lines of Eclipse with those of Herod or Matchem to produce a *first class racehorse and sire.* Chester was *both*, yet, as shown, he was persistently bred to Eclipse in nearly all his main lines. A little learning is said to be dangerous, and in the matter of pedigrees superficial knowledge is very misleading. If Lady Chester's pedigree is examined carefully it will discount considerably this apparent strong inbreeding to Eclipse. Whisker, though going in male line to Eclipse, was out of Penelope, by Trumpator (of the Matchem line), her dam Prunella, by Highflyer (Herod), and Highflyer from a Blank mare (Matchem). This explains why Whalebone and Whisker blood are equally valuable on either side of a pedigree. It is best described as a *pliable* strain. Now Emilius, again, though of the Eclipse line, had perhaps more God. Barb blood in his veins (twenty-one strains) than any of his contemporaries, except Melbourne and Harkaway, both bred very much in collateral lines to Matchem and Herod also. And we can easily understand that Stockwell (inbred to Penelope) crossed upon this combination would produce a mare like Lady Chester, eminently suited for a high-class brood mare, despite her (on paper) appearance of stoutness. This case will serve also to show, as before said, that it is very misleading to trust to a superficial glance through a pedigree, nor should a horse be condemned off-hand because he does not fit into some apparently well established theory.

I would also draw the attention of the stud master to the tendency of sires, inbred on both sides to Eclipse very strongly, and through sire figures, to *perpetuate* themselves. This phase is, indeed, one of the very strongest evidences of the soundness of the *sire* theory, as demonstrated by figures. But he will have ample opportunity to judge for himself out of the numerous tabulated pedigrees I propose to give. This power of perpetuation and sire potency is more marked when main branches of the *same* family have been inbred to themselves (or to a branch of another sire family), such, for instance, as Weatherbit (**12**), by Sheet Anchor (**12**); Sterling (**12**), the latter by Oxford (**12**). The sire and dam of Salvator (Am.) are from the **12** line. Newminster (**8**) by Touchstone (**14**), has left good sons; Musket (**3**) by Toxophilite (**3**); Chester (**8**) from Dr. of Stockwell (**3**); and Chester is by Yattendon (17), by Sir Hercules (**3**); Leamington (**14**), by Faugh-a-Ballagh (**11**). On the other hand, horses bred away from sire lines do not perpetuate, such as Gladiateur (5), by Monarque (19), by The Emperor (5). In the latter case (as shown) this weakness may be remedied by mating with mares *inbred* to sire lines. See (p. 60) Grandmaster's dam Celerrima (**14**), by Stockwell (**3**); Lord Gough's dam Battaglia (**12**) by Rataplan (**3**) from Espoir, by Liverpool (**11**); or the case of Blacklock (2) (by Whitelock (2), by Hambletonian 1) only able to perpetuate by means of the sire families. His best son Voltaire (**12**) is from a great sire family; so is Velocipede (**3**), Brutandorf (**11**), Belshazzar (**11**), and Buzzard (**8**). Later on I will refer to this at length. But the foregoing examples will serve to illustrate my contention that an inbreeding to Eclipse *through sire families* will be found on one side or other of *all great sires.*

When in England, in 1883, I saw Isonomy first at Lady Emily Peel's stud, and afterwards, when he changed hands for 9000 guineas, at Albert Gate. I had (at that time) not given this sire question so much consideration as it deserved, being more impressed with the value of the *running* lines, and I freely confess that, while I fully recognised the fact that he would, by virtue of his strong sire figures, leave *more than one good son* to carry on the male line, I thought it probable that this very strong inbreeding to the comparatively outside families of 19 and 12 might militate against his chances of proving a good *all-round* sire, unless mated with mares from the very best running families in his pedigree, also bred much more to Herod and Matchem than he was himself. I was both right and wrong; right as regards the blood he preferred, wrong as regards his not proving a good all-round sire. His pedigree is well worth studying, and is exceptionally stout on dam's side.

ISONOMY.

ISOLA BELLA. (19)		STERLING. (12)	
ISOLINE.	STOCKWELL. (3)	WHISPER.	OXFORD. (12)

Birdcatcher (11) — { Sir Hercules (2) ... { Whalebone (1) by Waxy (19). / Dr. of Wanderer, 11) by Gohanna, (24) }
{ Guiccioli (2) .... { Bob Booty by Chanticleer. (3) / Flight by Escape. }

Honey Dear .... { Plenipotentiary (6) by Emilius (28) by Orville. (8) / My Dear by Bay Middleton (1) by Sultan. (8) }

{ Camel (24) by Whalebone. (1) }
Touchstone (14)......{ Banter by Master Hy. (3) by Orville. (8,

Flatcatcher (3) { Decoy .... { Filho da Puta (12) by Haphazard (35), / Finesse by Peruvian by Sir Peter. (3) }

Silence { Melbourne (1) .... { Humphrey Clinker. (8) / Daughter of Cervantes. (8) }
{ Secret by Harkaway (15) by Velocipede (3) by Blacklock (2, 2, 1).

The Baron (24)... { Birdcatcher (11)... { Sir Hercules (2) by Whalebone. (1) / Guiccioli by Bob Booty. (23) }
{ Echidna .... { Economist (36) { Whisker. (1) / Dr. of Octavian. (8) } / Miss Pratt by Blacklock (2, 2, 1). }

Pocahontas .. { Glencoe (1)............ { Sultan (8) by Selim (2) by Buzzard, (3) / Trampoline by Tramp. (3) }
{ Marpessa .... { Muley (6) by { Orville (8) / Dr. of Whiskey. (2) } / Clare by Marmion by Whiskey (2) }

Ethelbert (12) .. { Faugh-a-Ballagh (11) { Sir Hercules (2) by Whalebone. (1) / Dr. of Bob Booty. (23) }
{ Espoir by Liverpool (11) by Tramp. (3) }

Bassishaw, ... { The Prime Warden (17) by Cadland. (12) / Miss Whinney by Sir Hercules (2) by Whalebone (1).

As in Chester's case, the four direct male ancestors of Isola Bella strain to Eclipse. Sterling is also strongly inbred to same source. It is somewhat singular that the two champion sires of England

F

and Australia a few years back (both dead) should be from Stockwell mares, and both are startling exceptions to the rule about crossing Eclipse male representatives on to females of the Herod and Matchem lines.   Here, indeed, is sufficient evidence of itself to start a theory in favour of the way these two great sires were bred ; so true is it that the stud books will provide ample evidence for countless theories.

A glance at Isonomy's pedigree discloses the fact that his main lines include four of my five *sire* figures (**3, 11, 12, 14**), *within the four top removes.*   I do not mean to assume the position that any horse with a similar combination of figures *must absolutely* be a success.   All I claim for the figures is that you must breed in this fashion if you wish to produce high-class sires.   I go even further and assert again (what may appear a paradox) that if a pedigree were built up so as to combine the great *running* lines (1, 2, 3, 4, 5, and 6) in the same profusion and positions as these *sire* figures occur in the pedigree of Isonomy, the result would be almost certain failure, even though a great racehorse resulted.   If any one of the prominent sires of the last half century are so bred then have I failed to discover it.

Col. Upton has laid it down as a law that the *male* should be *purer* and better bred than the female, if there is a choice to be made.   Doubtless this was by way of proving that because the majority of the best sires in the Stud Book are descended from the Darley Arabian, whom he considered superior to the Barbs and Turks, they must perforce have been purer bred than their mates, who hailed from Barb, Royal, and obscure sources.   My figures, however, prove the contrary.   They show clearly that the best and most prolific *dams* in the Stud Book as a rule come from three running lines (1, 2, 4)—origin, *pure Barb descent ;* whereas the best *sires* (as shown in the two last pedigrees of Chester and Isonomy) are a combination of families of *impure* origin, and this can be proved by scores of examples beyond any question.

Lord Lyon was very inbred to Nos. 1 and 2, and, though a brilliant racehorse, was a comparative failure at the stud. Peter, another wonder, a horse that could afford to stop dead in the middle

PETER.

LADY MASHAM. (9) — HERMIT. (5)

MAID OF MASHAM. — BRO. TO STRAFFORD. (**8**) — SECLUSION. — NEWMINSTER. (**8**)

Touchstone (**14**) { Camel (24) by Whalebone. (1)
{ Banter by Master Henry (**3**) by Orville. (**8**)

Breswing .... { Dr. Syntax (37) by Paynator. (18)
{ Dr. of Tomboy (**8**) by Ardrossan. (2)

Tadmor (**12** { Ion (4) by Cain (**8**) by Paulowitz (**8**) by Sir Paul. (**8**)

Miss Sellon ...... { Cowl (2) .... { Bay Middleton (1) by Sultan (**8**) by Selim. (2)
{ Crucifix by Priam. (6)
{ Belle Dame by **Belshazzar** (**11**) by Blacklock (**2**) by Whitelock. (**2**)

Y. Mel. (25) ...... { Melbourne (1) by Humphrey Clinker. (**8**)
{ Dr. of .... { Pantaloon. (17)
{ Dr. of Clenove. (1)

Dr. of .... { Gameboy (13) by Tomboy (**8**) by Jerry. (15)
{ Dr. of .... { Bay Middleton (1) by Sultan. (**8**)
{ Dr. of Whalebone. (1)

Don John (2) ...... { Waverley (2) by Whalebone. (1)
{ Dr. of Comus (25) by Sorcerer (6); Dr. of Stamford. (30)

Miss Lydia........ { **Belshazzar** (**11**) by Blacklock (**2**) by Whitelock. (**2**)
{ Dr. of Comus (25) by Sorcerer (6) by Trumpator. (**14**)

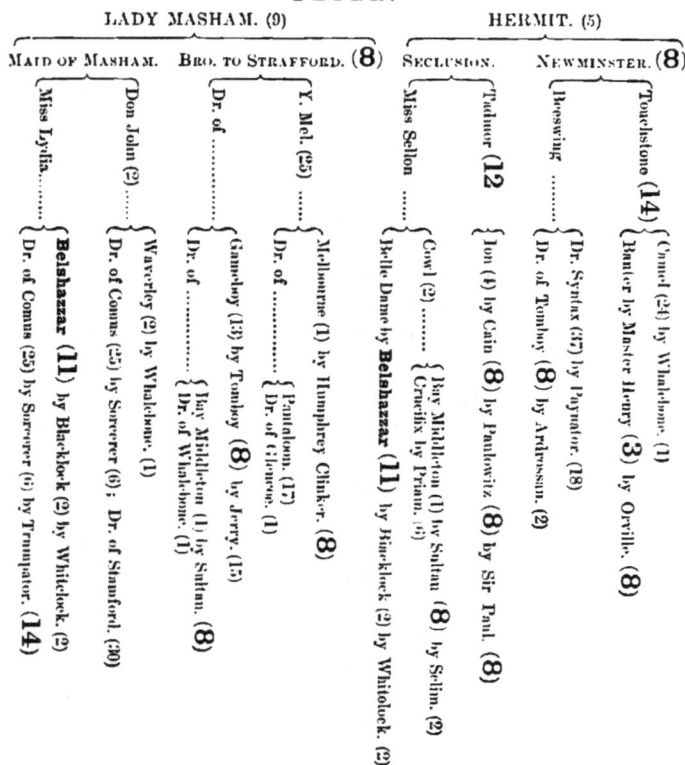

of a race, and then start away again and beat a field of first-class horses, is inbred very much on dam's side to pure, *i.e.*, running lines, and away from *sire* lines. He has fallen very short of what was expected when put to stud work, but his figures show that his dam was deficient in sire blood, and that his *inbreeding* was far more to the non-sire strains. Nos. 1, 2, and 4, which would have the effect of considerably reducing his sire potency.

The inbreeding was undoubtedly to Blacklock (through Belshazzar) and Bay Middleton. Out of the many horses whose names appear in this tabulation on dam's side, only two are in sire families in first four removes. On Hermit's side we have three sire figures in three removes. Clearly enough, Peter would, judged by the figure system, be a long way behind his sire as a getter of racehorses, and I think his greatest admirers must concede that he has proved a comparative failure. I have before stated the apparently paradoxical fact that the best running lines are far from being the best sire lines, yet it does not follow that a horse bred to the pure or running lines, like Peter, is incapable of producing a great racehorse if *properly* mated. Our standard of a great sire, I take it, implies that he will get racehorses from mares of quite distinct strains of blood, though it is notorious that even the best sires favour certain strains. When mating a horse bred like Peter away from stout sire blood, it is *imperative* that he should be crossed on mares such as daughters of Beadsman, or Isonomy to give him a strong infusion of sire strains as well as Stockwell, Birdcatcher, and Touchstone strains to counteract his Melbourne, Bay Middleton, Pantaloon, and Sorcerer blood. When I saw Peter at Newmarket in 1882, just retired from the turf, he had a lathy, shelly apppearance, which did not lead one to suppose he would develop into a high-class sire. His fillies should prove excellent brood mares because of this inbreeding to Blacklock and so much pure running blood. When Blacklock's figures are looked into one can in a measure sympathise with the much reviled Dr. Shorthouse, who was unfortunate enough to dub it the "accursed blood," whereas it has proved to be, and very justly so, the best strain in the Stud Book. The wonderful *concentration of running* strains in his pedigree makes the blood more potent and *further reaching* in its effects than any other strain, and when the figures are placed on the pedigree one can hardly fail to be convinced of this. But viewed in the light of a sire alone, it is easy to understand that those of his progeny descended from mares not in (or inbred to) sire families must have been indifferent performers,

BLACKLOCK.

- DR. OF (2)
  - WILDGOOSE.
    - Highflyer (13) by Herod (26) (see above).
    - Coheiress ......
      - Pot-8-os (38) by Eclipse **(12)** (above).
      - Manilla by Goldfinder. (1)
  - CORIANDER. (4)
    - Pot-8-os (38) ......
      - Eclipse **(12)** by Marske **(8)** by Squirt. **(11)**
      - Sportsmistress.
    - Lavender ......
      - Herod. (26)
      - Dr. of Snap. (1)
- WHITELOCK. (2)
  - ROSALIND.
    - Phenomenon (2)...
      - Herod. (26)
      - Frenzy by Eclipse. **(12)**
    - Atalanta by Matchem (4).
  - HAMBLETONIAN. (1)
    - King Fergus (6) by Eclipse **(12)** by Marske. **(8)**
    - Dr. of ....
      - Highflyer (13) by Herod. (26)
      - Dr. of Blank (15); Dr. of Regulus. **(11)**

and we will hope the worthy doctor's experience was confined to some of these. The pedigree of Blacklock is given above.

There is *no sire blood* till fourth remove; also the inbreeding to the pure figure of 2 is *direct, i.e.,* the 2 line is inbred to itself, as both his sire and dam descended from the Burton Barb Mare.

In cases of inbreeding there is a considerable difference in the

Breeding Racehorses by the Figure System.

potency of *direct* over collateral lines in favour of the former. It is only natural that it should be so, else the contention that families never lose their original characteristics would be without much value. In Blacklock's case we find not only his dam in 2 line, but his sire Whitelock also. Hence it is only reasonable to conjecture that Blacklock is the truest representative in the Stud Book of this almost superlative running line, especially when we find another

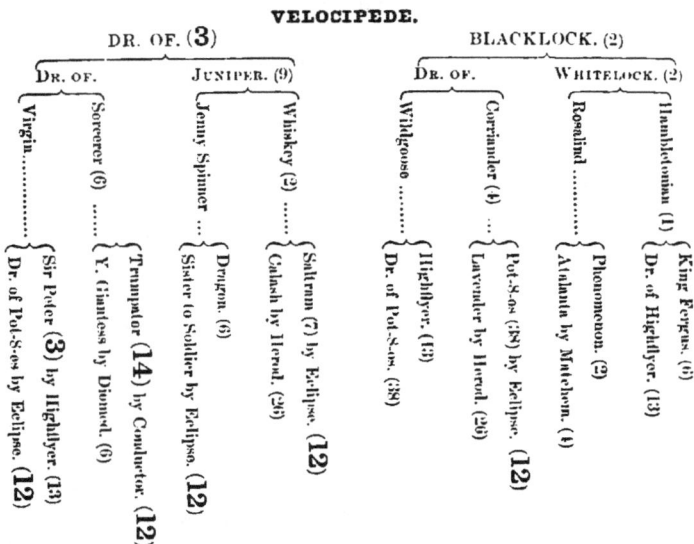

VELOCIPEDE.

DR. OF. (**3**) | BLACKLOCK. (2)

Dr. of. | Juniper. (9) | Dr. of. | Whitelock. (2)

Virgin ....
Sorcerer (6) ......
Jenny Spinner ...
Whiskey (2) ....
Wildgoose ....
Coriander (4) ...
Rosalind ....
Hambletonian (1)

Sir Peter (**3**) by Highflyer. (13)
Dr. of Pot-8-os by Eclipse. (**12**)
Trumpator (**14**) by Conductor. (6)
Y. Giantess by Diomed. (6)
Drogon. (6)
Sister to Soldier by Eclipse. (**12**)
Saltram (7) by Eclipse. (**12**)
Calash by Herod. (26)
Highflyer. (13)
Dr. of Pot-8-os. (38)
Pot-8-os (38) by Eclipse. (**12**)
Lavender by Herod. (26)
Phenomenon. (2)
Atalanta by Matchem. (4)
King Fergus. (6)
Dr. of Highflyer. (13)

close branch of the same line coming in through Whitelock's maternal grandsire Phenomenon. As a consequence of this close *line* breeding stud masters are finding the magic double and treble cross of Blacklock accountable for most of the phenomenal racehorses of the past twenty years, including cracks like Vedette, Galopin, Peter, Ormonde (four strains), Donovan, Bendigo, Barcaldine, Orme, Isonomy, La Flèche, and many others too numerous to particularise, and the blood of Blacklock may well claim to be quite equal, if not superior to, its great rival strain, Sir Hercules, hailing from the same (female) family, No. 2, by Whalebone, No. 1. I append the pedigrees of Velocipede's dam, the dams of Voltaire, Brutandorf, Belshazzar (Tranby, Laurel, and Buzzard), to show that Blacklock could not succeed without sire figures.

Velocipede's dam is from the sire line No. 3, the premier one of the five; and yet another strain comes in through Sir Peter, with additional sire strains through Trumpator and Eclipse.

Let us take Voltaire, and note how similar conditions prevail.

DAM OF VOLTAIRE.

DR. OF. (12)		PHANTOM. 6)	
DR. OF.	OVERTON. (11)	JULIA.	WALTON. (7)
Dr. of Ruler.	Walnut. (24)	Dr. of Herod. (26)	King Fergus (6) by Eclipse. (12)	Y. Giantess.	Whiskey (2) by Saltram. (7)	Dr. of Dungannon. (33)	Sir Peter. (3)

As in the previous pedigree, there is a strain of Whiskey of the same family as Blacklock (No. 2), but this nicking of No. 2 would have had no tendency to produce such great sires as Velocipede and Voltaire had they not been fortunate enough to be from dams in sire lines. Tranby, though coming from the 21 line, was from an Orville (8) mare, Laurel's dam, Wagtail, was by Prime Minister (12 from an Orville (8) mare of the 21 line, Buzzard was from an 8 mare. The pedigree of Brutandorf's dam Mandane is given on next page.

In five cases the successes were through mares directly from sire lines, and though there must have been scores of other sons throughout the Stud Book owning paternity to Blacklock, this remarkable truth is without dispute, that the blood is mainly valuable through four horses in the sire families, whose tabulations are given, and principally through Voltaire. The sons of this branch of the family, from Whitelock to Vedette, have shown a partiality for No. 2 blood. Blacklock, as shown, was the result of a union of three distinct branches of the 2 tap root. Voltaire's

MANDANE (Dam of **Brutandorf**).

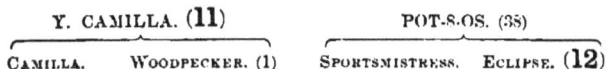

Y. CAMILLA. **(11)**   POT-8-OS. (38)

CAMILLA.   WOODPECKER. (1)   SPORTSMISTRESS.   ECLIPSE. **(12)**

MANUELLA (Dam of **Belshazzar**).

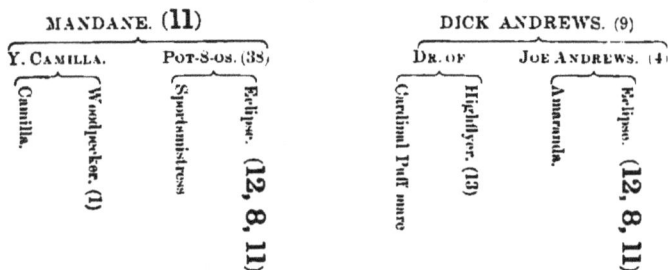

MANDANE. **(11)**   DICK ANDREWS. (9)

Y. CAMILLA.   POT-8-OS. (38)   DR. OF   JOE ANDREWS. (4)

Camilla.   Woodpecker. (1)   Sportsmistress   Eclipse. **(12, 8, 11)**   Cardinal Puff mare   Highflyer. (13)   Amaranda.   Eclipse. **(12, 8, 11)**

dam brought in another close strain through Whiskey (2), and Voltaire's best son, Voltigeur, was also in the 2 line. Voltigeur's main branch comes down to us in male line through Vedette of the 19 line, and his dam was by Birdcatcher **(11)**, a son of Sir Hercules (2) from Nan Darrell, by Inheritor (4) from Nell, by Blacklock (2), so that Vedette combined the double cross of Blacklock, as well as a strain of Sir Hercules. It is a remarkable pedigree, as being one of the first containing a double strain of

Blacklock. When the names of Blacklock and Eclipse occur I will, from this on, instead of giving their sires and grandsires, merely repeat the figures when space is curtailed. Both horses, in their own fashion, exercise such an influence in pedigrees that some distinctive mark is required to emphasise this fact to the student.

Taking into due consideration Vedette's strong inbreeding to No. 2 (a non-sire family) through Voltigeur, Blacklock (twice),

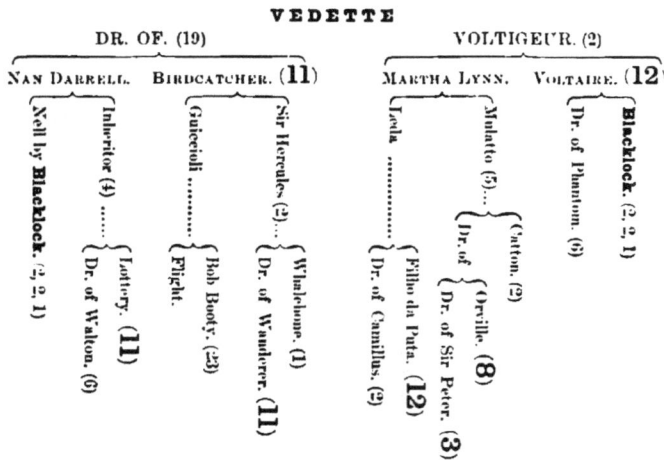

VEDETTE

DR. OF. (19)		VOLTIGEUR. (2)	
NAN DARRELL.	BIRDCATCHER. (11)	MARTHA LYNN.	VOLTAIRE. (12)

- Nell by **Blacklock.** (2, 2, 1)
- Interior (4)
  - Lottery. (11)
  - Dr. of Walton. (6)
- Guiccioli ....
  - Bob Booty. (23)
  - Flight.
- Sir Hercules (2)...
  - Whalebone. (1)
  - Dr. of Wanderer. (11)
- Iola ....
  - Dr. of Camillus. (2)
- Mulatto (5)...
  - Catton. (2)
  - Dr. of Sir Peter. (3)
  - Filho da Puta. (12)
  - Orville. (8)
- Dr. of Phantom (6)
- **Blacklock.** (2, 2, 1)

Sir Hercules, Catton, Phenomenon, and Whiskey, it is reasonable to suppose that this potent blood would dominate the few sire strains he possessed in his top removes, and as a very natural consequence he would require a profusion of sire blood in his mates to make any certainty of leaving *high-class* sons to carry on the family. Galopin was without question the best son he left behind.

Here we have in the dam, in four removes only, no less than five representatives of the great sire families, and this sire influence is rendered doubly intense through the fact of Flying Duchess coming direct from **3**, and sired by the Flying Dutchman of **3**. I may be met here with the oft-repeated assertion that Galopin was not got by Vedette, but until that can be proved to the satisfaction of the Messrs. Weatherby, Vedette must take the credit of siring one of the best all-round horses of modern days. The mantle

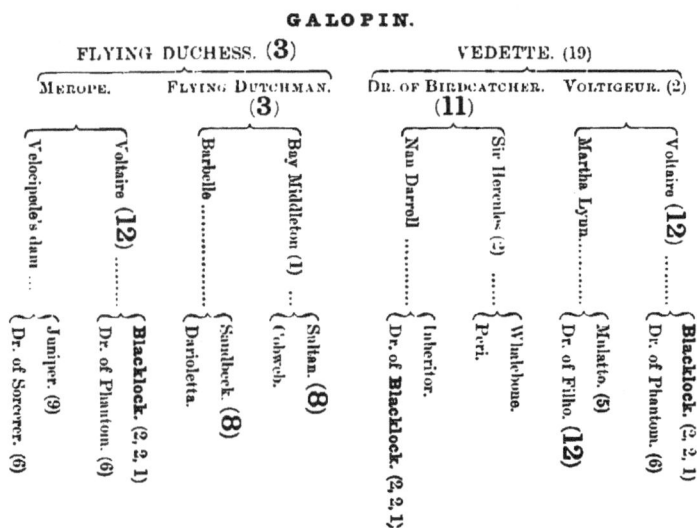

GALOPIN.

FLYING DUCHESS. (**3**)   VEDETTE. (19)

MEROPE.   FLYING DUTCHMAN. (**3**)   DR. OF BIRDCATCHER. (**11**)   VOLTIGEUR. (2)

Velocipede's dam ....{ Juniper. (9)
               { Dr. of Sorcerer. (6)

Voltaire (**12**) ....{ **Blacklock**. (2, 2, 1)
               { Dr. of Phantom. (6)

Barbelle ....{ **Sandbeck**. (**8**)
               { Darioletta.

Bay Middleton (1) ...{ **Sultan**. (**8**)
               { Cobweb.

Nan Darrell ....{ Inheritor.
               { Dr. of **Blacklock**. (2, 2, 1)

Sir Hercules (2) ......{ Whalebone.
               { Peri.

Martha Lynn ....{ Mulatto. (5)
               { Dr. of Filho. (**12**)

Voltaire (**12**) ....{ **Blacklock**. (2, 2, 1)
               { Dr. of Phantom. (6)

of Galopin has descended to his brilliant son St. Simon, who certainly would have won the Derby had his nomination not become void through the death of Prince Batthyany. He only ran at two and three years, and retired unbeaten. His pedigree is one that completely bears out the soundness of the figure system. A work of this character would not be complete without this champion sire as an illustration for or against, and it is therefore extremely gratifying to be able to use him as an example favourable to the figures.

Up to date his fillies have been higher class than his colts, notably La Flèche (L), Memoir (O and L), Mrs. Butterwick (O),

ST. SIMON.

ST. ANGELA. (11)		GALOPIN. (3)	

8th dam. Sister to **Regulus.**

ADELINE.
KING TOM. 3)
FLYING DUCHESS.
VEDETTE. 19)

Little Fairy ... {Lacerta by Zodiac (1) by St. George. (15)

Ion (4) ... {Horicea (15) by Velocipede (3) by **Blacklock.** (2, 2, 1)
{Dr. of Edmund (12) by Orville. (8)

Harkaway (2) .... {Cain (8) by Paulowitz (8) by Sir Paul. (8)
{Dr. of Nabocklish. (9

Pocahontas.......... {Glencoe (1) by Sultan (8) by Selim. (2)
{Marpessa by Muley (6) by Orville. (8)

Merope .... {Economist (36) by Whisker. (1)

Flying Dutchman (3) {Bay Middleton (1) by Sultan. (8)
{Barbelle by Sandbeck. (8)

Dr. of .... {Voltaire (12) by **Blacklock.** (2, 2, 1)
{Dr. of Juniper (9) by Whiskey. (2)

Voltigeur (2) .... {Voltaire (12) by **Blacklock.** (2, 2, 1)
{Martha Lynn by Mulatto. (5)

Dr. of .... {Birdcatcher (11) by Sir Hercules. (2)
{Dr. of .... {Inheritor (4) by Lottery. (11)
{Dr. of **Blacklock.** (2, 2, 1)

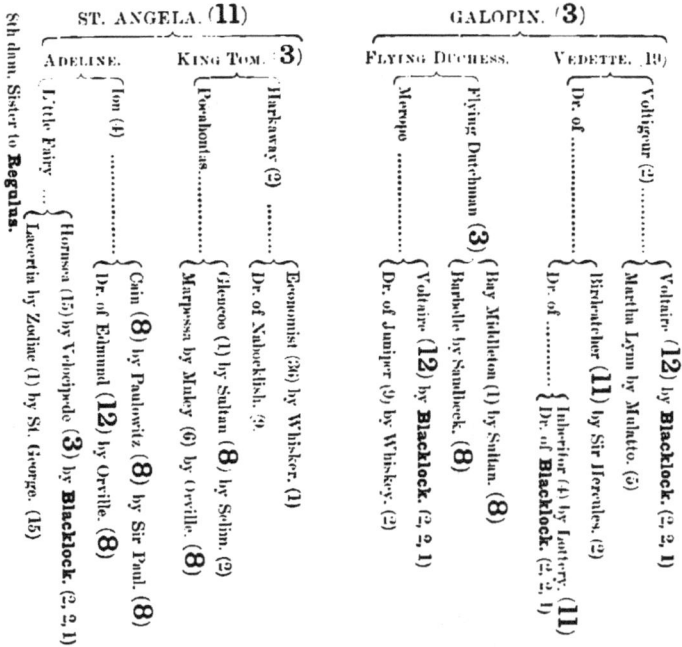

Amiable (1000). Later on I will endeavour to show where this tendency to throw good fillies comes from.

Speculum by Vedette was a long way from being so high class a horse as Galopin, nor did he develop so early. At the stud he was not anything like so successful, though many of his stock furnish into good handicap horses, and one (Sefton) managed to pull off the Derby in a rather weak year, the only horse of note in the race being Insulaire, to my mind a better horse than the winner.

It is only too apparent that when compared with St. Simon or Galopin, Speculum falls far short of the required inbreeding to sire figures, nor is his son Sefton better in this respect. They both require mates from the strong sire lines.   Progress, dam of

SPECULUM.

DORALICE. (1)		VEDETTE. (19)	
PRESERVE.	ORLANDO. (13)	DR. OF	VOLTIGEUR. (2)
Mustard — { Merlin (7) by Castrel. (2) } { Morel by Sorcerer. (6) }	Vulture — { Langar (7) { Selim. (2) } { Dr. of Walton. (6) } } { Kite ...... { Bustard. (35) } { Dr. of Sir Oliver. (13) } }	Dr. of ...... — { Inheritor (4) by Lottery. (**11**) } { Nell by Blacklock. (2, 2, 1) }	Martha Lynn — { Mulatto (5) by Catton. (2) } { Leda by Filho da Puta. (**12**) }
Emilius (29) — { Orville (**8**) by Beningbrough. (7) } { Dr. of Stamford. (30) }	Touchstone (**14**) — { Camel (24) { Whalebone. (1) } { Dr. of Selim. (2) } } { Banter ... { Master Henry. (**3**) } { Boudicca. } }	Birdcatcher (**11**) — { Sir Hercules (2) by Whalebone. (1) } { Dr. of Bob Booty. (23) }	Voltaire (**12**) — { Blacklock (2) by Whitelock. (2) } { Dr. of Phantom (6) by Walton. (7) }

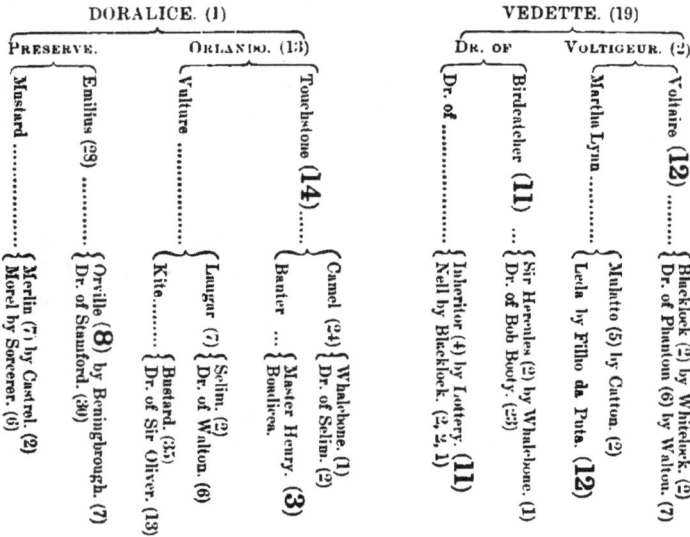

Penton, a good racehorse, by Speculum, is in the No. **8** line. Castlereagh's dam is by Birdcatcher (**11**), and she is also from the **8** family.   In Australia (imp.) Splendor, from Bathilde by Stockwell (**3**), is doing good service for the reputation of his sire, Speculum, at the stud farm of Mr. Frank Reynolds'.   I have pleasant recollections of going with his breeder, the late Mr.

Crowther Harrison, to see this colt saddled for the Middle Park Plate of 1882, won by Macheath by Macaroni. Splendor did not get a place, but won some races at three years, including, if I mistake not, the Payne Stakes. One of his sons, Jeweller, should have won the Melbourne Cup in 1893, but got pocketed in a large field, and was beaten (third) a half length from Tarcoola, the winner. He has since won the summer Cup at Sydney, carrying 9st. 5lbs. He comes from the No. 2 line, and in connection with this same race for the Melbourne Cup, out of the first five horses three, viz., Carnage (2nd), Jeweller (3rd), and Port Admiral (5th) are descended from No. 2, which worthily upholds its prestige no matter in what part of the world its descendants chance to be, as witness also two previous Melbourne Cup winners, Carbine and Malvolio (both No. 2), while that splendid specimen of a racehorse, The Admiral by Richmond, also claims the same female descent.

Having carried up the line of Blacklock through its main branch to the present day, we will now turn to the rival line of Sir Hercules, and see how it bears out the figure system. I have always been divided in my admiration for these two great horses, and while leaning towards Sir Hercules because of his great scion Stockwell, without doubt the best *all-round strain* in the Stud Book, there is hardly any question that Blacklock blood exercises a stronger influence when nicked. The reason has already been given, but will become more apparent after an analysis of the strains of Sir Hercules and some of his descendants down to Bend Or and Ormonde.

I have on page 58 given the pedigree of Whalebone in detail, showing the inbreeding three times to Snap (No. 1) through Whalebone's own line (1), also to the figure 4 through Squirrel and Matchem, both descending to the Layton Barb mare. I now propose to take his great son Sir Hercules and trace the line up.

Out of eight ancestors in the third remove Sir Hercules was bred three times to Eclipse in *main lines* and four times to Herod, also once

SIR HERCULES.

PERI. (2)   WHALEBONE. (1)

THALESTRIS.   WANDERER. (11)   PENELOPE.   WAXY. (18)

Rival ....

Alexander (13) ....

Catherine ....

Gohanna (24) ....

Prunella ....

Trumpator (14) ......

Maria ....

Pot-8-os (28) ....

{ Eclipse (12) by Marske (8) by Squirt (11) by B. Childers (6) by Darley Arabian.
{ Dr. of Sportsman by Cade (6) by Godolphin Barb.

{ Herod (26) by Tartar+ by Partner (9) by Jigg+ by Byerly Turk.
{ Lisette by Snap (1) by Snip (9) by Childers (6) by Darley Arabian.

{ Conductor (12) ... { Matchem (4) by Cade (6) by Godolphin Barb.
{ Brunette by Squirrel. (4)   { Dr. of Snap (1) by Snip (9) by Childers (6) by Darley Arabian.

Highflyer (13) ... { Herod (above).
{ Dr. of ....   { Blank (15) by Godolphin Barb.

Promise .... { Snap (1) by Snip (9) by Childers by Darley Arabian.
{ Julia by Blank (15) by Godolphin Barb.

Mercury (9) by Eclipse (12)   { Marske (8) by Squirt (11) by Childers (6) by D. Arab.
{ Spiletta by Regulus (11) by Godolphin Barb.

Dr. of Herod (26) ... { Tartar (see above).
{ Dr. of Matchem (4) by Cade (6) by Godolphin Barb.

Woodpecker (1) ... { Herod (26) (see above).
{ Dr. of Cade (6) by Godolphin Barb.

Camilla .... { Trentham (5) by Sweepstakes. (4)
{ Coquette............ { Compton Barb.
{ Sister to Regulus.

{ Eclipse (12)   { Marske (8) by Squirt (11) by Childers (6) by Darley Arabian.
{ Dr. of Regulus (12) by Godolphin Barb.

Dr. of Forester   { Forester.
{ Dr. of Coalition Colt by Godolphin Barb.

Sir Peter (3)   { Highflyer (13) (above).
{ Papilion by Snap. (1)

Hornet .... { Drone (4) by Herod.
{ Manilla by Goldfinder (1) by Snap. (1

to Matchem. There was a great deal of inbreeding to Godolphin Barb, as also in Guiccioli, the dam of Birdcatcher, given below.

Guiccioli had only one strain of Eclipse, all the rest go to Herod

GUICCIOLI.

FLIGHT. (11)   **BOB BOOTY. (23)**

Y. HEROINE   ESCAPE. (27)   IRENE.   CHANTICLEER. (3)

Woodpecker (1) ... { Herod (26) by Tartar + by Partner. (9)
{ Miss Ramsden by Cade (6) by Godolphin Barb.

Dr. of Eclipse (12) .... { Marske (8 by Squirt. (11)
{ Dr. of Regulus (11) by Godolphin Barb.

Bagot (41) .... { Herod (26) (above).
{ Marette .... { Matchem (4) by Cade (6) by Godolphin Barb.
{ Dr. of Traveller by Partner. (9)

Dr. of .... { Bustard (7) by Crab.
{ Cinnamon .... { Dr. of Regulus (11) by Godolphin Barb.

Patty .... { Tim (21) .... { Squirt. (11)
{ Miss Patch by Justice. { Dr. of Godolphin Barb.

Tom Tug (1) ...... { Herod. (26)
{ Legacy .... { Y. Snip.
{ Snap's dam.

Commodore (24) .... { Snurtnunoch (24) .. { Snap. (1)
{ Smallhopes .... { Sophia by Godolphin Barb.
{ Dr. of Blank by Godolphin Barb.

Highflyer (13) ... { Herod. (26)
{ Rachel .... { Blank (15) by Godolphin Barb.
{ Dr. of Regulus (11) by Cade (6)
{ by Godolphin Barb.

Dr. of .... { Shift .... { Sweetbriar.
{ Black Susan by Snap. (1)

Bagot (41) ...... { Herod (26) (above).
{ Marette by Matchem (4) by Cade (6) by Godolphin Barb.
{ Hero by Cade (6) by Godolphin Barb.

Heroine ...... { Sister to Regulus (12) by Godolphin Barb.

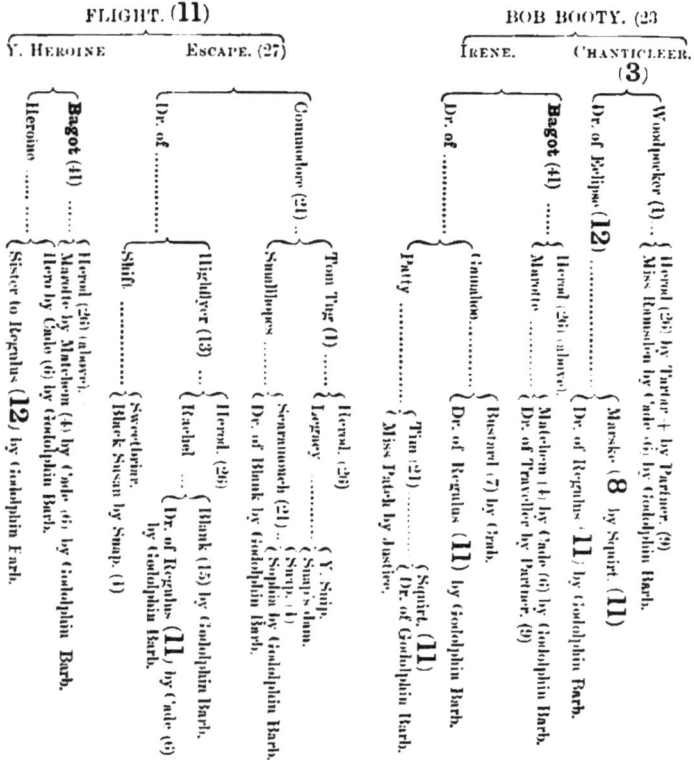

and God. Barb, the latter being especially strong at bottom of dam's pedigree, in some places incestuously. Except that she is from a sire line, **11** (and has two other sire strains close to the surface), there is very little inbreeding to sire blood, and **11** is evidently the strain she required a close return to. Sir Hercules, her mate, brought her this through his dam by Wanderer (**11**), of the Eclipse line in male descent, as also two other direct strains of Eclipse. Wanderer's

THE BARON.

ECHIDNA. (24)		BIRDCATCHER. (11)	
MISS PRATT.	ECONOMIST. (36)	GUICCIOLI.	SIR HERCULES. (2)

Galabout ...... { Orville (**8**) great grandson of Eclipse. (**12**) / Minstrel ...... { Sir Peter. (**3**) / Matron by Florizel (5)

Blacklock (9) { Whitelock (2)... { Hambletonian (1) g. son of Eclipse. (**12**) / Dr. of Phenomenon. (2) } / Dr. of Coriander. (4)

Florushe ...... { Octavian (**8**) by Stripling (2) by Phenomenon. (2) / Caprice by Anvil (9) by Herod.

Whisker (1)... { Waxy (18) by Pot-8-os (38) by Eclipse. (**12**) / Penelope by Trumpator (**14**) by Conductor. (**12**)

Flight by Escape (27) by Highflyer (13) by Herod.

Bob Booty (23) by Chanticleer (**3**).... { Woodpecker. (1) / Dr. of Eclipse. (**12, 8, 11**)

Peri............ { Wanderer (**11**) grandson of Eclipse. (**12, 8, 11**) / Dr. of Alexander (13) by Eclipse. (**12**)

Whalebone (1) { Waxy (18) by Pot-8-os (38) by Eclipse. (**12, 8, 11**) / Dr. of Trumpator. (**14**)

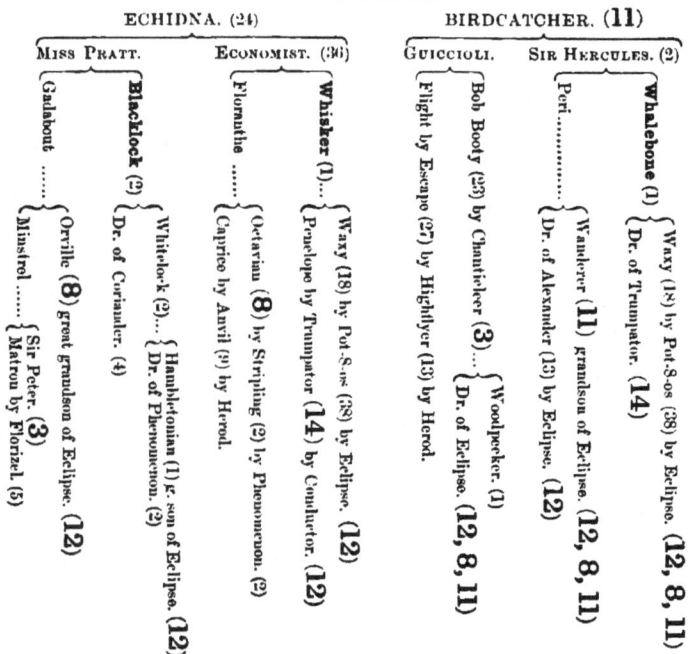

fourth dam, Sister to Regulus, was also the fourth dam of Guiccioli. In sire blood Eclipse occupies the same position that Blacklock later on took as the pre-potent running strain. When estimating its value in a pedigree like that of Birdcatcher, it must not therefore be gauged by its mere numerical strength, provided it has a channel like No. **11** to lift it to the surface, because for every appearance in any pedigree Eclipse brings into the combination no less than *four* sire figures, as

STOCKWELL.

POCAHONTAS. (**3**)   THE BARON. (24)

MARPESSA.   GLENCOE. (1)   ECHIDNA.   BIRDCATCHER. (**11**)

Clare ....

Malcy (6) ....

Trampoline ....

Sultan (**8**) ....

Economist (30) ......

Miss Pratt ....

Sir Hercules (2)...

{ Marmion (28) by **Whiskey** (2) by Saltram (7) by Eclipse. (**12**)
{ Gohanna (24) by Mercury (9) by Eclipse. (**12**)

{ Amazon ... { Driver (**11**) by Trentham. (5)
{ Dr. of Mercury by Eclipse. (**12**)

{ Harpliro ....

{ Eleanor by **Whiskey** (2) by Saltram (7) { Eclipse. (**12, 8, 11**)
{ Dr. of Snap. (1)

{ Orville (**8**) by Benningbro' (7) by King Fergus (6) by Eclipse. (**12**)

{ **Web** .... { Waxy (15) by Pot-8-os (28) by Eclipse. (**12**)
{ Penelope by Trumpator. (**14**)

{ Tramp (**3**) by Dick Andrews (10) by Joe A. (4) by Eclipse. (**12**)

{ Bacchante by Ditto (7) by Sir Peter. (**3**)

{ Selim (2).......... { Buzzard (**3**) by Woodpecker. (1)
{ Dr. of Alexander (13) by Eclipse. (**12**)

{ **Whisker** (1) by Waxy (18) by Pot-8-os by Eclipse. (**12**)
{ Dr. of Octavian (**8**) by Stripling (2) by Phenomenon. (2)

{ **Blacklock** (2, 2, 1) g. grandson of Eclipse. (**12, 8, 11**)
{ Dr. of Orville (**8**) g. grandson of Eclipse. (**12, 8, 11**)

{ **Whalebone** (1) by Waxy by Pot-8-os by Eclipse. (**12, 8, 11**)
{ Peri by Wanderer (**11**) grandson of Eclipse. (**12, 8, 11**)

{ Bob Booty (24) by Chanticleer (**3**). { Woodpecker. (**12**)
{ Dr. of Eclipse. (**12**)

Flight.

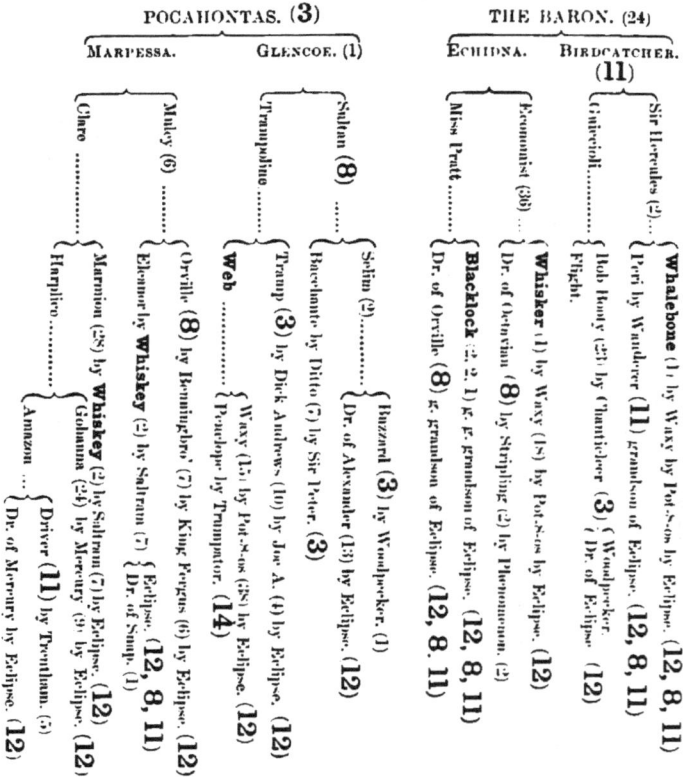

previously shown. For this reason the three strains of Eclipse we find in Sir Hercules outweigh in *potency* all the others combined

G

(they actually mean an inbreeding to *twelve* sire strains), backed
up as they are by four strains of Snap, a male descendant, also
of the Darley Arabian.   Nor must we forget that whenever the
name of Herod occurs it brings into the connection another close
strain of Childers, through Blaze, the sire of Herod's dam.   Let us
now examine the pedigree of The Baron, best son of Birdcatcher.

The Baron's dam, Echidna, did not contribute much in direct
sire strains, but in her second remove she had three out of four
lines coming in male descent from Eclipse.   But this of itself
was not nearly sufficient to make The Baron as good an all-round
sire as Birdcatcher, whose dam came directly from a sire line, and he
(The Baron) would therefore only succeed well with mares from
sire lines.   Pocahontas admirably suited him in this respect, and
the result of their union was Stockwell, the most successful sire of
modern days.   No pedigree of the present day is complete without
a strain of this great horse, and where it is absent such animal
should be mated with something in whose veins it courses.

The following table will give the student a better idea of the
combination of good families which go to make up the pedigrees of
those splendid sires Stockwell and King Tom.   By the way, St. Simon,
by Galopin from St. Angela by King Tom, comes from the **11** line,
but inherits all the strains of blood shown with the exception
of The Baron.   Pocahontas in female line is a direct descendant of
the dam of the Two True Blues.   Her sire Glencoe, and The Baron,
her mate, contained in their veins infusions of Sir Peter (**3**), Buzzard
(**3**), Chanticleer (**3**), and Tramp (**3**), all four of which trace back
to the same descent as herself in female line, and three of them
through Miss Belsea by Regulus (**11**), and her daughters Rosebud,
Hyæna, and Curiosity, all by Snap (**1**), while the fourth horse,
Sir Peter, is out of Papillon by Snap (**1**), from Miss Cleveland by
Regulus (**11**).   Woodpecker (**1**) also plays a conspicuous part in the
table.   Stockwell may therefore claim to have had a curious
inbreeding to perhaps the best family in the Stud Book (**3**), also to

DAM OF THE TWO TRUE BLUES. (3)

Dr. of Byerley Turk.

Dr. of Honeywood Arabian.

Dr. of Bartlett's Childers. (6)

Miss Belsea by Regulus. (11)

Midge by Bay Bolton.

Miss Cleveland by Regulus. (11)

Papillion by Snap. (1)

SIR PETER (3) by Highflyer (3) out dam by Regulus. (11)

Roselmd by Snap. (1)

Dr. of Eclipse. (12)

CHANTICLEER (3) by Woodpecker. (1) Chanticleer was a full brother to Stockwell's seventh dam.

Curiosity by Snap. (1)

Misfortune by Dux. (7)

BUZZARD (3) by Woodpecker. (1)

Hyæna by Snap. (1)

Everlasting by Eclipse. (12)

Dr. of Woodpecker. (1)

Flaxinella by Trentham. (5)

TRAMP (3) by Dick Andrews. Tramp's second dam was full sister in blood to Chanticleer.

Hyæna by Snap. (1)

Everlasting by Eclipse. (12)

From Dr. of Regulus. (11)

Sister to Goldfinch by Woodpecker. (1)

Fractious by Mercury. (9)

Amazon by Driver. (11) his dam from sister to Regulus).

Harpalice by Gohanna (24) grandson of Eclipse (12) from Dr. of Regulus. (11)

Clare by Marmion (28) g. grandson of Eclipse (12) from Dr. of Regulus. (11)

Marpessa by Muley (6) g.g. grandson of Eclipse (12) from Dr. of Regulus. (11)

Pocahontas by Glencoe. (1) { Sultan (8) by Selim (2) by BUZZARD (3) (above). Trampoline by TRAMP. (3)

STOCKWELL (3) by The Baron. (24)

KING TOM (3) by Harkaway. (2)

G 2

the five celebrated Snap mares, all from Regulus mares (four from Miss Belsea), as well as large infusions of Eclipse, bringing in each time another strain of Regulus and the strong inbreeding to sire blood. It is no wonder that Stockwell stands out conspicuous amongst his contemporaries as a splendid exponent of both sire and running strains, which was the real secret of his being so catholic in his matings. St. Simon owes his excellence to much the same strains as Stockwell with the addition of Ion (4), Vedette (19), Flying Dutchman (3), Harkaway (2), and it is reasonable to

BRIBERY (Dam of **St. Albans**).

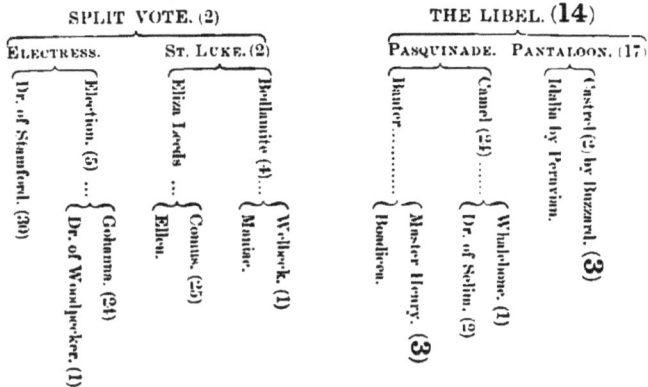

SPLIT VOTE. (2)				THE LIBEL. (14)		
ELECTRESS.		ST. LUKE. (2)		PASQUINADE.		PANTALOON. (17)
Dr. of Stamford. (30)	Election. (5) — Gohanna. (24), Dr. of Woodpecker. (1)	Eliza Leeds ... Comus. (25), Ellen.	Bellhunite (4) ... Welbeck. (1), Manfac.	Banter ... Master Henry. (3), Boadicea.	Camel (24) ... Whalebone. (1), Dr. of Selim. (9)	Castrel (2) by Buzzard. (3), Idalia by Peruvian.

suppose that, coming direct in female descent from "Sister to Regulus," he is the greatest living representative of that choice progenitor, and like him is a better sire of fillies than colts.

Bearing in mind Stockwell's pedigree, we will glance at those of Bribery and Marigold, the dams of St. Albans and Doncaster, and students can judge for themselves through which the Stockwell male line is most likely to descend.

Neither of these mares give Stockwell much return in sire blood, nor have their respective sons, St. Albans and Doncaster, shone very brilliantly at the stud as compared with their sire, which is only to be expected, seeing that they have very much less in proportion of the sire element than he had.

True it is that St. Albans got a brilliant son in Springfield, because in this mating the dam brought in a large infusion of **12**, a crack sire family.

It may be well asked why Springfield has not been a greater success, owing to double cross of **12**, and seeing that his dam brought to the union such a profusion of sire blood? The reason is not far to seek.

MARIGOLD (Dam of Doncaster).

DR. OF (5)		TEDDINGTON. (2)	
DR. OF	RATAN. (9)	MISS TWICKENHAM.	ORLANDO. (13)

- Dr. of Phantom (6) by Walton (7).
- Melbourne (1) ... { Hy. Clinker. (8) / Dr. of Cervantes (8) }
- Dr. of Picton. (9)
- Buzzard. (8) ... { Blacklock. (2, 2, 1) / Dr. of Delpini. (30) }
- Dr. of Election. (5) by Gohanna (24)
- Rockingham. (1). { Hy. Clinker. (8) / Medora. }
- Vulture .... { Langar. (7) / Kite. }
- Touchstone (14) { Camel. (24) / Banter by Master Hy. (3) }

A close analysis of his pedigree will show that he is bred in his main lines very much to flashy Herod blood, Castrel and his brothers. Stockwell, on the other hand, has only *one* strain of the brothers through Glencoe, and this was closely nicked in Bribery (dam of St. Albans). Her sire, The Libel, was inbred closely to Castrel and Selim, giving St. Albans three strains altogether. Viridis (dam of Springfield) was again persistently inbred to the brothers; Orlando having three strains, Pyrrhus 1. two strains, and Palmyra two more, or ten all told.   Besides these, there are eight strains of Whalebone, Web, and Whisker in Springfield, and, as I have before pointed out, when Whalebone is strongly associated with the male line of Herod or Matchem, it is apt to be dominated by them, and thus lose its characteristic stoutness.   Springfield by his breeding is essentially a sprinter, and his racing proved this to some extent.   His most meritorious win was the Champion Race (one and a quarter miles),

VIRIDIS.

MAID OF PALMYRA. (12)

PALMYRA.

- Hester............
- Sultan (8) by Selim (2) by Buzzard. (3)
- Camel (24) { Whalebone. (1) / Dr. of Selim. (2)
- Dr. of Maley (6) by Orville. (8)

PYRRHUS I. (3)

- Fortress............
- Epirus (13)............
- Langar (7) by Selim. (2)
- Olympia by Sir Oliver. (13)
- Defence (5) { Whalebone. (1) / Dr. of Rubens. (2)
- Dr. of Moses (5) by Whalebone (1)

MARSYAS. (12)

DR. OF.

- Dr. of Octavian. (8) Stripling (2)
- Whisker (1) ......

ORLANDO. (13)

- Vulture............
- Touchstone (14) { Camel (24)... { Whalebone. (1) / Dr. of Selim. (2) / Banter by Master Henry. (3)
- Langar (7) by Selim. (2)
- Kite by Bustard, by Castrel. (2)
- Waxy (18) by Pot.Sou. (28)
- Penelope by Trumpator. (14)

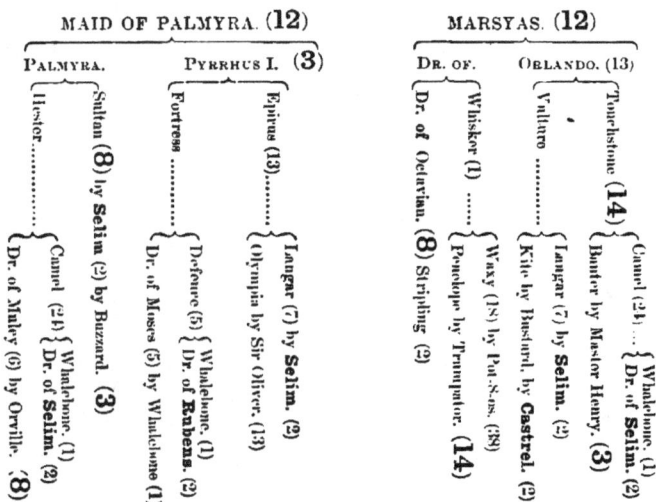

about the end of his tether.   He is bred, as shown, by a double cross of the **12** line, with back breeding to No. 2 through Castrel and Selim, with **3** as his best sire figure.   Nothing could be happier than his mating with the beautifully bred Sanda (dam of Sanfoin, Derby winner) of the 2 family, by Wenlock (4) from Sandal, by Stockwell (**3**).   This union gave him a double strain of Stockwell and Rataplan, the whole combination of dam's blood being of a stout Eclipse character. In other words, it was a meeting of *opposite temperaments* with an inbreeding to same *good* ancestors, Stockwell and Touchstone, through the pure channel of the 2 family. Taking up the Stockwell male line through Doncaster, the pedigree of Ormonde is given below for five removes, but will be treated in detail later on.

Anticipating that hypercritical readers may take up the position that, if Bend Or was out of Clémence it would render

ORMONDE.

LILLY AGNES. (16)		BEND OR. (1)	
POLLY AGNES.	MACARONI (**14**)	ROUGE ROSE.	DONCASTER. (5)

Miss Agnes .... {
The Cure (6). {
Dr. of .... {
Sweetmeat (21) {
Ellen Horne {
Thormanby (4) {
Marigold .... {
Stockwell (**3**) {

Agnes by Clarion. {
Birdcatcher (**11**) by Sir Hercules. (2) {
Morsel by Mulatto. (5) {
Physician (21) by Brutandorf. (**11**) {
Banter by Master Henry. (**3**) {
Pantaloon (17) by Castrel. {
Dr. of {Dr. of Blacklock. (2, 2, 1) {
Voltaire (**12**) by Blacklock. (2) {
Gladiator (23) by Partisan. (1) {
Delhi by Plenipo. (6) {
Red Shank (15) by Sandbeck. (**8**) {
Alice Hawthorn by Muley Moloch. {
Windhound (**3**) by Pantaloon. (17) {
Dr. of Fatau (2) by Buzzard. (8) {
Teddington (2) by Orlando. (3) {
Pocahontas by Glencoe. (1) {
The Baron (24) by Birdcatcher. (**11**) {

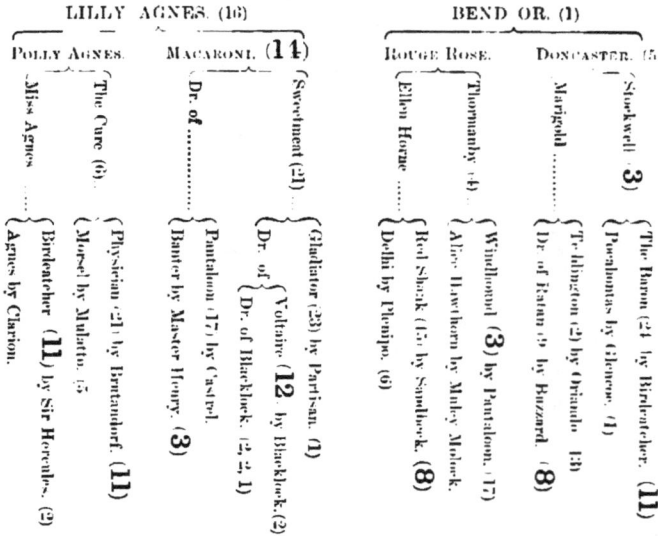

the above pedigree of less value as an example, I have thought it better to insert both, and let students draw their own deductions. With regard to the winning of Bend Or's Derby in 1880, I may state that I had the previous season (in Australia) examined the pedigrees of all the winning two-year-olds of important events, and was very confident that Bend Or and Robert the Devil would fill the first and second positions in the order named, partly on their superior two-year-old running, but mainly because they both came from the No. 1 family.   I backed my opinion to the extent of a level £5 with a friend who took considerable interest in pedigrees and racing but was somewhat sceptical of the soundness of the Figure system.   When the cable reached Australia announcing the fact that Bend Or had beaten Robert the Devil by a head, and my money was won, I naturally enough felt very jubilant, and picked Illuminata (1) and another filly (whose name I forget) in the same family to win the Oaks, betting my friend double or quits, with a start, of course.   When the detailed account of the race reached us neither of the fillies had started.   While I write Illuminata's son * Ladas is first favourite for the Derby of 1894, having already placed the Two Thousand Guineas to Lord Rosebery's credit.   In Silvio's year, 1877, when the cable informed Australians of the result of the 2000 Guineas — Chamant, Brown Prince, and Silvio—I ran out their respective pedigrees, and finding them to be Chamant (3), Brown Prince (21), and Silvio (1), I stated confidently to friends that Silvio would win the Derby, and if there were any other No. 1 horses in the race they would fill the places ; also that the same would happen in the Oaks ; and, failing Nos. 1, that the Nos. 2 would fill the first places.   The result of the Derby was some thirteen starters, and *only three* No. 1 horses, and they ran into the three first places in the following order : Silvio, Glen Arthur, and Rob Roy.   The Oaks did not contain a No. 1 representative, but Placida, the only No. 2, won the ladies' race.   I have previously stated that I attached rather too much importance at that time to the animal coming *direct* from the great winning lines, but I have since then had reason to modify my opinions by seeing repeated instances, such as the particular one of Ormonde, where an animal may be descended in female line from a

---

* He subsequently won the Derby.

comparatively outside family and yet contain in his veins far more strains of the potent 1, 2, **3**, 4, and 5, than another horse from one of these lines *direct*. When the doubt cropped up about which mare was really the dam of Bend Or, I was met with the remark, " If

ORMONDE.

LILY AGNES. (16)   BEND OR. (2)

POLLY AGNES.   MACARONI. **(14)**   CLÉMENCE.   DONCASTER. 5

Miss Agnes ......

The Cure (6) ...... { Physician (24) by Brutandorf (11) by Blacklock. (2, 2, 1)
                    { Morsel by Mulatto (5) by Catton. (2)

Dr. of .... { Birdcatcher (11) by Sir Hercules. (2)
                 { Clarion. (6)

Sweetmeat (24) ... { Agnes ...... { Charion. (6)
                                  { Annette ...... { Priam (6) Emilius. (28)
                                                   { Dr. of Don John.* (2)

                   { Gladiator (24) by Partisan. (1)
                   { Lollipop ...... { Voltaire **(12)** by Blacklock. (2, 2, 1)
                                     { Dr. of Blacklock. (2, 2, 1)

Pantaloon (17) ... { Castrel. (2)
                   { Idalia.

Hunter .... { Master Henry **(3)** by Orville. **(8)**
                 { Boudicea.

Eulogy .... { Euclid (7) by Emilius (28) by Orville. **(8)**
                 { Martha Lynn by Mulatto (5) by Catton. (2)

Newminster **(8)** { Touchstone **(14)**
                   { Beeswing.

                   { Camel (24) by Whalebone. (1)
                   { Banter by Master Henry. **(3)**

Marigold......... { Teddington (2) ... { Orlando (13) by Touchstone. **(14)**
                                       { Miss Twickenham.

                  { Dr. of Ratan (9) by Buzzard **(8)** by Blacklock. (2, 2, 1)

Stockwell **(3)** ... { The Baron (24) by Birdcatcher (11) by Sir Hercules. (2)
                      { Pocahontas by Echidna. { Economist.
                                                { Dr. of Blacklock. (2, 2, 1)

Bend Or turns out after all to be in an outside family, how about your theory?" With some trepidation, I confess, I hunted up Clémence, and found to my satisfaction that she was in the No. 2 line, and I think it will be admitted that the pedigree reads

* This error has been previously noticed, Don Juan, not Don John, being the maternal grandsire of Annette.—W. A.

very much better than the accepted one. Looking back at Bend Or's figures (in accepted pedigree), it will be seen that he was deficient in sire figures, only two in three top removes. The pedigree on preceding page is a considerable improvement in this respect.

Lily Agnes has three strains of Blacklock, one of Birdcatcher, one each of Mulatto, Emilius, and Banter, to nick with Bend Or's two strains of Blacklock, one each of Birdcatcher, Mulatto, and Emilius, and two of Banter. On the figures I should be disposed to favour the Clémence theory. It is to be regretted that any doubt has arisen over the pedigree of such a high-class racehorse, though it was eminently satisfactory to me personally to find that in either case Bend Or descends from one of the two premier winning lines of the Stud Book, thus fulfilling the conditions required for a successful mating with Lily Agnes. Lily Agnes was not likely to make a hit with any horse deficient in *running* families in the first three removes, because in her own pedigree table *none* are to be found until we reach Partisan and Castrel in the *fifth* remove. Her back breeding is to Blacklock (2), Sir Hercules (2), Catton (2), and Castrel (2). Under these conditions a horse from the No. 2 line was eminently fitted to be her mate, to nick with and revitalise all this latent but splendid blood. Bend Or, if from Rouge Rose's family, was a combination of Nos. 1, **3**, 5, and 2 (Teddington) and Thormanby (4), so that my figure theory was not really affected, only somewhat strengthened, by the change from Rouge Rose to Clémence. Further on I will show that some of the running figures 1, 2, **3**, 4, or 5, *must* be on either side of table in three top removes in the pedigrees of modern racehorses.

Whether Ormonde is destined to take precedence in the male line of Stockwell, as against Springfield, St. Albans, Robert the Devil, Craig Millar, Silvio, &c., is still an open question. Of one thing I am convinced, so far as the figures can be relied upon as a test, that he will score his greatest successes with mares that bring to his embrace a *large infusion* of his *best sire blood* No. 3. I do not wish it to be understood that any good racehorse (even that gigantic failure, Gladiateur) must of necessity be condemned because he is scantily favoured with the five sire lines of **3, 8, 11, 12, 14**. What I contend for, and am prepared to prove, is that some of these families *must* be on one side or other of the table inside the third

ORME.

SISTER TO ST. SIMON. (11)		ORMONDE. (16)	
ST. ANGELA.	GALOPIN. (3)	LILY AGNES.	BEND OR. (1

ST. ANGELA:
- King Tom (3)
  - Harkaway (9) by Economist (36) by Whisker, (1)
  - Pocahontas by Glencoe (1) by Sultan. (8)
- Dr. of Ion (4) by Cain (8) by Paulowitz (8) by Sir Paul. (8)

GALOPIN. (3):
- Vedette (19)
  - Voltigeur (2) by Voltaire (12) by Blacklock, (2, 2, 1)
  - Dr. of ....
    - Inheritor (4) by Lottery. (11)
    - Dr. of Blacklock, (2, 2, 1)
- Dr. of ....
  - Flying Dutchman (3) by Bay Middleton. (1)
  - Dr. of Voltaire (12) by Blacklock, (2, 2, 1)

LILY AGNES:
- Macaroni (14) by Sweetmeat (24) with two strains of Blacklock, (2, 2, 1)
- Polly Agnes:
  - The Cure by Physician, grandson of Blacklock, (2, 2, 1)
  - Miss Agnes by Birdcatcher (11) by Sir Hercules. (9)

BEND OR. (1:
- Doncaster (5) by Stockwell (3) by The Baron. (24)
- Rouge Rose by Thormanby (4) by Windhound. (3)

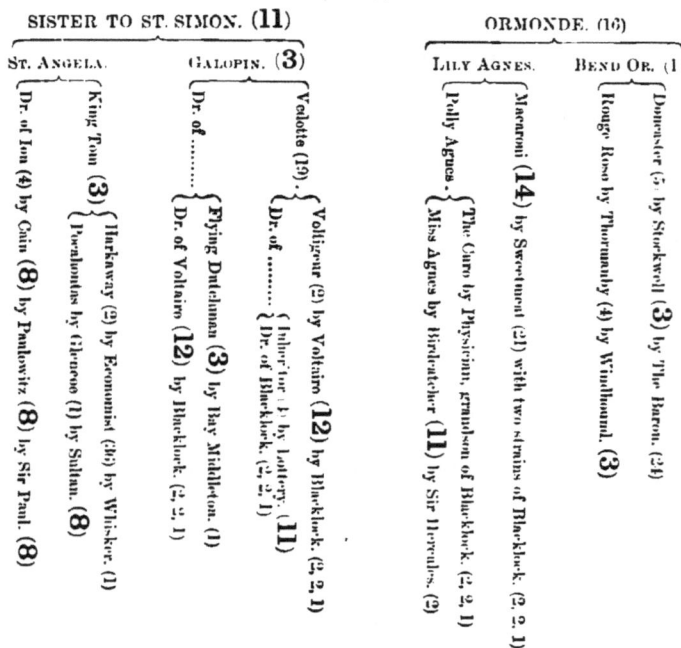

remove, and, if possible, there should be an inbreeding to sire figures. Take the example given of Orme for proof to show that Ormonde requires a *strong* inbreeding to sire figures in his mates, to correct his deficiency in that respect.

Another good son of Ormonde is Sorcerer, whose dam Crucible is, like Orme's dam, very prolific in sire blood.

CRUCIBLE (Dam of **Sorcerer**).

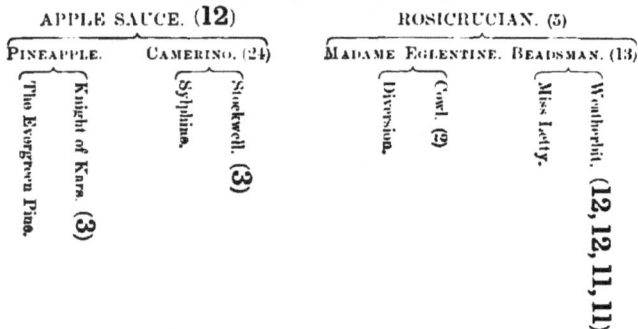

APPLE SAUCE. (12)   ROSICRUCIAN. (5)

PINEAPPLE.   CAMERINO. (24)   MADAME EGLENTINE.   BEADSMAN. (13)

- The Evergreen Pine.
- Knight of Kars. (3)
- Sylphine.
- Stockwell. (3)
- Diversion.
- Cowl. (9)
- Miss Letty.
- Weatherbit. (12, 12, 11, 11)

THISTLE (Dam of **Goldfinch**).

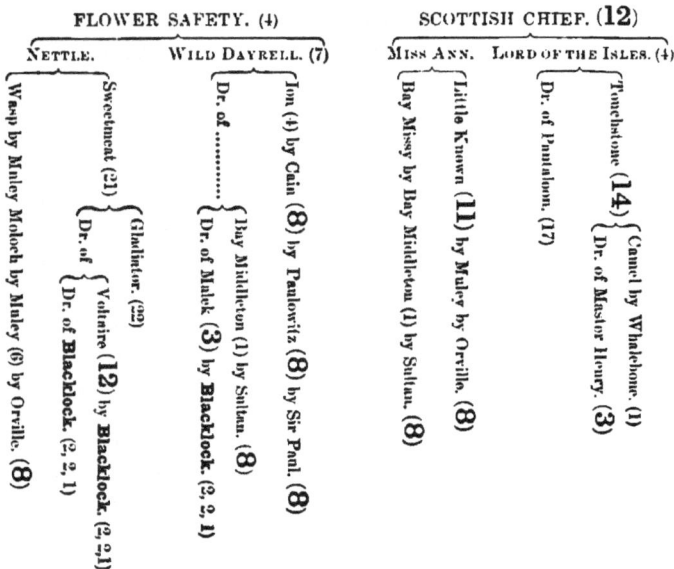

FLOWER SAFETY. (4)   SCOTTISH CHIEF. (12)

NETTLE.   WILD DAYRELL. (7)   MISS ANN.   LORD OF THE ISLES. (4)

- Wasp by Muley Moloch by Muley (6) by Orville. (8)
- Sweetmeat (21)
- Gladiator. (22)
- Dr. of ....
- Jon (4) by Cain (8) by Paulowitz (8) by Sir Paul. (8)
- Bay Middleton (1) by Sultan. (8)
- Dr. of Malek (3) by **Blacklock.** (2, 2, 1)
- Voltaire (12) by **Blacklock.** (2, 2, 1)
- Dr. of **Blacklock.** (2, 2, 1)
- Dr. of Pantaloon. (17)
- Little Known (11) by Muley by Orville. (8)
- Bay Missy by Bay Middleton (1) by Sultan. (8)
- Touchstone (14)
- Camel by Whalebone. (1)
- Dr. of Master Henry. (3)

It was my privilege when in California to accompany Mr. W. B. Macdonough on more than one occasion to view the peerless Ormonde at the Menlo Park Ranch. If twenty years' experience judging bloodstock in the show rings of New South Wales counts for anything, Ormonde (in my opinion) combines nearly everything to be desired in a racehorse. He has size without any suspicion of coarseness or unnecessary lumber, all his parts fit together as though fashioned by a master hand, and his temper is excellent. I have seen most of the best English, American, and Australian horses, but, to my mind, there never was a more commanding animal or more perfect galloping machine than Ormonde. Like Carbine, he is high on the leg and short in the back, and his hind legs are inclined to be straight, which is an immense advantage to a racehorse, for when fully extended the hind legs never get too far back, and are always working well under and forward. Such horses will give a good, honest run over a mile of ground when only half fit, because they do not tire so quickly as the bent legged ones. My chief regret is that I never saw Ormonde gallop home to any of his victories.

Mr. Macdonough is to be envied the possession of such a perfectly shaped animal.

I have at page 65 given an extended pedigree of Isonomy, and will take it only in some lines to the sixth remove, that being sufficient to show the working of the figures, and will be less confusing than a mass of names.

I have remarked elsewhere that from the absence of Nos. 1, 2, and 4 in four top removes Isonomy would *mate best* with mares in these lines direct or inbred to them. His son Common (Derby) comes from Thistle (4) by Scottish Chief (**12**), by Lord of the Isles (4); and the second dam, Flower Safety, is by Wild Dayrell (7) by Ion (4). His great daughter, Seabreeze (winner of the Oaks and Leger), comes also *direct* from this running line (4) (with a Barb origin), and her dam, St. Marguerite, is by Hermit (5) from Devotion, by Stockwell (**3**), from Alcestes by Touchstone (**14**). Again, take Isinglass (Two Thousand Guineas, Derby, and Leger), his dam Deadlock is in the **3** family, and by Wenlock (4) from Malpractice, by Chevalier d'Industrie (2) from a Flying Dutchman mare (**3**). So far Isinglass is his best son, and it must be admitted that he is a splendid exponent of the Figure system, inasmuch as his dam is not

ISONOMY.

ISOLA BELLA. (19)   STERLING. (**12**)

ISOLINE.   STOCKWELL. (**3**)   WHISPER.   OXFORD. (**12**)

Bassishaw ....

Ethelbert (**12**)

Pocahontas by Glencoe (1) by Sultan.

The Baron (24) ...

Silence ....

Flatcatcher (**3**) ...

Honey Dear ......

Birdcatcher (**11**) { Sir Hercules. (2 { Guiccioli.

The Prime Warden. (17)

Dr. of **Sir Hercules.** (2

{ Dr. of Liverpool. (11)

Faugh-a-Ballagh (**11**) by **Sir Hercules.** (2)

Echidna.

Birdcatcher (**11**) by **Sir Hercules.** (2)

Melbourne. (1)

Secret by Horneea by Velocipede. (**3**)

Touchstone. (**14**)

Decoy.

Plenipotentiary (6)

My Dear.

Sir Hercules. (2

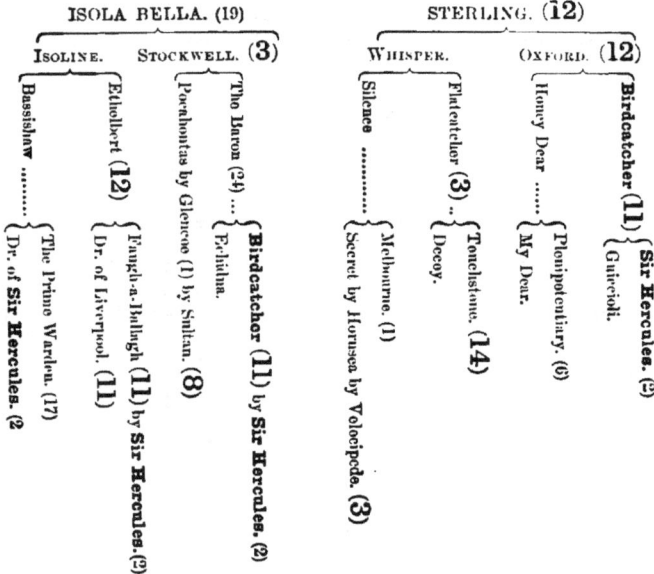

only in a great running line, but his second and third dams come from the 2 and **3** lines, and Deadlock was therefore admirably suited as a mate for Isonomy by the rules I have laid down and explained. I look to Isinglass to carry on the male line from Isonomy.

When we see a sire showing a decided partiality (as Isonomy did) for any particular female line (4) amongst his numerous matings, it is safe to infer that this effect is traceable to some cause. As I have shown, Isonomy is strongly and persistently bred to Sir Hercules, and if we are to accept the theory of heredity he was the truest representative of that fine strain of blood to be found. Perhaps an examination of Sir Hercules' pedigree in detail will disclose Isonomy's liking for the 4 family.

SIR HERCULES.

PERI. (2)

WHALEBONE. (1)

THALESTRIS.

WANDERER. (11)

PENELOPE.

WAXY. 1.

Rival ....
Alexander (12) ... { Eclipse. (12)
{ Dr. of Forester. (2)
{ Sir Peter. (3)
{ Hornet .... { Drone. (4)
{ Dr. of Goldfinder. (1)

Catherine ....
Gohanna .... { Mercury (9) ... { Eclipse. (12)
{ Dr. of Herod: Dr. of **Matchem**. { Dr. of Tartar.
{ Dr. of Matchem. (4)
Woodpecker, (1)
Camilla by Trentham (5) { **Sweepstakes.** (4)
{ Dr. of South: Dr.
of **Cartouch**. 4)

Prunella by Highflyer. (13)

Trumpator (14) { Conductor (12) by **Matchem**. (4)
{ Brunette by Squirrel. (4)

Maria .... { Herod. (26)
{ Dr. of Snap. (1)

Pot-8-os (38) ... { Eclipse. (12)
{ Sportsmistress.

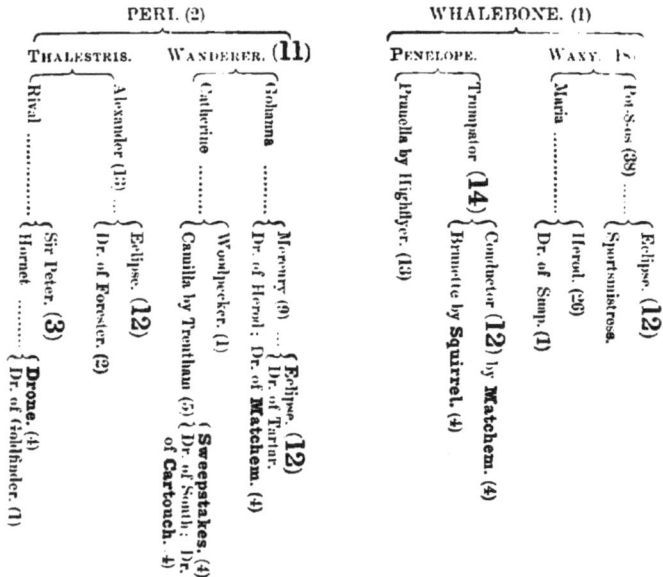

Tramp occurring twice in Isonomy's pedigree brings in *each* time six *close* strains of No. 4 family through Joe Andrews, Omnium, Cardinal Puff, *Matchem, Sweepstakes*, and *Cartouch*, all hailing from the same female line, or twelve strains, of No. 4; while Sir Hercules *alone* repeated four times contributes *twenty-four* infusions of the same family, mostly through same horses.

Having as far as space will admit traced the Blacklock and Sir Hercules' branches of Eclipse in England, I now propose to follow Leamington across the herring pond to America, whither he was taken by my old friend Sir Roderick Cameron, who has earned the thanks of every true horse loving American for importing the best

LEAMINGTON.

DR. OF. (14)				FAUGH-A-BALLAGH. (11)		
DAPHNE.		PANTALOON. (17)		GUICCIOLI.		SIR HERCULES. (2

Dr. of .... { Dr. of Orville (8) great-grandson of Eclipse. (12, 8, 11) / Champion (32) ... { Selim. (2, 3, 1) / Pedigru. } }

Laurel (21) ... { Dr. of Prime Minister. (12) / Blacklock (2, 2, 1), g.g. grandson of Eclipse. (12, 8, 11) }

Idalia .... { Musidora by Meteor. (7) / Peruvian (27) by Sir Peter. (3) }

Castrel (2) ... { Dr. of Alexander (13) by Eclipse. (12, 8, 11) / Buzzard (3) by Woodpecker (1) by Herod. }

Flight by Escape by Highflyer. (13)

Bob Booty (20) by Chanticleer (3) by Woodpecker. (1)

Dr. of Wanderer (11) by Gohanna (24), grandson of Eclipse. (12, 8, 11)

Whalebone (1) ... { Penelope by Trumpator. (14) / Waxy (18) by Pot-8-os by Eclipse. (12, 8, 11) }

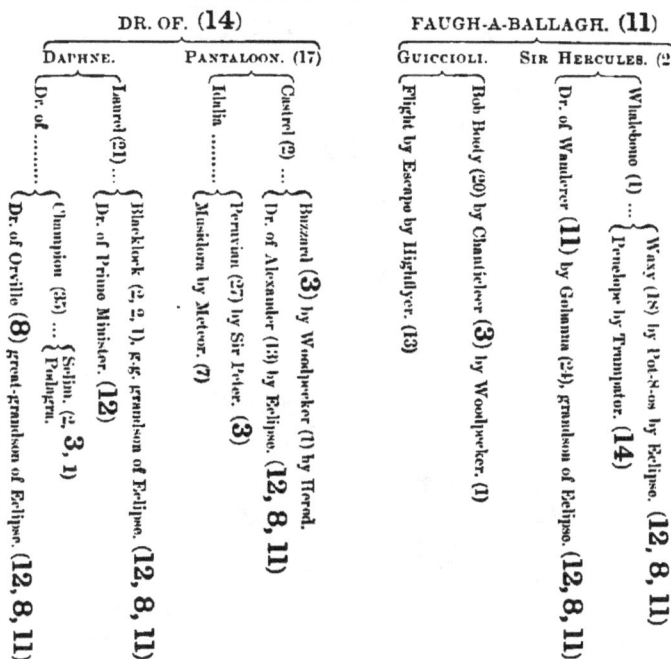

strain of blood and best representative of Eclipse ever landed on American shores. It may not be generally known, even amongst Americans, how much this gentleman has done towards building up their great stud of thoroughbreds, and had fortune favoured him his

COMMON

No. 1. RUNNING LAMB.

intended importations would have contributed yet a larger share; but, unhappily, in crossing the Atlantic about thirty-four out of thirty-eight head were thrown overboard owing to rough weather. Fortunately Leamington was landed safely to beget Iroquois, who fought and won another Bunker's Hill for his country on classic Epsom Downs in 1881.

The most captious pedigree student can find very little room for suggestion in Leamington's pedigree as a sire, and he was especially suited for America, where sire blood was the exception if we except

IROQUOIS.

MAGGIE B.B. +   LEAMINGTON. (14)

MADELINE.   AUSTRALIAN (imp.). (11)   DR. OF.   FAUGH-A-BALLAGH. (11)

- Magnolia .... { Glencoe (1) by Sultan. ('8) / Myrtle by Mameluke. (3
- Boston (40) by Timoleon. (41)
- Emilia .... { Y. Emilius. (1) / Dr. of Whisker. (1)
- W. Australian (7) { Melbourne. (1) / Dr. of Touchstone. (14)
- Daphne .... { Laurel. (2) / Maid of Honour.
- Pantaloon (17) { Castrel. (2) / Idalia.
- Gniccioli .... { Bob Booty. / Flight.
- Sir Hercules (2) ... { Whalebone. (1) / Dr. of Wanderer. (11)

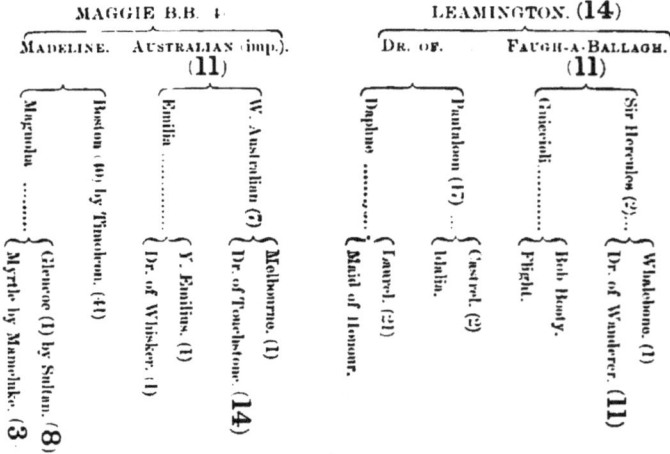

the Levity family (12). This very sire influence accounts for the wonderful success of that family on the race tracks of America, because, as a fact, in England the 12 family has not been amongst the successful running ones. Iroquois' brilliant victories in the Derby and Leger and other races single him out as Leamington's best son. Pedigree above.

H

Maggie B.B. has only one sire line in her first four removes, and was therefore well suited by a horse whose sire and dam both came from sire lines. Maggie B.B. comes from the family of the Layton Barb mare (4), and was in other respects very full of running blood.

As pointed out in the case of Peter, the many running (and non-sire) strains in the dam somewhat weakened the sire influence of Iroquois, as compared with his father, though it gave him a far

TAMMANY.

TULLAHOMA. (12)   IROQUOIS. (4)

BLINK BONNIE.   GREAT TOM. (11)   MAGGIE B.B.   LEAMINGTON. (14)

Dr. of ....

Bonnie Scotland (9) ....

Woolcraft ....

King Tom (3) ....

Madeline ....

Australian (11) ....

Dr. of ....

Faugh-a-Ballagh (11)

Volga by Glencoe from Vandal's dam.

Lexington. (12)

Queen Mary.

Iago by Don John. (2, 2, 2)

Dr. of Camel. (24)

Voltigeur. (2)

Pocahontas by Glencoe. (1)

Harkaway. (2)

Magnolia (1) by Glencoe.

Boston. (40)

Dr. of Y. Emilius. (1)

West Australian. (7)

Dr. of Blacklock. (2, 2, 1)

Pantaloon. (17)

Dr. of Bob Booty.

Sir Hercules. (2)

larger share of the vitality which makes great racehorses. If the Figure system is not at fault, he requires a lot of **3, 8, 11, 12, and 14** in his mares to produce high class animals, though his inbreeding to 1, 2, and 4 would ensure his being a fairly good sire from all kinds of mates. His best son was undoubtedly Tammany, who defeated everything in his day, and proved himself one of the highest class animals ever saddled in America. I look to him to carry on the principal branch of Leamington. He is descended in female line from the Levity (**12**) family, and his dam, Tullahoma, is by Great Tom (**11**) (brother to English Kingcraft, Derby), from Blink Bonnie by Bonnie Scotland (10), from daughter of Lexington (**12**), from Volga by Glencoe (1), from Vandal's dam by Tranby (21), son of Blacklock (2). Great Tom is by King Tom (**3**).

SALVATOR.

SALINA. (**12**)		PRINCE CHARLIE. (**12**)	
LIGHTSOME.	LEXINGTON. (**12**)	EASTERN PRINCESS.	BLAIR ATHOL. (10)

Levity .... { Trustee (7) ... { Catton. (2)
                                   { Dr. of Whisker. (1)
         { Dr. of Tranby (21) by Blacklock (2, 2, 1)

Glencoe (1) ... { Sultan (8) by Selim. (2)
                      { Dr. of Tramp. (3)

Alice Carneal ... { Sarpedon (41) by Emilius. (22)
                         { Dr. of Sumpter (4 by Sir Archy. (41)

Boston (40) ... { Timoleon (41) { Sir Archy. (41)
                                { Dr. of Saltram.
             { Dr. of Ball's Florizel.

Tomyris .... { Neustria. (12)
                      { Dr. of Glaucus. (3)

Surplice (2) ... { Touchstone. (14)
                      { Crucifix.

Blink Bonny ... { Melbourne. (1)
                    { Queen Mary.

Stockwell (**3**) { The Baron. (21)
                      { Dr. of Glencoe. (1)

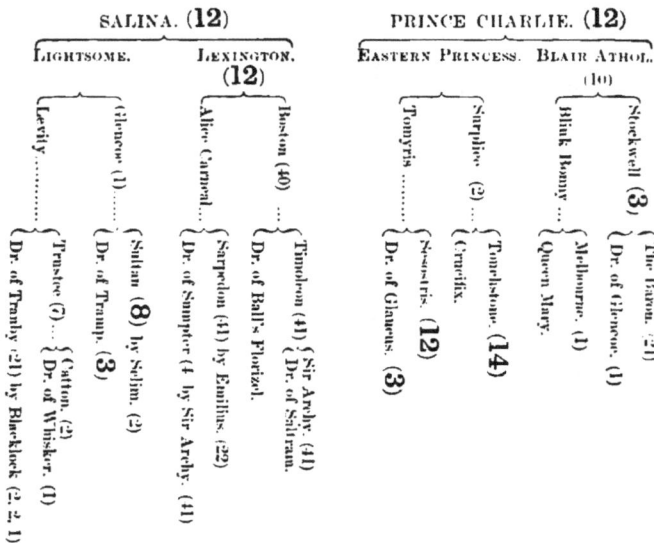

On the opposite page is the tabulated pedigree of Tammany. Time alone will prove whether he is capable of acting up to the traditions of the great sire families represented in his personality, but, judged by pedigree and performance, there is little cause to fear the result, and he is directly descended both in male and female lines from Eclipse.

Besides Iroquois, Leamington has left behind him those good sons, Eolus (6) (sire of the crack Morello), Onondaga (**12**) (sire of Dr. Rice and others), Longfellow (26), and Enquirer, so that the line is not in danger of breeding out. Iroquois has been more than once at the head of American sires with a large number of winners to his credit. Longfellow left a great son in Leonatus, (**12**) line.

While on the subject of American sires, it will not be out of place to treat of another branch of Sir Hercules imported to that country, viz., Prince Charlie, winner of the Two Thousand Guineas, and dubbed "The Prince of the T.Y.C." He cannot be said to have been a success in England.* One of his best sons was Prestonpans, now at the Del Paso Stud, near Sacramento. Prince Rudolph, another good horse by him, and inbred, like Salvator, to the **12** line, remains alone in England to represent him. But the air of America appeared to have rejuvenated Prince Charlie, and he sired a magnificent racehorse in Salvator, credited with running the straight mile against time in 1min. 35½sec., and one and a quarter miles in 2min. 5sec. He is a beautifully turned chestnut with four white legs, and reminds one very strongly of portraits of Eclipse, as well he might, seeing his repeated inbreeding to Eclipse's line (**12**). The figures indicate that he will have a successful stud career if mated to 1, 2, **3**, and 4 families.

---

* Owing to the prejudice of insular studmasters against a roarer, he never had a fair chance in England.—W.A.

CHAPTER VI.

THE LINE OF WHISKER.

THE line of Eclipse through Whisker is deserving of more than a passing notice, although he is not nearly so largely represented as Whalebone, probably through the misfortune of never being mated with such high class mares. If we can judge by old portraits of Whisker, he was better looking and of more substance than his brother Whalebone, and, according to some authorities, was even a superior performer on the track. He is represented in England by King Tom.

Harkaway furnishes another strong link in the chain of evidence as regards sire blood. He is curiously deficient in sire blood, though plentifully supplied with running strains, especially through Whisker (1), Stripling (2), and Phenomenon (2), his own dam being direct from the 2 line. How is it that we have no male representatives of this great racehorse other than King Tom, whose dam was from the great sire family of 3? Idle Boy is the next best son of Harkaway, and though his dam is in the 6 line, her sire is by Sir Hercules (2) (from a Wanderer (11) mare) from a Sultan (8) mare, from a Cervantes (8) mare. The second dam of The Bard is by Idle Boy. In Australia imported Ace of Clubs was by Stockwell (3) from Irish Queen (of the 8 line), by Harkaway; and, indeed, I cannot find any instance where Harkaway made a bit outside of mares direct from sire lines or very inbred to them. King Tom blood can hardly be overrated, especially through his daughters, and this may be attributed principally to the large infusions of God. Barb back in Harkaway's pedigree, which were conveyed to the surface through the medium of Nos. 2 and **3** lines. King Tom claims the honour of siring the dams of St. Simon, Royal Hampton, Poste Restante, Chislehurst, Romany King, and Town Moor. In Australia one of the prominent sires, Neckersgat (2), is from Miss Giraffle by King Tom.

KING TOM.

POCAHONTAS. (**3**)   HARKAWAY. (2)

MARPESSA.   GLENCOE. (1)   DR. OF   ECONOMIST. (36)

- Harpflee ....
- { Maley (6) by Orville, (**8**) great grandson of Eclipse. (**12, 8, 11**)
- { Gohanna (24) by Mercury (9) by Eclipse. (**12**)
- { Amazon by Driver. (**11**)
- { Dr. of Tramp (**3**) by Dick Andrews (9) by Joe Andrews (4) by Eclipse. (**12**)
- { Su'tan (**8**) by Selim (2) by Buzzard (**3**) by Woodpecker. (1)
- Dr. of Teddy the Grinder (5) by Asparagus (15) by Pot-8-os (38) by Eclipse. (**12**)
- { Nabocklish (9) ....
- { Ruganino.+
- { Dr. of Master Bagot (9) by Bagot (41)
- Dr. of Octavian (**8**)
- { Dr. of Oberon (9) ... { Highflyer, (13)
- { Queen Mab by Eclipse. (**12**)
- { Stripling (2) .... { Phœnomenon, (2)
- { Laura by Eclipse. (**12**)
- Whisker (1) ....
- { Waxy. (18)
- { Penelope .... { Trumpator. (**14**)
- { Prunella.

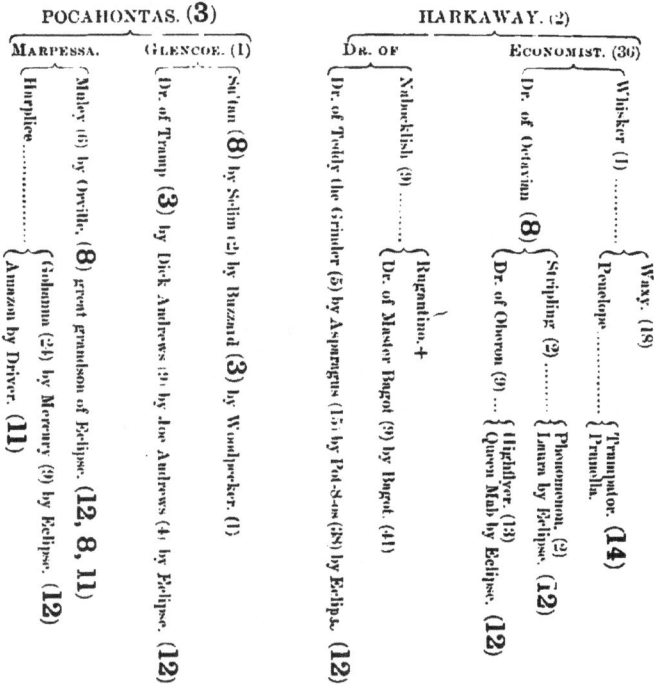

In the year 1839 Mr. Kater, of Australia, imported Cap-à-pie by The Colonel (second to Cadland for the Derby, and winner of the Leger), son of Whisker. Cap-à-pie's companion *en royage* (also owned by Mr. Kater) was Paraguay, by Sir Hercules, probably the best mare that ever left the shores of England, and certainly the best mare sired by Sir Hercules, if one may judge her by her figures and the family she founded in Australia. Unfortunately she only threw two sons Sir Hercules

SIR HERCULES. (Aus.)

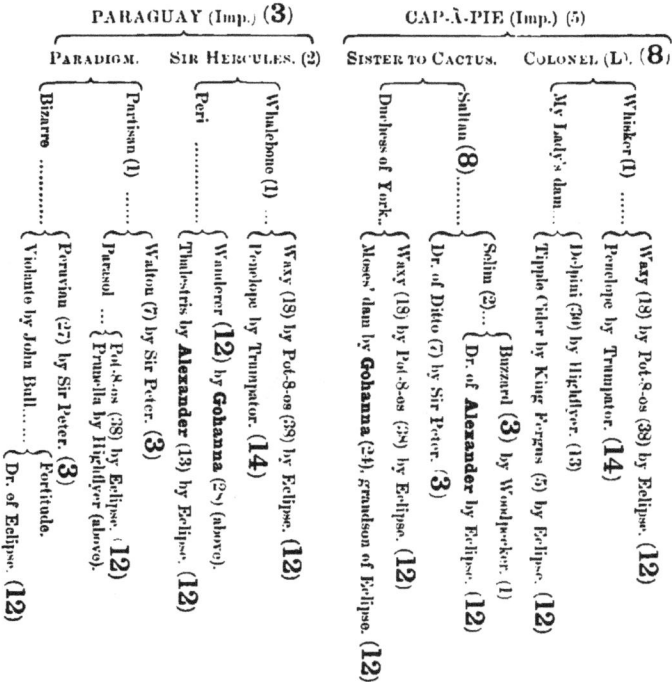

```
PARAGUAY (Imp.) (3)                         CAP-À-PIE (Imp.) (5)

PARADIGM.    SIR HERCULES. (2)     SISTER TO CACTUS.    COLONEL (L). (8)

Whisker (1) ...... { Waxy (18) by Pot-8-os (38) by Eclipse. (12)
                   { Penelope by Trumpator. (14)

My Lady's dam ... { Delpini (30) by Highflyer. (13)
                  { Tipple Cider by King Fergus (5) by Eclipse. (12)

Sultan (8) ....... { Selim (2) ... { Buzzard (3) by Woodpecker. (1)
                                   { Dr. of Alexander by Eclipse. (12)

Duchess of York.. { Dr. of Ditto (7) by Sir Peter. (3)
                  { Waxy (18) by Pot-8-os (34) by Eclipse. (12)
                  { Moses' dam by Gohanna (24, grandson of Eclipse. (12)

Peri ............ { Wanderer (12) by Trumpator. (14)
                  { Thalestris by Alexander (13) by Eclipse. (12)

Whalebone (1) ... { Waxy (18) by Pot-8-os (38) by Eclipse. (12)
                  { Penelope by Trumpator. (14)

Partisan (1) .... { Walton (7) by Sir Peter. (3)
                  { Parasol ... { Pot-8-os (38) by Eclipse. (12)
                                { Prunella by Highflyer (above).

Bizarre ......... { Peruvian (27) by Sir Peter. (3)
                  { Violante by John Bull...... { Fortitude.
                                                { Dr. of Eclipse. (12)
```

(Aus.) and Whalebone (Aus.), leaving no daughters to carry on the female line. The tabulated pedigree here given shows her son Sir Hercules to have inherited all the best strains in the Stud Book, besides being closely inbred to Whalebone and Whisker at three removes. His blood bears favourable comparison with that of Stockwell, whose only advantage was in having a strain of Blacklock.

YATTENDON.

CASSANDRA. (17)		SIR HERCULES. (3)	
ALICE GREY.	TROS (12) (imp.)	PARAGUAY.	CAP-A-PIE. (5)

Gulnare (imp.) ....

Rous's Emigrant (4) ....

Ally ....

Priam (6) ....

Sir Hercules (2) ....

Dr. of ....

Dr. of Saltan (8) by Selim (2) by Buzzard (3) by Woodpecker, (1)

Colonel (8) by Whisker (1) { Waxy by Pot-8-os (34) by Eclipse, (12) / Penelope. { Trumpator, (14) / Prunella by Highflyer.

Whalebone, (1)

Peri by Wanderer (11) by Gohanna, (24)

Partisan (1) .... { Walton by Sir Peter, (3) / Parasol by Pot-8-os by Eclipse, (12)

Bizarre by Peruvian (27) by Sir Peter, (3)

Emilius (28) by Orville (8) by Beningbro', grandson of Eclipse (12)

Cressida by Whiskey (2) by Saltram by Eclipse, (12)

Partisan (1) .... { Walton, (7) / Dr. of Pot-8-os by Eclipse, (12)

Jerd by Waxy (18) by Pot-8-os by Eclipse, (12)

Whiskey (2) grandson of Eclipse, (12) / Prunella.

Pioneer (1) ....

Ringtail .... { Buzzard (3) by Woodpecker, (1) / Dr. of Trentham.

Y. Gohanna (3) by Gohanna (24) by Mercury (9) by Eclipse, (12, 8, 11

Ultima .... { Hollyhock by Evergreen (3) by Herod. / Dr. of Satellite (4) by Eclipse, (12)

In 1828 the late Admiral Rous, then stationed on the Australian coast, did that country a signal service by importing a very beautifully bred horse called Emigrant (4) (known in New South Wales as Rous's Emigrant to distinguish him from another of the same name). This horse was by Pioneer, a son of Whiskey and Prunella. Later on, about 1840, a horse called Tros (**12** was brought to the colonies. His breeding was by Priam from Ally by Partisan, grandson of Prunella. From a union of (Aus.) Sir Hercules and Cassandra (the latter bred from these two strains of Emigrant and Tros) sprang Yattendon, a great racehorse and a magnificent sire. Cassandra, his dam, was the best race mare of her day. She threw two other good sons, Ramornie and Kiogle, and ended her days in the stud of Mr. C. G. Tindal, of Ramornie, Clarence River, the breeder of Yattendon and his half-brothers.

Yattendon's dam does not bring into this connection a great show of sire blood, but it will be observed that she is very much inbred to Eclipse, and Tros being from the same female line as Eclipse, it may be reasonably inferred that he brought into operation all the latent back strains and sire influence of his great progenitor far more strongly than if he had descended from the **14. 8**, or **3** line. It will be seen also that Partisan and Pioneer were closely related, so that Yattendon was strongly inbred to No. 1 through the best representatives, Whalebone, Whisker, Partisan (twice), and Pioneer, a son of the much prized Whiskey (2). Rous's Emigrant combined the figures 4 (in main line). 1 twice, also 2 and **3**. (Aus.) Sir Hercules (**3**) in main line, with three strains of 1 close up, and two of No. 2 very close, thus giving Yattendon a larger share of running blood (through best sources) than will generally be found in sires of the first water. As a result he suited mares of totally opposite strains. If they were deficient in running blood he supplied it; if in sire, he was equally fitted to fill the want. I have dwelt somewhat at length on this pedigree, as it will be a useful one for students to study, in view of the fact that

Yattendon not only left at least two great sons behind him to carry on the fortunes of the Whisker branch of Eclipse, but from this very inbreeding to running figures his mares are most invaluable as brood mares, many of the best racehorses in Australia to-day being the produce of his daughters (as previously stated), notably Trenchant (the A.J.C. Derby winner, 1893), Lady Trenton (Sydney Cup, 1894), Paris (Metropolitan, 1893), and Brockleigh (Epsom, 1893). Those who have followed me so far will have naturally inferred that Yattendon's sons, which have proved so successful at the stud, are descended from sire families if my theory is consistent. I have at page 62 given the pedigree of Chester, his most successful son at the stud, and will not repeat it here, more than to say that his dam, Lady Chester, came direct from the **8** family, and she was a daughter of Stockwell (**3**), from Austry, by Harkaway (**2**). A more perfect pedigree is rarely met with, and Australia owes a considerable debt of thanks to the late Edward King Cox, of Fernhill, for importing such a mare, and also for his splendid judgment in selecting Yattendon to preside over his choice harem of mares. Mr. Cox was also the breeder of the unbeaten Grand Flaneur (by Yattendon), coming from the **14** line, his dam, First Lady, was by St. Albans (**2**) by Stockwell (**3**). Chester has left more than one son likely to carry on the male line, Abercorn (the rival of Carbine) and Dreadnought (another classic winner) were both from the **3** family. Carlyon (**11**) is another promising son full of sire blood, through Adventurer and Stockwell. Few better looking horses of the big sort can be seen than Cranbrook (winner of the Newmarket Handicap (6 furlongs), at Flemington, with 8st. 12lb. up, three years), the property of my friend Mr. Henry C. White, of Havilah, who bids fair to become as successful a breeder as his brother, the late Mr. James White. Cranbrook is from La Princess by Cathedral (**8**), from Princess of Wales by Stockwell (**3**), and is therefore well supplied with sire blood. All he requires is to be crossed upon the Sweetmeat and Blacklock strains, through mares in the running families, to counteract his double strain of Melbourne. Cranbrook, though on the large side, has grown into a well-proportioned horse, without coarseness, notwithstanding his immense bone and grandly developed quarters, and in stud condition has lost the appearance of weakness of loin which he had in training. Macaroni mares would have corrected this admirably with their short backs and generally small size.

I must be excused for lingering so long upon this branch of Whisker, as I have a great love for the old (Australian Sir Hercules strain, and when on the Clarence River in 1862-63 spent many a half hour sitting on the top rail of Yattendon's exercise yard admiring the aristocratic looks and wonderful quality of the then yearling and last foal of grand old Cassandra, whose last days were spent in slings in the vain effort to prolong her days. She was twenty years old when she dropped Yattendon, and, if I mistake not, Sir Hercules was over twenty years when he sired him, thus disproving the theory about the evil effects of crossing old sires on to old mares.

The line of Whisker has played a conspicuous part in America, seeing that Foxhall comes from that male line. Also (imp.) King Ban (sire of Ban Fox and many good horses). Imported King Ernest is another son of King Tom. Imported Phaeton, grandsire of Foxhall, was also sire of Ten Broeck, a great performer. In securing these highly bred representatives of the hitherto much neglected line of Whisker, the Americans are to be congratulated. Both King Ban and King Ernest come in female descent from the **3** line (dam of the Two True Blues), and must on that account alone prove of immense service to cross upon the old American pedigrees which have so little of it, except through Medley and American Eclipse, both **3**. No stud can be said to be complete without many strains of this celebrated family, from which emanated, as we have seen, such horses as Sir Peter, Stockwell, Galopin, Flying Dutchman, and scores of other wonders. Foxhall is, so far, the greatest production of the American Whisker line. As a racehorse, he ranked in the very first flight, but, so far, has not distinguished himself at stud work, nor is he likely to do so unless mated to mares from sire lines, No. **3** for preference, and inbred to Stockwell and Galopin.

Later on, when dealing with the causes which produce phenomenal racehorses, Foxhall's pedigree will be given in an extended form. King Alfonso traces to an American source, while his sire, Phaeton (9), springs from a line singularly unprolific of high class sires, though many racehorses of note hail from it, Peter to wit.

Before closing this chapter I will give some American sires of early days (and later), also the pedigrees of Sir Modred and Darebin, both of which were selected by me for Mr. J. B. Haggin for his Del Paso ranch. Sir Modred was a splendid racehorse, and considered one of the best looking ever bred in Australia, or, rather, New Zealand, where he was born. He was one (the second) of four celebrated brothers: Betrayer (N.Z. D), Sir Modred (N.Z. D), Idalium (now at San Francisco), Cheviot (sire of Rey el Santa Anita, the winner of this year's American Derby), in the stud of Mr. Charles Reed, of America, and July, owned by Mr. Barnes, of New South Wales, Australia. Sir Modred was undoubtedly the king of them all, both as regards looks and performances.

We will now examine the pedigree of Foxhall, and note how he comes through the ordeal of the figures and other conditions essential to a stud horse.

His dam is descended from a family which has produced some excellent racehorses during its career. Hornsea, Soothsayer, Jerry, Sealskin, Skylark, Harvester (dead heat for the Derby with St. Gatien), &c., but in the list there have not been any good sires. Harvester sold lately for £800, and Skylark has been a failure. Apart from the want of prestige of the family, there is a very scanty infusion of sire families in Foxhall's pedigree, and where it does appear is associated with effeminate and running blood, and very little strong inbreeding to Eclipse, the majority of main branches going to Herod. It is only necessary to turn back to Isonomy, Stockwell, Chester, Galopin, or St. Simon and make comparisons to convince the stud master that Foxhall is not likely to make a great

FOXHALL.

JAMAICA (15)   KING ALFONSO.+

FANNY LUDLOW. LEXINGTON. (12)   CAPITOLA.   PHAETON. (9)

King Tom (3) { Harkaway. (2)
{ Dr. of Glencoe. (1)

Merry Sunshine by Storm (20) by Touchstone. (14)

Vandal (12) { Glencoe by Sultan. (8)
{ Dr. of Tranby (21) by Blacklock. (2, 2, 1.

Dr. of Margrave (2) by Muley (6) by Orville. (8)

Boston (40) { Timoleon by Sir Archy. (41)
{ Dr. of Ball, Florizel.

Dr. of Sipedon (41 by Emilius (28) by Orville. (8)

Eclipse (4) (Imp.) { Orlando (33) by Touchstone. (14)
{ Dr. of Bay Middleton. (1

Mollie Jackson { Vandal (12) { Glencoe. (1)
{ Dr. of Tranby (21) (son of
{ Blacklock.
Dr. of Margrave (2) (above).

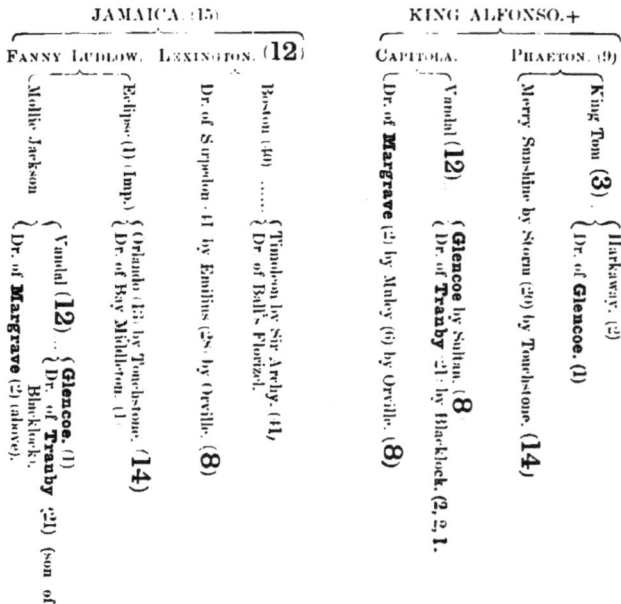

name at stud work, unless he is mated with very stoutly bred mares in sire families and a return to Blacklock, such as Galopin mares or mares inbred to Stockwell.

CHAPTER VII.

SOME AUSTRALIAN SIRES.

Also Genealogical Tables of some of the Principal Male
Descendants of Darley Arabian, Byerly Turk, and
Godolphin Barb.

Before quitting the subject of sires it will be of interest to see how
the figures work out in Australia. The pedigrees of Sir Hercules,
Yattendon, and Chester have been given as successful sires from sire
families or inbred very much to them. Chester's great rival,
Musket, imported from England, is given opposite, with his greatest
son, Carbine.

It will be seen on examination that Knowsley's dam and
Musket's dam are half-sisters, so that Musket got a return of his
dam's most potent strain, Blacklock, with Stockwell and Newminster
thrown in.

The double return of the Matchem line direct through Melbourne
and Dr. Syntax evidently strengthened the combination, and gave to
the sporting world one of the equine wonders of this century.
Indeed, I doubt if we shall ever see another horse capable of
emulating Carbine's feat of winning the Melbourne Cup (two miles)
against an aristocratic field of thirty-nine runners in the remarkably
fast time of 3min. 28½sec., with 10st. 5lb. (145lb.) in the saddle.
His temper was most peculiar. In his quiet dominant way
he would often, when being taken to the starting post, stop
dead and gaze about, and, probably, no amount of beating
would have induced him to move a yard. Fortunately he was

MUSKET.

DR. OF. (**3**)   TOXOPHILITE. (**3**)

BROWN BESS. WEST AUSTRALIAN. (7)   DR. OF.   LONGBOW. (21)

WEST AUSTRALIAN branch:
- Melbourne (1) ... { Hy. Clinker. (**8**) / Dr. of Cervantes. (**8**) }
- Mowerina .... { Touchstone. (**14**) / Dr. of Whisker. (1) }
- Camel (24) .... { Whalebone (1) / Dr. of Selim. (2) }
- Dr. of Brutandorf (**11**) by **Blacklock**. (2, 2, 1)

TOXOPHILITE branch:
- Ithuriel (2) .... { Touchstone. (**14**) / Dr. of Velocipede. (**3**) by Blacklock. (2, 2, 1) }
- Miss Bowe....... { Catton. (2) / Dr. of Orville. (**8**) }
- Pantaloon (17) ... { Castrel. (2) / Idalia. }
- Dr. of Filho da Puta. (**12**)

MERSEY (Dam of Carbine).

CLEMENCE. (2)   KNOWSLEY. (**3**)

EULOGY. NEWMINSTER. (**8**)   DR. OF.   STOCKWELL. 3)

NEWMINSTER branch:
- Beeswing .... { Dr. of Syntax. (37) / Dr. of Ardrossan. (2) }
- Touchstone (**14**) { Camel (24) / Banter. }

EULOGY branch:
- Euclid (7) .... { Emilius. (28) / Maria (Sister to Emma). }
- Martha Lynn ...... { Mulatto. (5) / Dr. of Filho da Puta. (**12**) }

STOCKWELL branch:
- The Baron (24) ... { Birdcatcher. 12 / Echidna. }
- Pocahontas ...... { Glencoe. (1) / Marpessa. }
- Orlando (13) ...... { Touchstone. (**14**) / Vulture. }

DR. OF. / Brown Bess branch:
- Brown Bess ... { Camel. (24) / Dr. of Brutandorf (**12**) by Blacklock. (2, 2, 1) }

in the hands of a clever, capable trainer, who humoured his
fancies, and coaxed him to do what was required. But for
this, it is quite possible he would have developed bad temper.
At the starting post he behaved admirably, seemed to be well aware
of what was *always* expected of him by his popular owner, Mr.
Donald Wallace, and it was a real treat to see him extend himself for
a hard finish, knowing the whereabouts of the winning post just as
well as his jockey. Truly, racing is a noble sport when carried out
under such conditions. Inbreeding like this is mostly accompanied
by abnormal speed, and when, as in this case, the courage is not
injured by bad temper, such horses can *stay* by reason of the very
ease with which they gallop alongside of their opponents, prepared to
make any post a winning post. The old time stayer, as a rule, was
a poor performer over a sprint course. Favoured with condition, he
started off for a three mile-race at about 1.55 pace, keeping this
up till the best conditioned and most enduring of his opponents
were left to make a fairly strong finish with him. It was
rather unfortunate that, for the sake of time tests, Carbine and his
great rival, Abercorn (a year older), never had a strong pace made
for them in any of their three-mile races, as it is quite probable they
would have run the distance under 5min. 20sec.

Carbine has yet to prove himself at the stud, but he cannot fail
to be a success, and his fillies should be worth their weight in gold
as dams. He stands about 16.1½ hands, with light looking barrel
and straight hind legs. The pedigrees of the dams of Nordenfeldt
and Trenton are given here, both sons of Musket, and doing
remarkably well at stud work. Nordenfeldt has sired a classic
winner, Strathmore (V.R.C. Derby and Leger), and many good
runners.

The pedigree of Trenton includes some of the best old Australian
blood on dam's side. He is from the celebrated Frailty (dam of
Niagara, Trenton, Cissy, Cuirassier, &c.) by Goldsborough (13), from
Flora McIvor by New Warrior (24), from Jo by Sir Hercules (**3**)

(Aus.), from Flora Melvor by (imp.) Rous's Emigrant (4), from Cornelia by Grasshopper, from Manto (imp.) by Soothsayer. Trenton has a great liking for the Yattendon Sir Hercules blood, and has already sired an A.J.C. Derby winner (Trenchant) from a Yattendon mare.

I give the pedigree of the (imp.) English horse St. Albans, along

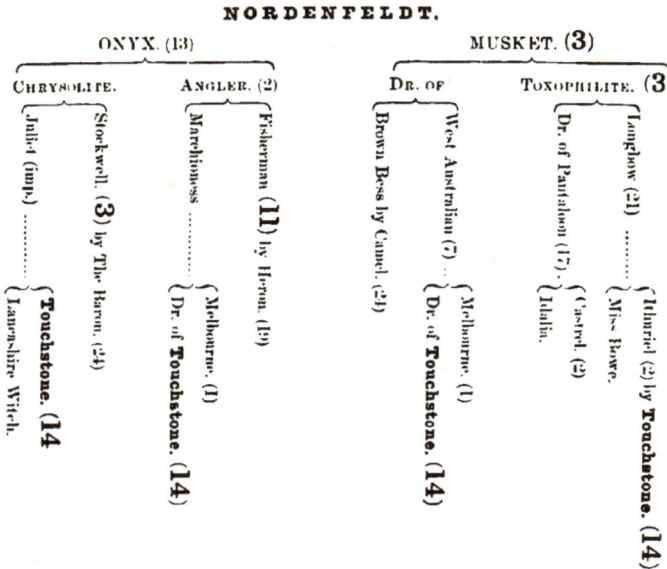

NORDENFELDT.

ONYX. (13)		MUSKET. (3)	
CHRYSOLITE.	ANGLER. (2)	DR. OF	TOXOPHILITE. (3
Stockwell. (3) by The Baron. (2) { **Touchstone. (14** / Lancashire Witch.	Fisherman (11) by Heron. (19) { Melbourne. (1) / Dr. of **Touchstone. (14)**	West Australian (7) ... { Melbourne. (1) / Dr. of **Touchstone. (14)**	Longbow (21) .... { Ithuriel (2) by **Touchstone. (14)** / Miss Bowe.
Juliet (imp.)	Marchioness	Brown Bess by Camel. (2)	Dr. of Pantaloon (17). { Castrel (2) / Idalia.

with the dam of his best son, Malua, winner of the Melbourne Cup in 1884 with 9st. 9lb. up, besides many other important races.

St. Albans was a failure until bought by Mr. John Field and put to his mares, most of which were similar in breeding to Edella (3), and consequently well suited for a horse not strong in sire blood, and wanting mares from the same strain as his best blood, Stockwell (3). He sired another good runner and winner of Melbourne Cup, viz.,

1

Sheet Anchor, whose dam was by Castle Hill, from Edella (3)
(above). Except for the luck of getting into this choice Tasmania
harem, so suitable to him, he would in all probability have been
bracketed with the already too large list of failures at the stud. I

MALUA.

EDELLA. (3) — ST. ALBANS. (28)

EDELLA. (3):
- RESISTANCE.
- PETER WILKINS. (3)

ST. ALBANS. (28):
- PANDORA.
- BLAIR ATHOL. (10)

RESISTANCE.
- Bay Middleton (1)
- Dinus

PETER WILKINS. (3)
- Flying Dutchman. (3)
- Dr. of

PANDORA.
- Polydora
- Cotherstone (7)

BLAIR ATHOL. (10)
- Blink Bonny
- Stockwell (3)

Stockwell (3) .... { The Baron (24) by Birdcatcher. (11)
                            { Pocahontas by Glencoe. (1)

Blink Bonny .... { Melbourne (1) by Hr. Clinker. (8)
                          { Queen Mary by Gladiator. (22)

Cotherstone (7) .... { Touchstone (14) by Camel. (24)
                           { Emma by Whisker. (1)

Polydora .... { Priam (6) by Emilius. (29)
                          { Manto by Tiresias.

Flying Dutchman. (3) ... { Bay Middleton. (1)
                           { Barbelle.

Dr. of ... { Plenipotentiary (6) . { Emilius (29) by Orville. (8)
           {   { Dr. of Pericles.
           { Marpessa, Dr. of Mulcy (6) by Orville. (8)

Bay Middleton (1) .... { Jersey by Blacklock. (2, 2, 1)
                           { Dr. of .... { Bay Middleton. (1)
                                                 { Dr. of Whalebone. (1)

Dinus .... { Peter Fin (13) by Whalebone. (1)
                           { Curiosity .... { Buffalo.
                                                    { Edella. (imp.)

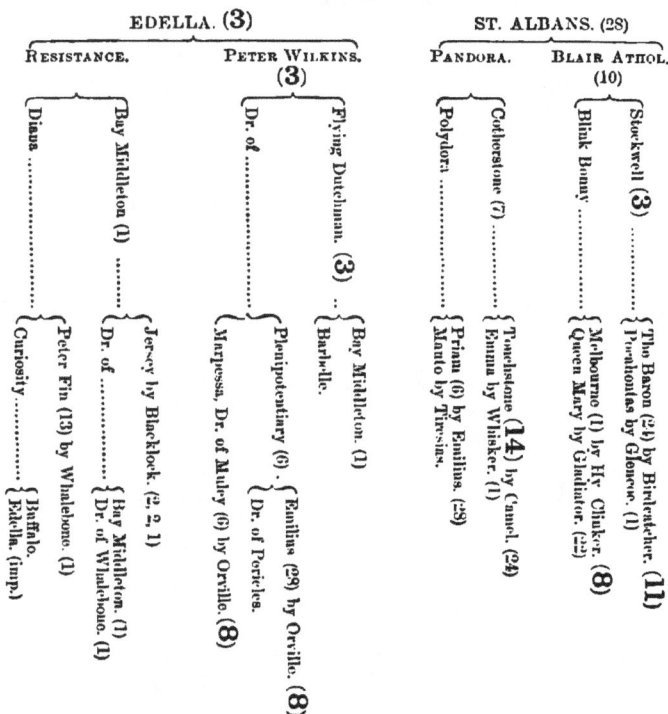

may add that Castle Hill (imp.) was a splendidly bred horse, by
Voltigeur (2) from Bab-at-the-Bowster, by Annandale (4) (son of
Touchstone) from Queen Mary.

Malua has begun stud life well by siring the Melbourne Cup winner of a few years back—Malvolio, of the 2 family. Provided he gets anything like the same chances his father enjoyed, he should make a far better all-round sire.

Next to Carbine, the most phenomenal horse bred in Australia was The Barb, a poor stud horse, in spite of his beautiful proportions

THE BARB.

YOUNG GULNARE. (4)		SIR HERCULES. (3)	
GULNARE.	THE DOCTOR. (9) (imp.)	PARAGUAY. (imp.)	CAP-À-PIE. (5) (imp.)

Deception ...... { Theorem (1) by Merlin. (8) / Cutty Sark. (imp.)

Golanna (17)...... { Rous' Emigrant (4) (imp.) by Pioneer. (1) / Gulnare (imp.) by Golanna. (24)

Y. Johannah Southcote { Walton (7) by Sir Peter. (3) / Johannah Southcote by Bunningborough. (7)

Physician (21) ... { Brutandorf (11) by Blacklock. (2, 2, 1) / Dr. of Prime Minister. (12)

Paradigm ...... { Partisan. (1) / Dr. of Peruvian. (27)

Sir Hercules (2) .. { Whalebone. (1) / Peri by Wanderer. (11)

Dr. of Sultan (8) by Selim. (2)

Colonel (8) by Whisker. (1)

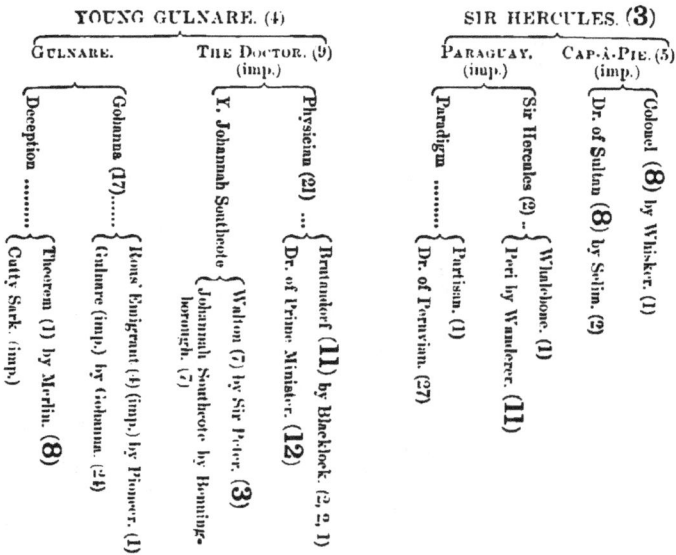

and marvellous racing powers. He was a very shapely black horse, with a wonderful turn of speed, and could stay any distance. He won the Sydney Cup twice, on the last occasion carrying 9st. 10lb. two miles.

Young Gulnare, though rich in running strains, was very deficient in sire blood. What Sir Hercules brought into the connection was sufficient to produce a great racehorse, but not enough to warrant his son being regarded as anything like his equal as a producer of racehorses, and so it turned out, to the disappointment of his owners. His only racehorses of merit were Tocal, from a mare of the **3** family, and The Barber, from a Middlesex (**14**) (imp.) mare. The latter horse brought a lot of sire blood into the mating, as he came from the **14** family, and was by Melbourne (**1**) from a daughter of Touchstone (**14**). The Barb's merit, however, has asserted itself in the second generation through his mares, many of which proved to be good dams.

One of the most valuable stud horses ever imported to Australia was Panic (**14**) by Alarm (**19**) (by Venison, **11**). Panic was from Queen of Beauty by Melbourne (**1**) (by Humphrey Clinker, **8**), from Birthday (by Pantaloon, **17**), from Honoria by Camel (**24**), son of Whalebone (**1**). Panic was well supplied with sire blood, and his best running strain being No. 1, it was only natural that he should have sired a high class horse, Wellington (V.R.C. Derby) from (imp.) Frou Frou (**1**) by Macaroni (**14**), Macaroni by Sweetmeat (**21**), son of Gladiator (**22**) (son of Partisan, **1**), with two strains of Blacklock in his dam. Panic was also sire of a long distance horse, Commotion (**9**). His dam was Evening Star by Lord Clifden (**2**) (by Newminster, **8**), from Maid of Derwent by Flatcatcher (**3**), from daughter of Belshazzar (**11**) by Blacklock (**2**). Commotion was a failure at stud, notwithstanding his sire blood, but he had the misfortune to come from a family (**9**) which rarely ever produced a good sire from amongst its roll of many splendid sons.

Imported Fisherman, the hero of many scores of hard-fought fights, in which he generally worsted his opponents, appears in the pedigrees of so many first class racehorses in Australia that this chapter would not be complete without a record of some of his best efforts in the land of his adoption. He was taken to Australia in 1860 by Mr. Charles B. Fisher, a name which carries with it the admiration and esteem of all good sportsmen at the Antipodes who, like himself, race for the honour and glory of the sport. Few men have done more to build up the name and fame of Australian studs. At a time in the colonies when the name of Stockwell carried little or no significance, except to a few enthusiasts who kept touch with English racing, Mr. Fisher secured some valuable brood mares, including Marchioness, by Melbourne (winner of the Oaks); Gildermire, by Flying Dutchman (dead heater for the Oaks); and better than either, the peerless Juliet, by Touchstone. Marchioness (2) and Juliet (13), after landing, dropped respectively Rose of Denmark by Stockwell, and Chrysolite by Stockwell. These original mares, with several other highly bred ones, including Omen (imp.) by Melbourne, and Rose de Florence by the Flying Dutchman, formed a harem for Fisherman as choice as any he would have got in England, had he remained there. From Marchioness (2) he sired the flying Fishhook, who put The Barb down in the Leger. Also Angler (Leger), who proved to be one of his best sons at stud, and was the sire of Onyx, dam of Nordenfeldt (Derby) (by Musket) and Robinson Crusoe. Fisherman's best son at stud was Maribyrnong. His pedigree is given in conjunction with Richmond's dam. Richmond was a classic winner, and is the sire of a high class horse, The Admiral.

Richmond was a small horse of wonderful speed and staying power. It is absurd to suppose that such excellence was the result of a nick of Whisker at five and six removes, the only return within these limits of any common ancestor. We must therefore conclude that the *inbreeding* of the **3** line to itself was accountable for the success. It is a parallel case with Salvator (whose pedigree has been elsewhere commented upon), Blacklock, Queen of Trumps, and many others to be treated of later on. Richmond's best son is The Admiral, of the **2** line, who seems destined to carry on the Fisherman (Herod) line, especially if mated with mares strongly inbred to the best representatives of Eclipse —daughters of Isonomy or Sterling would suit well. Fisherman's

daughter Sylvia, from Juliet (13) by Touchstone, has proved a great
brood mare, throwing Martini Henry (by Musket), a winner of the
double of Melbourne Derby and Cup, also Goldsborough (L) (son
of Fireworks), a sire of classic and Melbourne Cup winners, viz.,
Melos and Arsenal. A glance back at Fisherman's pedigree shows

RICHMOND.

THE FAWN. (3)				MARIBYRNONG. (3)			
MELESINA.		THE PREMIER. (4)		ROSE DE FLORENCE.		FISHERMAN. (11)	
Puteen		Torboy (4)		Boarling School Miss		Heron (19)	Bustard (35) by Castrel. (2)
			Tomboy. (8)		Marpessa		Dr. of Orville (8) by Benningborough. (7)
			Bessy Bedlam by Filho da Puta. (12)				
Harkaway (2)		Baroness by Leopold (12) by Camillus. (2)		Flying Dutchman (3)	Bay Middleton. (1)	Manibrace	Sheet Anchor (12) by Lottery. (11)
					Barbelle by Sandbeck. (8)		
	Economist (32) by Whisker. (1)				Plenipotentiary. (6)		Bay Middleton. (1)
	Dr. of Nabocklish. (2)					Dr. of	Whisker. (1)
Brandy Bet.	Y. Blacklock (17) by Blacklock. (2, 2, 1)						Dick Andrews. (9)

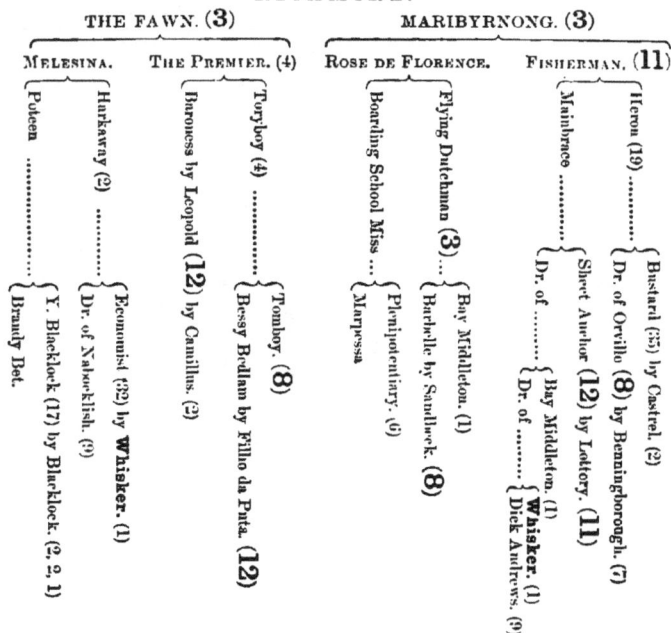

that his top lines are not wanting in sire blood, but are mostly bred
to the non-running lines of **11**, **12**, 19, 18, and 35, so that he was
well mated with such mares as Marchioness of the 2 line, and
Rose de Florence of the **3** line, and it is through these first class
lines his name will survive in male line.

Take another of America's great racehorses, Spendthrift. His most meritorious sons are undoubtedly Lamplighter and Kingston, whose dams furnish, in a very *remarkable* degree, those elements without which it would be unlikely for him to sire a horse of the

LAMPLIGHTER.

TORCHLIGHT (imp.) (14)

MIDNIGHT.
- King Tom (3)
  - Harkaway (2) by Economist. (36)
  - Dr. of Glencoe (1) by Sultan. (8)
- Starlight...........
  - Kremlin (12) by Sultan. (8)
  - Evening Star by Touchstone. (14)

SPECULUM. (1)
- Violette (19)
  - Voltigeur (2) by Voltaire (12) by Blacklock. (2,2,1)
  - Dr. of Birdcatcher (11); Dr. of Inheritor (4);
- Dr. of ....
  - Dr. of Blacklock. (2,2,1)
  - Orlando (33) by Touchstone. (14)
  - Dr. of Emilius. (28)

SPENDTHRIFT. +

AEROLITE.
- Lexington (12)
  - Boston (10) by Timoleon + Sir Archy. (41)
  - Dr. of Sarpedon (41) by Emilius. (29)
- Dr. of ....
  - Glencoe (1) by Sultan. (8)
  - Dr. of Medoc. +

AUSTRALIAN (imp.) (11)
- West Aus. (7)
  - Melbourne (1) by Hy. Clinker. (8)
  - Dr. of Touchstone. (14)
- Dr. of ....
  - Y. Emilius (1) by Emilius (29) by Orville. (8)
  - Dr. of Whisker (1) by Waxy. (1s)

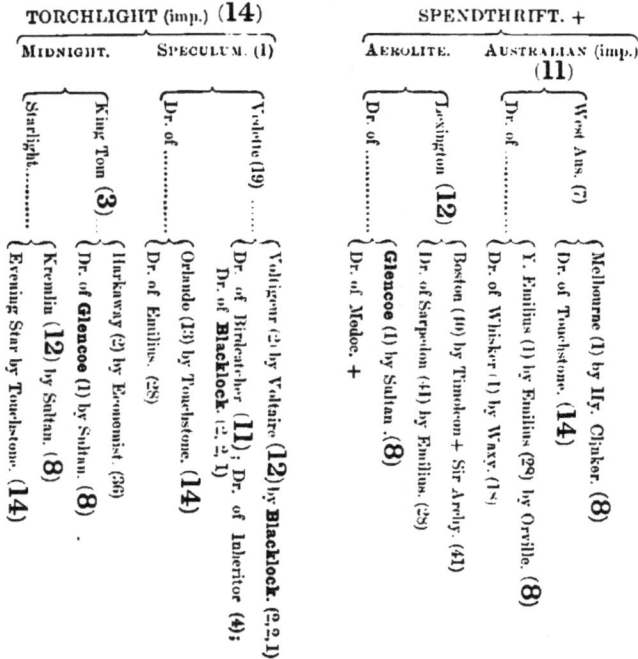

highest class, especially as his dam comes from an unknown family in English Stud Books.

His other great son, Kingston, shows the partiality Spendthrift has for sire strains.

As might be supposed from a horse bred like Spendthrift, he responded readily with a mare carrying double Blacklock through sire lines, as in the case of Lamplighter above.

Lexington has played such an important part in the turf history of America that no book on the subject of breeding racehorses would be complete without a reference to him. As a racehorse he was the very best of his day, and though he once suffered defeat from

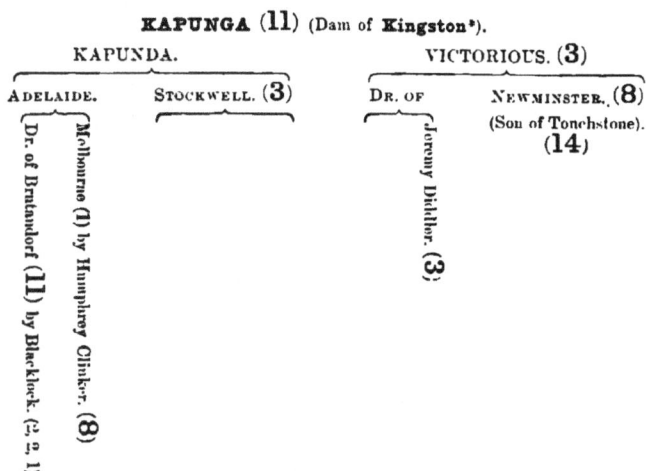

KAPUNGA (11) (Dam of **Kingston**).

KAPUNDA.		VICTORIOUS. (3)	
ADELAIDE.	STOCKWELL. (3)	DR. OF	NEWMINSTER. (8) (Son of Touchstone). (14)
Dr. of Brutandorf (11) by Blacklock. (2, 2, 1) — Melbourne (1) by Humphrey Clinker. (8)		Jeremy Diddler. (3)	

Lecompte in a four-mile heat race, it was attributed to the jockey pulling up at the end of the third mile under the impression that the race was over, and the owner of Lecompte refused to accept a challenge to run it again. Mr. S. D. Bruce, of New York, speaks of him in his excellent "Breeders' Handbook" as "the best racehorse America ever produced, and the king of stallions."

The pedigree of Boston discloses only one sire figure in the

---

* Kingston ran 129 races, four times unplaced. Ran 1¼ miles in 2min. 35½sec.; car. 125lb.

LEXINGTON.

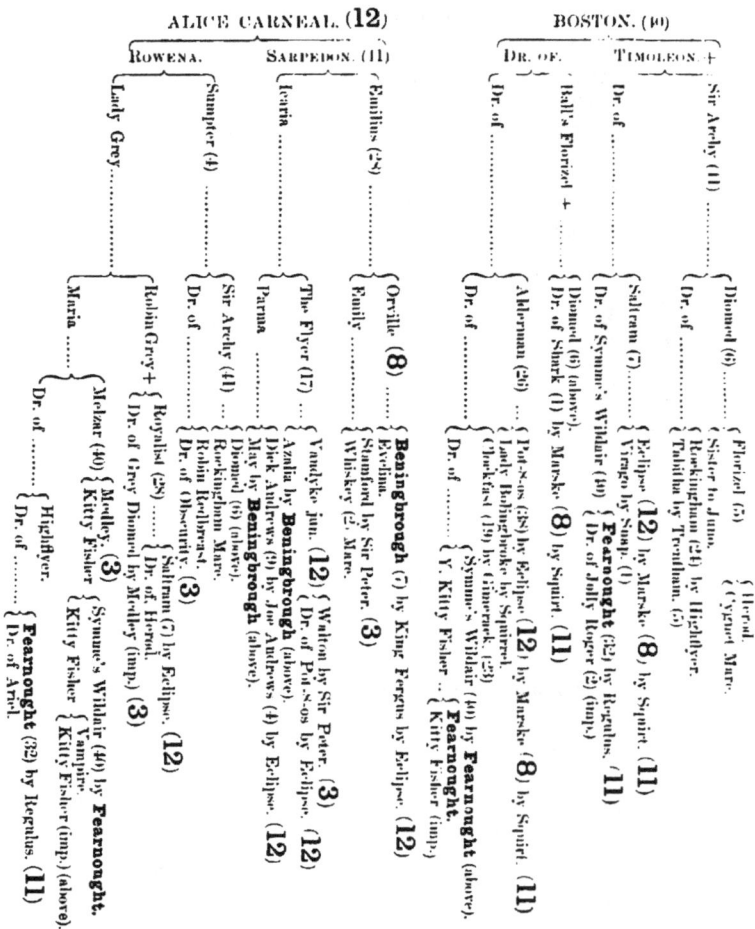

ALICE CARNEAL. (12)

BOSTON. (10)

ROWENA.   SARPEDON. (11)   DR. OF.   TIMOLEON. +

first five removes, and then we get Eclipse. Judged by the Figure standard, he could only sire superior racehorses by mating with mares from sire families, like Alice Carneal (**12**), or else from mares in running strains as an alternative, for he was very deficient in these families as well. That Boston himself was in his day a phenomenal horse on the turf is beyond doubt, but it is somewhat difficult to get any accurate line of comparison between such horses and those of to-day, where training and other conditions are so dissimilar. A first class horse in these times has to prove himself against tremendous odds in the numbers of highly trained animals pitted against him (in races from six furlongs to one and a half miles), and the facility with which all the very best are brought together. In three and four mile heats it was very often purely a matter of training and endurance, the factor of *high* speed being as often as not absent. Personally, I look upon these long heat races as simply barbarous and unsportsmanlike. Two miles (one event) is quite enough to test the stamina of race-horses. Most of the Australian champion races (three miles) are mere farcical canters until the last six furlongs. In 1894, when Portsea broke a record in 5min. 23½sec., three of the leading horses were put into the vet.'s hands just after the race.

It has been a common sight to see this race run in such *slow* time as 6min. by very high class animals, capable of doing the distance in 5min. 30sec. and under ; but owners will not injure their future chances by running it from end to end fast, unless compelled by some time limit, such as they have now in Melbourne, where the champion race must be run under 5min. 40sec. Therefore I contend that it is much safer to gauge the past heroes by their records at the stud than by these wonderful four-mile heat races they have won While admitting freely that Boston was a remarkably good horse on the track, as also his sons Lexington and Lecompte, he has failed to perpetuate himself, except through Lexington, and that horse (like the rest of the Herod line) stands a fair show of fading gradually out of existence in male line. A look into the pedigree will show why. Where I have placed a cross it denotes either some English obscure family which has never won a classic race or one tracing to obscure American, Australian, or French origin. Now, the great bulk of Lexington's blood traces to outside or obscure origin. Take

DUKE OF MAGENTA.

MIRIAM. +		YORKSHIRE. (2) (imp.)	
MINERVA ANDERSON.	GLENCOE. (1)	MOSS ROSE.	ST. NICHOLAS. (6)

Dr. of ....

Luxborough (6) (imp.) ....

Dr. of ....

Sultan (8) ....

Dr. of ...

Tramp (3) ....

Sea Mew ....

Emilius, (29) ....

Sir Charles + ...
Dr. of Brunner ......

Ditto (7) by Sir Peter. (3)
Dr. of Dick Andrews (9); Eleanor by Whiskey. (2)

Selim (2) by Buzzard (3) by Woodpecker. (1)
Dr. of Ditto (7) by Sir Peter. (3)

Tramp (3) (above).
Web by Waxy. (18)

Sancho by Herod. (26)
Dr. of Coriander. (4)

Dick Andrews (9) by Joe Andrews. (4)
Gohanna. (24)
Dr. of Woodpecker. (1)

Beningbrough. (7)
Dr. of Highflyer.

Commander by Hambletonian. (1)

Stamford (26) by Sir Peter. (3)
Dr. of Whiskey. (2)

Orville. (8)

Sir Archy. (41)
Dr. of Citizen.
Mendoza by Medley. (3)
Dr. of Medley. (3)

such names as Boston (40), Sir Archy (41), Sarpedon (41), Timoleon (+), Wildair (40) (four times), Fearnought (32) (seven times), Rockingham (24) (twice), Melzar (40) (once), Royalist and Emilius (28) (once each), Robin Grey (+), Ball's Florizel (+)

(once), Alderman (26) (once).   Every time that Lexington is introduced into a pedigree at the present day, and inbred to, as we see so frequently in American pedigrees, all this dead weight of *outside* blood is brought to the surface.   Fortunately, while crossing Lexington upon itself it is, in the vast majority of cases, accompanied by the two splendid strains of Glencoe (1) and Yorkshire (2), which made the name of Lexington something to conjure with in the past when his stock were sweeping the boards.   Take Glencoe and Yorkshire away, and where would he have been?   Take Penelope away, and where else of consequence do we find the much vaunted Waxy?   Examine the two pedigrees of Glencoe and Yorkshire, and mark the contrast of running figures which are so conspicuous by their absence in Lexington's pedigree.   I give the dam of Duke of Magenta, one of his best sons, as she includes strains of both Yorkshire and Glencoe.

No less than twenty-five of the horses included in those given here are from the running families of Nos. 1, 2, **3**, 4, 6, and 7. Figure **3** occurs eight times, and nothing could be happier for Lexington, whose best back strains on dam's side are Sumpter (4), Robin Redbreast (**3**), also inbred to **3** through Sir Peter, his sire. There are five strains of the No. 1 family, four of the No. 2, and three of No. 4.   To the student who has followed me closely this will be more convincing than many pages of argument.   Boston's great son, Lecompte, and the only conqueror of Lexington, should be no exception to the above if there is any soundness in my Figure system.

Reel, though herself in an outside line, has strong inbreeding to the four premier running families; Gallopade is closely inbred to No. 2 through Catton and Camillus, and another close strain comes to Reel through Glencoe's grandsire Selim.   It will be observed also that Glencoe, Woodpecker (three times), and Hambletonian all hail from No. 1, also Joe Andrews and Matchem No. 4 (the latter four times) are from same line.   Withal, there is no lack of good sire blood up close, and it is no wonder that Lecompte was equal to putting Lexington down. It is quite probable from his breeding that over a reasonable distance of ground, and up to two miles, he (Lecompte)

REEL (Dam of **Lecompte**).

GALLOPADE (23) (imp.)		GLENCOE. (1)	
CAMILLINA.	CATTON. (2)	TRAMPOLINE.	SULTAN. (8)

GLENCOE. (1)

SULTAN. (8)
- Selim (2)
  - Buzzard (3) by Woodpecker. (1)
  - Dr. of Alexander (13) by Eclipse. (12, 8, 11)
- Bacchante by Ditto (7) by Sir Peter. (3)

TRAMPOLINE.
- Tramp (3)
  - Dick Andrews (9) by Joe Andrews (4) by Eclipse (12, 8, 11)
  - Dr. of Gohanna (29) { Mercury by Eclipse. / Dr. of Woodpecker. (1) }
- Web
  - Waxy (18) by Pot-8-os (38) by Eclipse. (12, 8, 11)
  - Penelope by Trumpator. (14)

GALLOPADE (23) (imp.)

CATTON. (2)
- Golumpus (11)
  - Gohanna (24) { Mercury (9) by Eclipse. (12, 8, 11) / Dr. of ... { Herod. (26) / Minikin by Matchem. (4) } }
  - Catherine { Woodpecker. (1) / Camilla by Trentham. (5) }
- Dr. of
  - Timothy (23) { Delpini (20) / Cora by Matchem. (4) }
  - Lucy { Florizel. (6) / Frenzy by Eclipse. (12, 8, 11) }

CAMILLINA.
- Camillus (2)
  - Hambletonian (1) by King Fergus (6) by Eclipse. (12, 8, 11)
  - Faith { Precolt (9) by Blank. / Atalanta by Matchem. (4) }
- Dr. of
  - Smolensko (18) by Sorcerer. (6)
  - Miss Cannon { Orville. (8) / Dr. of ... { Weathercock. / Cora by Matchem. (4) } }

would have proved himself the better of the two. I have before remarked that the peerless Glencoe blood made the fortunes of Lexington, backed up as it was by the Yorkshire strain. It would not serve any purpose, therefore, to follow his career further, except as he comes into American pedigrees. Boston, his sire, ran forty-five races and won forty. Of these, thirty were four-mile

HARRY BASSET.

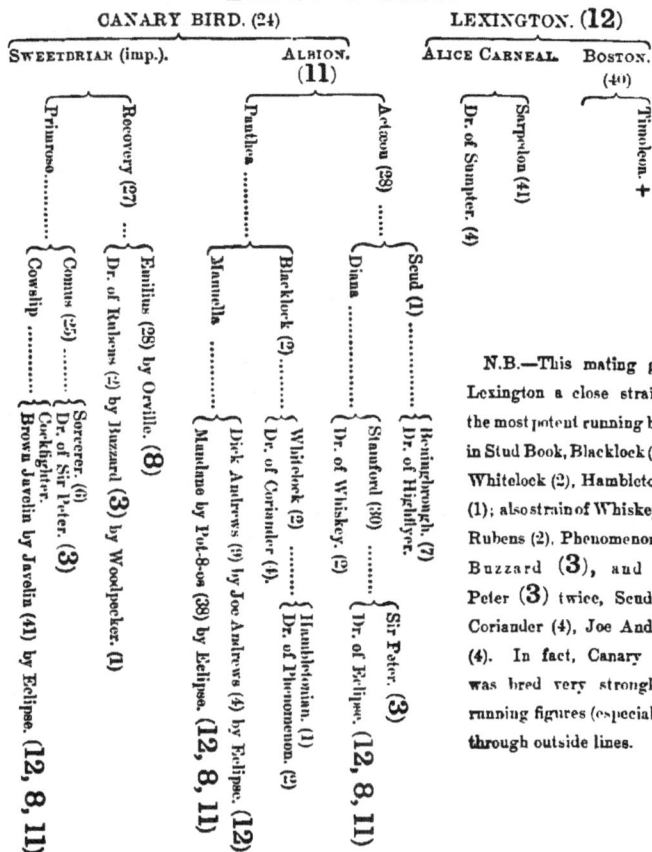

CANARY BIRD. (24)

LEXINGTON. (12)

SWEETBRIAR (imp.).

ALBION. (11)

ALICE CARNEAL.

BOSTON. (40)

Recovery (27)

Actæon (28)

Dr. of Sumpter. (4)

Sarpedon (41)

Timoleon. +

Primrose.........

Pantlea ....

Scud (1) ....

Æmilius (28) by Orville. (8)

Dr. of Rubens (2) by Buzzard (3) by Woodpecker. (1)

Blacklock (2) ....

Diana ....

Mantua by Pot-8-os (38) by Eclipse. (12, 8, 11)

Manuella. ....

Dick Andrews (2) by Joe Andrews (4) by Eclipse. (12)

Whitelock (2) ....

Dr. of Coriander (4).

Stamford (38) ....

Dr. of Whiskey. (2)

Beningbrough. (7)

Dr. of Highflyer.

Comus (25) ....

Dr. of Sir Peter. (3)

Sorcerer. (6)

Corkflighter.

Cowslip ....

Brown Javelin by Javelin (41) by Eclipse. (12, 8, 11)

Hambletonian. (1)

Dr. of Phenomenon. (2)

Sir Peter. (3)

Dr. of Eclipse. (12, 8, 11)

N.B.—This mating gives Lexington a close strain of the most potent running blood in Stud Book, Blacklock (2) by Whitelock (2), Hambletonian (1); also strain of Whiskey (2), Rubens (2), Phenomenon (2), Buzzard (3), and Sir Peter (3) twice, Scud (1), Coriander (4), Joe Andrews (4). In fact, Canary Bird was bred very strongly to running figures (especially 2) through outside lines.

heats; nine, three-mile heats; and one race of two-mile heats. Lexington, as remarked before, was only beaten once in his remarkable turf career.

In case I should be met with the contention that Harry Basset, probably the best racehorse ever sired by Lexington, has no Glencoe and Yorkshire blood in his dam, it may be well to insert his dam's pedigree.

Probably the best example of the Lexington male line is old Grinstead, the once pride of Lucky Baldwin's Santa Anita ranch, Southern California. It is rather a sad sight to see the old horse wandering about his inclosure very aged and impotent, yet well cared for by his owner. He was a good racehorse and a first class sire. Three Derby winners, if I mistake not, spring from his loins, and many good stake horses. He was by Gilroy (4) (by Lexington, **12**, from Dr. of Glencoe, 1) from sister to Rurie (**12**), by (imp.) Sovereign (17) (son of Emilius, 28) from Levity, by Trustee (7) (by Catton, 2) from Vandal's dam, by Tramby (21) by Blacklock 2, 2, 1. Grinstead's best son is Gano, one of the Santa Anita sires. It will be seen that Grinstead was the result of a double cross of the No. **12** line. Vandal by Glencoe (1) also descends from this line (**12**). He was successful both at track and stud, and undoubtedly the best sire Glencoe produced. Vandal left a useful son in Virgil (20), sire of Virgilian (4), the latter from a Lexington (**12** mare. Virgil was from Hymenia by (imp.) Yorkshire (2), from Little Peggy by Cripple (4), and therefore had both sire and running blood of best kind in his pedigree.

I give the pedigrees of both Sir Modred and Darebin. Sir Modred last season (1893) was deprived of the great honour of heading the list of winning sires of America by the enormous sum in stakes won by Himyar's son Domino. Darebin, through lack of suitable mares, has been a partial failure, though he sired a high class horse over all distances, the Australian Peer, before leaving Australia; and likewise the half season of Sir Modred (in New South

Wales) produced two nearly first class animals, Sir William and Antaeus.

While neither sire or dam are in sire lines there is a steady

SIR MODRED.

IDALIA. (17) | TRADUCER. (20)

DULCIBELLA. | CAMBUSCAN. (19) | ARETHUSA. | THE LIBEL. (14)

Priestess ....
{ The Doctor ..... { Dr. Syntax. (37) / Dr. of Lottery (11) by Tramp. (3) }
The Biddy ...... { Birni (1) by Hy. Clinker. (8) / Idalia by Peruvian (27) by Sir Peter. (3) } }

Voltigeur (2) ....
{ Voltaire (12) by Blacklock. (2, 2, 1) / Martha Lynn by Mulatto. (5) }

The Arrow ....
{ Slane (25) ... { Royal Oak (5) / Dr. of Orville. (8) } / Southdown by Defence (5) by Whalebone. (1) }

Newminster (8) ....
{ Touchstone (14) { Camel (28) by Whalebone. (1) / Dr. of Master Henry. (3) } / Beeswing ...... { Dr. of Syntax. (37) / Dr. of Ardrossan. (2) } }

Languril ......
{ Cain (8) by Paulowitz (8) by Sir Paul (8) by Sir Peter. (3) / Lydia by Pouton by Sir Peter. (3) }

Elis (13) by Langar (7) by Selim (2) by Buzzard. (3)

Sister to Touchstone ... { Camel (28) by Whalebone. (1) / Dr. of Master Henry (3) by Orville. (8) }

Pantaloon (17) .... { Castrel (2) by Buzzard. (3) / Dr. of Peruvian by Sir Peter. (3) }

inbreeding to sire blood all through the pedigree, and perhaps more Sir Peter (3) than any horse in America. At the same time, he is strong in Eclipse, especially on dam's side. With so much Sir

No. 3. RUNNING AND SIRE FAMILY.

LA FLÈCHE

Peter (**3**) at bottom of pedigree it is only natural to suppose that mares from the **3** line would suit him, or else, failing this, mares by horses of **3** line, such as Stockwell. He has hit well with Glenelg, a grandson of Stockwell. Perhaps his best sons, from a stake horse point of view, are Sir Excess, who showed himself a first class two-year-old last season, and his full brother, Connoisseur, a big winner in 1894. His dam is Dixianne by King Ban of the **3** line, and King Ban is by King Tom, also of the **3** line. King Ban is from Atlantis by Thormanby (4), who was again by Windhound of the No. **3** line. The breeding of this colt looks more like Derby form than anything I have seen by Sir Modred, and the mare comes from a great winning line, No. 1.

Dr. Hasbrouck by Sir Modred is the champion sprinter of America. His dam is a short pedigree mare with only one strain of the brothers Castrel and Selim, through Virgil, Vandal, and Glencoe, She would of course be well served by a horse descending from the *male* line of Castrel, especially as she brings to him a return of Blacklock. Virgil's inbreeding is to Tramp, a **3** horse, through Glencoe (1) and Yorkshire (2), all extremely favourable conditions, but I will enlarge upon this pedigree later on.

Plaything, the dam of Tournament, another good son of Sir Modred, is by Alarm, son of (imp.) Eclipse (1) and Maud, by Stockwell (**3**) from a Lanercost (**3**) mare from a Velocipede mere (**3**), and the latter horse, being by Blacklock (2), would give Alarm a double strain of this excellent blood to nick with Sir Modred's grandam, Dulcibella, by Blacklock's son Voltiguer (2). One can well appreciate the good result likely to accrue from such a mating. I look upon the Blacklock strain, carried through mares inbred to the **3** family, as being the orthodox mating for Sir Modred, Galopin blood to wit.

Sir Modred, as before remarked, sired only a few horses in Australia, as I purchased him for Mr. J. B. Haggin in the early part of his first season at the stud. Only four of his stock were raced out of about half a dozen foaled, and two, Antæus and Sir William, were nearly first class. Antæus won a mile race in Sydney last season in good company with 10st. 7lbs. (147lbs.) up. He is from Millie by (imp.) Grandmaster (**14**) (whose pedigree is given at page 60), from Vesper by Barbarian (4) (son of Sir Hercules (Aus.), from Dr. of Kingston (imp.), a horse of No. 1 line. Grandmaster (**14**) is from a Stockwell (**3**) mare, and Australian Sir Hercules is from the same family (**3**) as Stockwell. The mare is also inbred to Blacklock (two strains). Sir William is out of Vesper above. For his inches (he stood about fifteen hands) it was astonishing how he could carry big weights over a two-mile course in the best of company.

Antæus has grown into a very shapely horse, but as a two-year-old he was very much on the plain side ; and when his present owner, Mr. H. C. White, of Havilah, near Sydney, Mr. Thomas Cook, of Turanville, New South Wales, also a large breeder, and myself awarded him first prize at the Singleton show in his class, his breeder and then owner, Mr. Ben Richards, was very disappointed at our placing him over Camden, another son of Sir Modred, subsequently proved to be a duffer. We rejected Camden because he was *too neat*, and did not look like furnishing into a big weight carrier. A "pretty" youngster, whether equine or human, rarely grows into a handsome horse or man.

Darebin won the V.R.C. Derby, also Sydney Cup, four years, carrying 9st. 5lbs. He is a typical Melbourne horse, and would be a very valuable outcross in England for the ever recurring Stockwell and Blacklock. He descends in female line from a noted sire family (**14**). His pedigree is given below in conjunction with the dam of Australian Peer, a first-class racehorse over all distances. I cannot give him any higher praise than to record that on the first eight occasions he met Abercorn (by Chester), both three years (at weight for age), they each won four times at all distances. This was excellent form, seeing that Abercorn (four years) defeated Carbine (three years) three times at weight for age.

Darebin being inbred to Matchem and Herod in his main lines was well suited with a mare having no less than four strains of Blacklock, one coming through Stockwell.

AUSTRALIAN PEER.

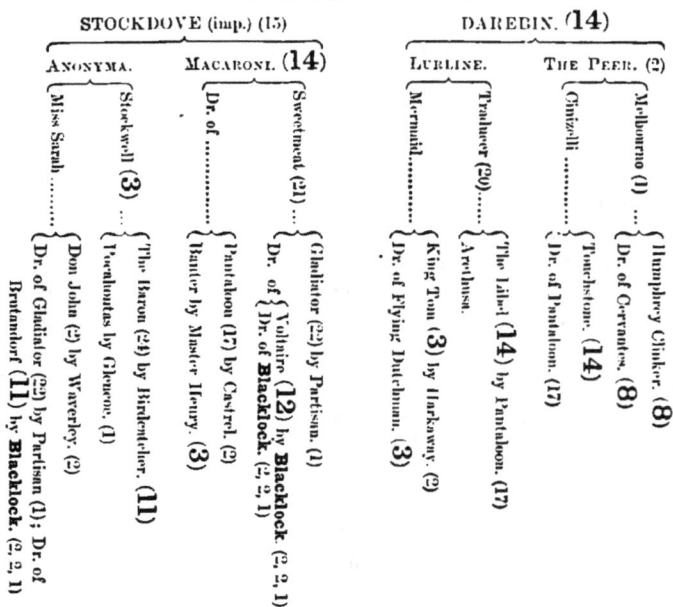

STOCKDOVE (imp.) (15)   DAREBIN. (14)

ANONYMA.   MACARONI. (14)   LURLINE.   THE PEER. (2)

Melbourne (1) ... { Humphrey Clinker. (8) / Dr. of Cervantes, (8)

Touchstone. (14) { Dr. of Pantaloon. (17)

Chinzelli ....

Archduke.

Trducer (20) ...... { The Libel (14) by Pantaloon. (17)

Mermaid. .... { King Tom (3) by Harkaway. (2) / Dr. of Flying Dutchman. (3)

Sweetmeat (21) ... { Gladiator (22) by Partisan. (1) / Dr. of { Voltaire (12) by **Blacklock**. (2, 2, 1) / Dr. of **Blacklock**. (2, 2, 1)

Dr. of .... { Pantaloon (17) by Castrel. (2) / Banter by Master Henry. (3)

Stockwell (3) ... { The Baron (24) by Birdcatcher. (11) / Pocahontas by Glencoe. (1)

Miss Sarah ...... { Don John (2) by Waverley. (2) / Dr. of Gladiator (22) by Partisan (1); Dr. of Brutandorf (11) by **Blacklock**. (2, 2, 1)

While the Rancho del Paso mares, both in good looks and breeding, hold their own with any stud in America, there are very few suitable as mates for a horse bred like Darebin. His best hit has been with Lou Lanier by Lever (12) (Lexington), a son of Levity by (imp.) Trustee, whose dam, Emma, was by Whisker (1).

K 2

Levity was out of Vandal's dam by (imp.) Tranby (21), son
of Blacklock (2).   Lou Lanier's second dam, Re-Union, was
incestuously bred to Glencoe (1), Sultan (8), Selim (2), and Woodpecker (1).   It is easy to imagine that Lou Lanier, inbred to
Glencoe, Blacklock, and Whisker, all quality blood, would throw
speedy racehorses like Kildeer and Lucky Dog to Darebin.

The Rancho del Paso stud has yet another Australian sire,
Maxim* (12, by Musket (3) from Realization, by Vespasian (19)
from a Stockwell (3 mare) from Hopeful Duchess by the Flying
Dutchman (3).   Many good judges considered him the equal of
Carbine, but as they never measured strides (so far as I remember)
Carbine is entitled to be called the better horse on his Melbourne
Cup performance alone.

Maxim is a big brown horse of the Musket type, and must make
his name at stud work, suitably mated, for he is rich in sire strains
and good running blood also.   His inbreeding to the 3 family should
prove an excellent nick on American mares, especially the Monday
and Norfolk strains and Sir Modred fillies.

As it would be tedious to go through all the principal sires of
the Eclipse, Matchem, and Herod lines, I have inserted comparative
tables of descent showing the curious consecutive following of the
sire figures, and it will be found that wherever the sire figures are
thickest the best results were obtained.

* Died in August of this year, 1894.

(28) Pot-8-os.

(18) Waxy. (26)

(1) Whalebone. (14)

(2) Sir Hercules. (11)

(11) Birdcatcher.

(24) The Baron. (36)

(12) Oxford. (6)

(12) Sterling. (3)

(19) Ismony. (3)

(3) ISINGLASS. (4)

Also by Ismony.

(4) COMMON. (12

(24) The Baron. (36)

(3) Stockwell. (1) 8)

(16) Blair Athol. (1 8)

(1) Silvio. (12, 11)

(2) The Marquis. 14)

(3) Newminster. (14, 3)
(Aus.)

(2) St. Albans. (14)

(12) Springfield. (12,

(2) Sainfoin. (4)

'3 ORME. 3)

(24) The Baron. (36)

(3) Stockwell. (1)

(5) Doncaster. (2)

(1) Bend Or. (4)

(16) Ormonde. 14)

(5) Doncaster. (2)

(16) Muncaster. (8, 14)

(14) SARABAND. 12, 14)

(28) St. Albans. (5, 6)
(imp.)

3) Malua. (3, 3)
(Aus.)

(12) Prince Charlie. (: 12)
(imp.)

(12) SALVATOR. 12) (6
(Am.)

(12 Prince Rudolph (1) 3, 12)

11 Faugh-a-Ballagh brother to Birdcatcher.

(14) Leamington. (17)

(4) Iroquois. (11)

+ ENQUIRER. (12, 3

(15) INSPECTOR B. + (12) (14) TAMMANY. (11)

Other sons of Leamington.

(24) LONGFELLOW. 3, 3)

(12 ONONDAGA. (12 (1)

(4) POWHATTAN. 12 (1)

(12 SENSATION. 12 (1)

(12 Leonatus, (3)
al-a

(12 THE BARD. (2

Note.—The author has sometimes given the numbers of the dam's sire and his sire; sometimes of the dam's sire and of the second dam's sire.   W. A

THE DARLEY ARABIAN MALE LINE (through Touchstone).

N.B.—The right hand figures are those of maternal grandsire and great grand-dice. Left hand figures denote family from which the horse is descended.

+ A family which has never won an English classic event.

.˙. This line might also have been given to include Orlando, Teddington, Marsyas, and Albert Victor.—W. A.

(6) Bartlett's Childers.

(11) Squirt.

(8) Marske.

(12) Eclipse. (11)

(38) Pot-8-os.

(18) Waxy. (26)

(1) Whalebone. (14)

(24) Camel. (2) (3)

(14) Touchstone. (3, 12)

(8) Newminster. (37) (3)

(2) Lord Clifden. (1) (8, 12)

(10) Hampton. (3, 3)

(8) AYRSHIRE. (3) (19)

Other sons of Hampton are:
(11) ROYAL HAMPTON. (3)
(22) MERRY HAMPTON. (10)

(2) Hurriel. (3)

(21) Longbow. (2)

(3) Toxophilite. (17, 2)

(3) Musket. (7, 1)

(2) CARBINE. (3) (Aus.)

Other sons of Musket:
(2) PETRONEL. (6) (12)
(19) NORDENFELDT. (2) (3) (Aus.)
(18) Trenton. (13, 24) (Aus.)

(8) TRENCHANT. (17) (3)

(10) LIGHT ARTILLERY. (10) (3) (Aus.)

(5) Hermit. (12) (2)

(22) ST. BLAISE. (12) (Am.)

(23) Zealot. (3)

(2) Castor. (12, 12) (N.Z.)

(4) ST. HONORAT. (3, 14)

(2) Lord Clifden. (1) (8, 12)

(10) Petrarch. (13, 9)

(19) Cambuscan. (25)

(12) Adventurer. (38, 1)

(10) Pretender. (11) (1)

(2) Camballo. (13)

THE DARLEY ARABIAN MALE LINE (through Blacklock).

(6) Bartlett's Childers.

(11) Squirt.

(8) Marske.

(12) Eclipse. (11)

(6) King Fergus.

(1) Hambletonian.

(2) Whitelock. (2, 4)

(2) Blacklock. (4, 13)

(3) Velocipede. (9)

(11) Brutandorf. (8, 1)

(2) Hetman Platoff. (25) (3)

(1) COSSACK. (6) (8)

(12) Voltaire. (6, 7) (3)

(2) Voltigeur. (5) (8)

(11) Belshazzar.

(21) TRANBY. (8)

(19) Vedette. (11) (6) (11)

(3) Galopin. (3, 12)

(11) St. Simon. (3) (4)

(16) Thirlthorpe. (6) (11)

(2) MATCHBOX. (11, 12)

(5) SIMONIAN. (4, 19)

(19) CHILDWICK. (3, 3)

(8) ST. SERF. (4) (3)

THE DARLEY ARABIAN MALE LINE (through Whisker).

N.B.—The right hand figures are those of maternal grandsire and great-grandsire. Left hand figure denotes family from which the horse is descended.

+ A family which has never won an English classic event.

(6) Bartlett's Childers.

(11) Squirt.

(8) Marske.

(12) Eclipse. (11)

(38) Pot-8-os. +

(18) Waxy. (26)

(1) Whisker. (14)

(36) Economist. (8)

(2) Harkaway. (9)

(3) King Tom. (1) (8)

(11) KINGCRAFT. (2) (12)

Other sons of King Tom are :

(3) King Ban. (4) (3)

(12) Restitution. (25, 2)

(3) King Ernest. (14, 8)

(9) Phaeton. (20) (14)

+ King Alfonso. (12) (2)

(15) FOXHALL. (12) (1)

(19) King Cole. (2) (12)

NELSON. (17) (3) (N.Z.)

(8) The Colonel. (30)

(5) Cap-à-Pie (imp.) (8)

(3) Sir Hercules. (2, 1)

(17) Tattendon. (12) (4)

(8) Chester. (3) (2)

(3) Abercorn. (13, 4)

Other sons of Chester are :

(3) Dreadnought. (10) (3)

(11) Carlyon. (10) (3)

(13) Cranbrook. (8, 3)

(9) Camoola. (13, 2)

(14) Grand Flaneur. (2) (3)

(5) PATRON. (3)

MALE LINE OF BYERLY TURK.

N.B.—The right hand figures are those of maternal grand-sire and great-grand-sire. Left hand figures denotes family from which the horse is descended.

+ A family which has never won an English classic event.

+ Jigg. (6)

(9) Partner. +

+ Tartar. (6)

(26) Herod. + (6)

(13) Highflyer. (15) (11)

(3) Sir Peter. 1) (11)

(1) Woodpecker. (6, 4)

(3) Buzzard. (7, 1)

(7) Walton. (33) (12)

(8) Sir Paul. (17)

(2) Castrel. (13)

(2) Selim. (13) (12)

(1) Partisan. (38) (12)

(8) Pantaloon. (13)

(17) Pantaloon. (3)

(8) Sultan. (7) (3)

(11) Venison. (1?

(8) Cain. (18) (14)

(3) Windhound. (14)

(1) Bay Middleton. (6) (7)

(12) Kingston. (25) (8)

(4) Ion. (8, 8)

(4) Thormanby. (9, 6)

(3) Flying Dutchman. (8)

Dutch Skater.

(1) Man-at-Arms. (2) (14)

(2) Wild Dayrell. (1) (8)

(1) CHARIBERT. (27) (11)

(4) Mosquetaire. (2) (3)

(14) Buccaneer. (37) (3)

(14) The Libel. (24. 1)

(1) Glencoe (Am.) (3)

(2) Castrel (above). (13)

(4) KISBER. (3) (11)

(29) Traducer. (13) (8)

(12) Vandal. (21)

(35) Bastard. (21) (12)

(5) Florizel. (6)

(17) Sir Modred. (19) (8)

(10) Virgil. (2)

(19) Heron. (8)

(6) Diomed. (1, 15)

(1) CONNOISSEUR. (3, 3)

(24) Hindoo. (12, 12)

(11) Fisherman. (12, 12)

(11) Sir Archy. (28)

(15) Hanover. (10) (12)

(3) Marlburnug. (3) (1)

+ Tumbleon. (7) (12)

(3) Richmond. (4, 4)

(40) Boston. + (6)

(2) THE ADMIRAL. (2,9)

(12) Lexington. (11) (6)

(12) Monarchist. (1) (8)

(12) Lever. (7)

(9) TRIDENT. (1)

+ Norfolk. (1) (8)

+ Emperor of Norfolk. (3)

(4) Gilroy. (1) (8)

+ Duke of Magenta. (2, 1)

(13) Robinson Crusoe. (3)

(2) Angler. (1, 8)

(12) Kingston. (25)

(1) Kingston. (11, 14) (imp.)

+ Kingsborough. (3) (Aus.)

(12) Grinstead. (17)

Gann.

MALE LINE OF GODOLPHIN BARB (through Melbourne).

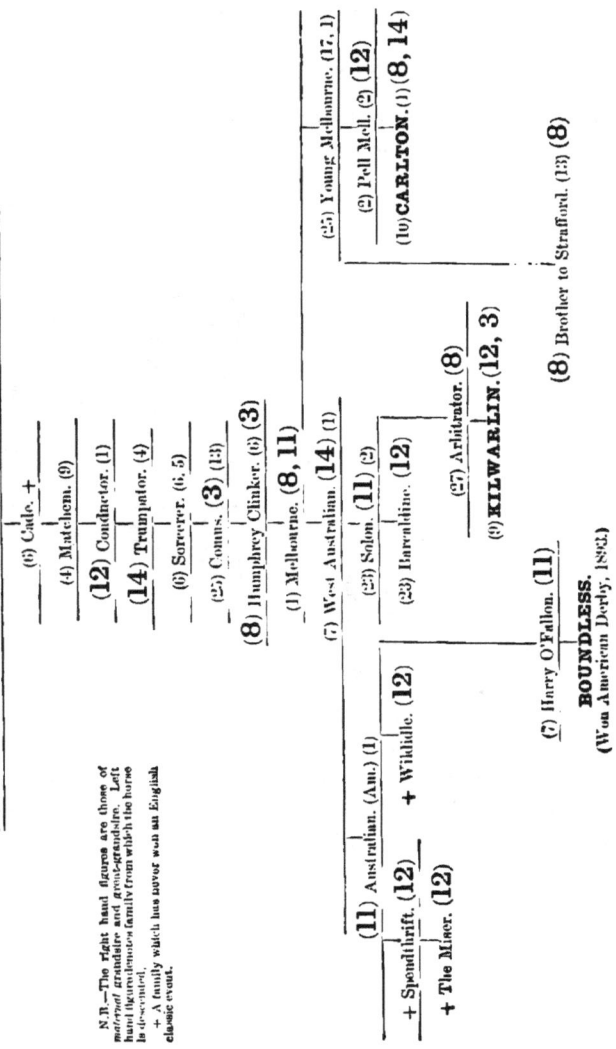

N.B.—The right hand figures are those of *maternal* grandsire and great-grandsire. Left hand figures denote family from which the horse is descended.

+ A family which has never won an English classic event.

(6) Cade. +

(4) Matchem. (9)

(12) Conductor. (1)

(14) Trumpator. (4)

(6) Sorcerer. (6, 5)

(2) Comus. (13)

(2) Comus. (3) (13)

(8) Humphrey Clinker. (6) (3)

(1) Melbourne. (8, 11)

(7) West Australian. (14) (1)

(27) Solon. (11) (2)

(23) Barcaldine. (12)

(27) Arbitrator. (8)

(9) KILWARLIN. (12, 3)

(25) Young Melbourne. (17, 1)

(2) Pell Mell. (2) (12)

(10) CARLTON. (1) (8, 14)

(8) Brother to Strafford. (13) (8)

(7) Harry O'Fallon. (11)

BOUNDLESS.
(Won American Derby, 1888.)

(11) Australian. (Am.) (1)

+ Spendthrift. (12)

+ The Miner. (12)

+ Wildidle. (12)

CHAPTER VIII.

THE RUNNING LINES AND HOW TO USE THEM.

HAVING in the last chapters dealt almost exclusively of sires and how to choose them, I now propose to treat of the running lines, and how they should be utilised in the building up of successful pedigrees. I have before remarked that by *themselves* 1, 2, 4, 5, and 6 are not

KINCSEM.

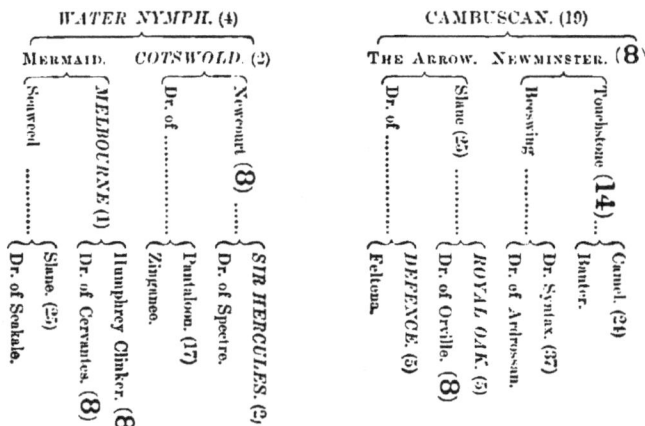

of value without the sire lines **3, 8, 11, 12,** and **14**; nor are the latter valuable without the aid of the former.

Take, for example, the case of Kincsem, the Hungarian mare, acknowledged to be the best mare of modern days—a winner of some sixty odd races at all distances, and never beaten.

No running blood is found in Cambuscan nearer than the fourth remove. After that he has no lack whatever of it. He is quite well provided with sire blood. What he required was a profusion of 1, 2, **3,** and 4 in his mates, and *close* up to the surface, as in Water Nymph, who comes in direct descent from a great filly line (4); while her sire Cotswold is from the 2 line, and her dam by a horse of the 1 family.

I have found very few exceptions to this rule—viz., that some of

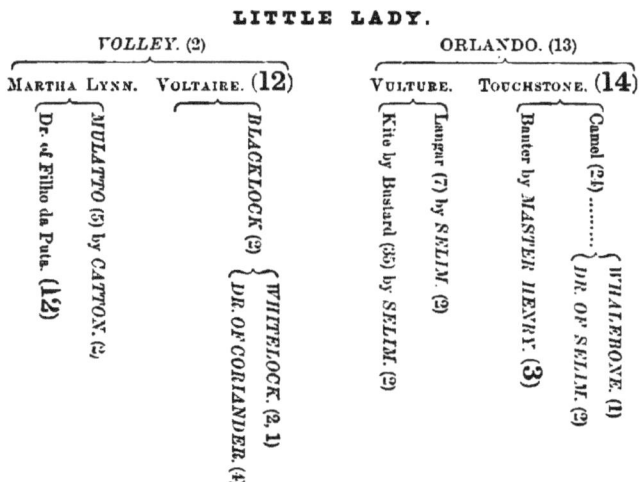

LITTLE LADY.

VOLLEY. (2)   ORLANDO. (13)

Martha Lynn.   Voltaire. **(12)**   Vulture.   Touchstone. **(14)**

- Dr. of Filho da Puta. **(12)**
- *MULATTO* (5) by *CATTON.* (2)
- *BLACKLOCK* (2)
- *WHITELOCK.* (2, 1)
- *DR. OF CORIANDER.* (4)
- Kite by Bustard (35) by *SELIM.* (2)
- Langar (7) by *SELIM.* (2)
- Banter by *MASTER HENRY.* **(3)**
- Camel (24) .... *WHALEBONE.* (1)
- *DR. OF SELIM.* (2)

the running families 1, 2, **3,** and 4 *must* appear in the first *three* removes. The only exceptions are where the pedigrees of both dam and sire have a *large* accumulation of pure or running strains *under* the third remove, as in the case of Peter, page 67, where *only one* pure figure is reached on either side of pedigree table until the fourth remove. As pointed out, there is then quite a plethora of 1, 2, **3,** and 4, principally through that far-reaching blood Blacklock.

To those familiar with English horses, it is hardly necessary to give Camballo's pedigree to confirm the foregoing. He was probably the next best animal sired by Cambuscan. His dam, Little Lady, was by Orlando, a horse inbred three times, and very closely to Selim and Castrel of the 2 line, and his great-grandsire, Whalebone, was of the 1 line. As though this were not enough to fill Cambuscan's requirements, Volley, the dam of Little Lady, was sister to Voltigeur, a shining light of the 2 family.

See Idalia, dam of Sir Modred, for another instance. She was from Dulcibella, a *Voltigeur* mare. Her brother Onslow was, like his sister, a first-class horse, beating Cremorne on one occasion.

WHEEL OF FORTUNE.

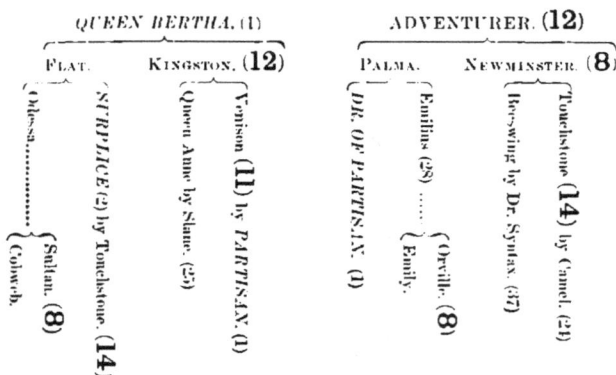

The same conditions exist in the case of that "flying filly" Wheel of Fortune, whose portrait I saw hanging upon the walls of kindly old Mat Dawson's snug library at Heath House, Newmarket, in 1883. She won the Oaks in 1879.

Adventurer has no running blood above the fourth remove, while Queen Bertha is from the 1 family direct, and her dam is by Surplice of the 2. Of course all the other conditions were in accordance with the figures. Indeed, most of the late Lord

Falmouth's matings were very scientifically arranged. The in-breeding here was to Touchstone at three and four removes, and Partisan at four removes. Adventurer sired another classic winner, Pretender. His dam is given below.

Here, again, the mare's pedigree was built up very much on running lines, as both Selim and Blucher were inbred to 1, 2, **3**,

FERINA.

PARTIALITY. (10)		VENISON. (11)	
FAVOURITE.	MIDDLETON.* (3)	FAWN.	PARTISAN. (1)

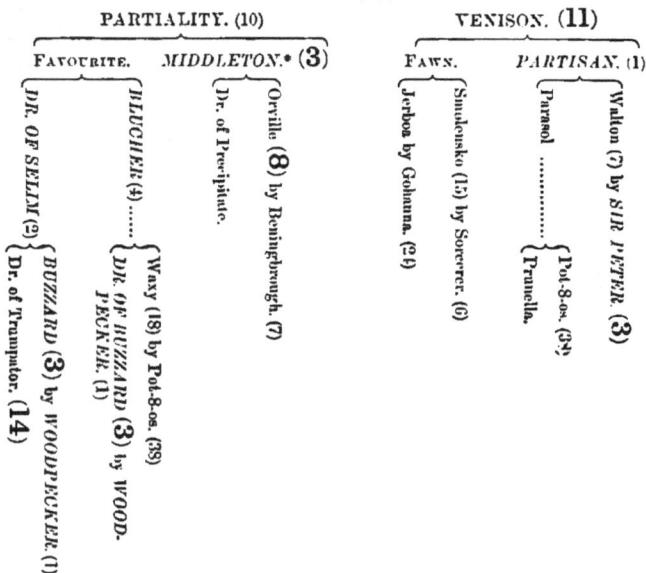

- *DIR. OF SELIM* (2) { *BUZZARD* (3) by *WOODPECKER*. (1) / Dr. of Trumpator. (14)
- *BLUCHER* (4)...... { Waxy (18) by Pot-8-os. (38) / *DIR. OF BUZZARD* (3) by *WOOD-PECKER*. (1)
- Dr. of Precipitate.
- Orville (8) by Beningbrough. (7)
- Jerboa by Gohanna. (24)
- Smolensko (12) by Sorcerer. (6)
- Parasol { Pot-8-os. (34) / Prunella.
- Walton (7) by *SIR PETER* (3)

and 4, and on top of this we get Partisan (1). Pretender, so bred, though a good racehorse, would make an indifferent sire, and this has been his record. He would only have succeeded with such bred mares as a sister of Isonomy, for instance. A mare so bred would

---

* The author here had taken the wrong Middleton's pedigree. Middleton, sire of Ferina, was of No. 1 family, by Phantom, of No. 6; and the reason, therefore, why Pretender should not succeed as a sire becomes still more obvious on these corrected figures.—W. A.

bring back the stoutness he lacked, as well as the sire blood necessary to make him father winners.

Another instance of Adventurer's partiality for the 1, 2. **3**, and 4 families was his greatest filly, Apology, winner of the Oaks and Leger (1874), from the 4 family, her dam by Rataplan (**3**). Bal Gal is given.

APOLOGY.

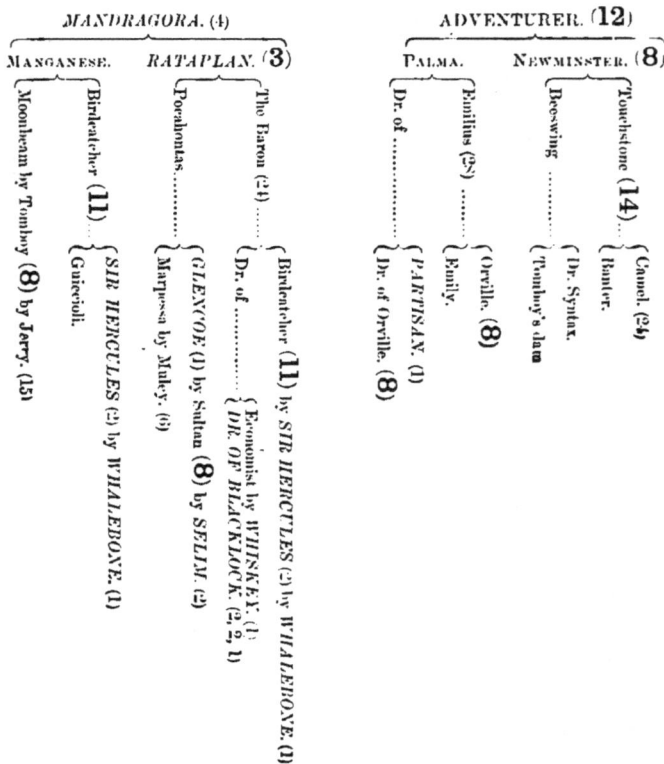

Bal Gal was one of the greatest flyers Lord Falmouth ever bred. Her dam, Cantiniere, descended from the No. 2 line, and was inbred to it through Blacklock (twice).   It seemed as if Adventurer could not possibly sire a high class animal without a return to the pure figures he was bred away from.   Another case in point is the dam of Ishmael, whose breeding is admirably suited for Adventurer, viz., Lina by Stockwell (**3**), from Dr. of Orlando (13), from a Velocipede mare (**3**), Blacklock (2, 2, 1), from Dr. of Whisker (1).   Here is running blood in profusion.   Lina hails from the 7 family.

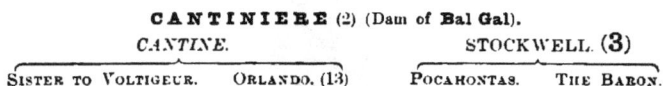

CANTINIERE (2) (Dam of **Bal Gal**).

CANTINE.		STOCKWELL. (**3**)	
SISTER TO VOLTIGEUR.	ORLANDO. (13)	POCAHONTAS.	THE BARON.

See also Cheviot, imported to Australia.   His dam inbred to Stockwell and Blacklock.   Jongleur, a French horse that won the Cambridgeshire some years back with a big weight up, was bred like the foregoing.

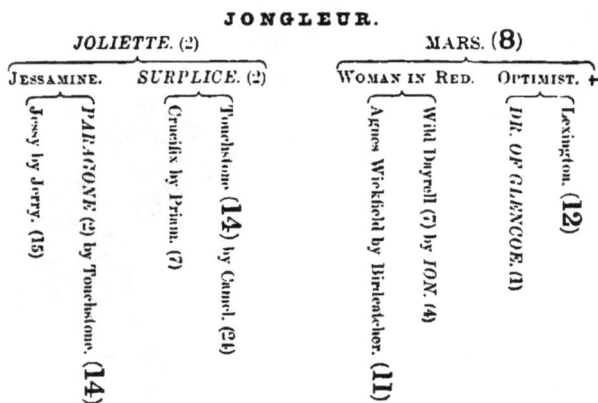

JONGLEUR.

JOLIETTE. (2)				MARS. (**8**)			
JESSAMINE.		SURPLICE. (2)		WOMAN IN RED.		OPTIMIST. +	
Jessy by Jerry. (15)	PARAGONE (2) by Touchstone. (14)	Crucifix by Priam. (7)	Touchstone (14) by Camel. (20)	Agnes Wickfield by Birdcatcher. (11)	Wild Dayrell (7) by ION. (4)	Lexington. (12)	DR. OF GLENCOE. (1)

On Mars' side no running blood in three top removes, and he was very well mated with a mare so remarkably inbred to No. 2.

Peregrine (Two Thousand Guineas) is another instance of a horse bred in this way. His sire, Pero Gomez, being bred away from the running lines in top removes.

A better illustration of the phase of mating now under con-

PEREGRINE.

ADELAIDE. (9)		PERO GOMEZ. (27)	
DR. OF.	Y. MELBOURNE (25).	SALAMANCA.	BEADSMAN. (13)

ADELAIDE. (9)

DR. OF.
- Dr. of .... { DON JOHN (2) by WATERLY (2) by WHALEBONE (1) / Dr. of Belshazzar (11) by BLACKLOCK. (2, 2, 1)
- TEDDINGTON (2) { Orlando (13) by Touchstone (14) by Camel (24) by W. (1) / Valture by Langar (7) by SELIM. (2)

Y. MELBOURNE (25).
- DR. OF GLENCOE (1) by Sultan (8) by SELIM. (2)
- Dr. of Pantaloon (17) by CASTREL. (2)
- MELBOURNE (1) by Hy. Clinker. (8)

PERO GOMEZ. (27)

SALAMANCA.
- Bravery .... { Gauerboy (13) by Tomboy. (8) / Emma .... { BAY MIDDLETON. (1) / DR. OF VELOCIPEDE (3) by BLACKLOCK. (2, 2, 1)
- Student (8) .... { Chatham (12) by Colonel. (8) / Dr. of Laurel (21) by BLACKLOCK. (2, 2, 1)

BEADSMAN. (13)
- Mendicant .... { Touchstone (14) by Camel (24) by Whalebone (1). / Dr. of Tramp (3) by Dick Andrews. (9)
- Weatherbit (12) { Sheet Anchor (12) by Lottery. (11) / Miss Letty by Priam. (6)

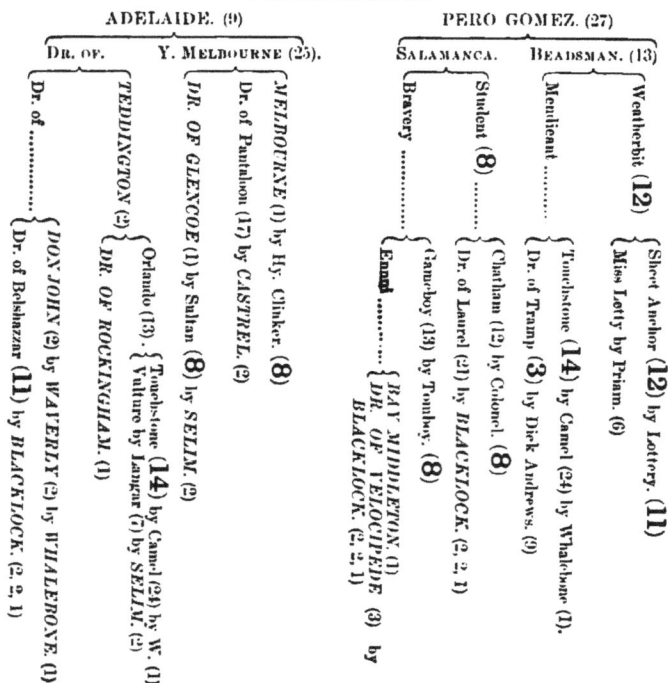

sideration could hardly be cited. Here we have the sire Pero Gomez with sufficient sire blood to make him a success if properly mated, *but* bred right away from the *running* families in his main lines. Practically, we find none till the fifth remove. On the other

L

146   *Breeding Racehorses by the Figure System.*

hand, we get in Adelaide totally opposite conditions. She has little
or no *sire* blood, and would only succeed with a horse inbred to it.
Her inbreeding to the running figure 2 is most persistent, and when
we bear in mind that Orlando himself has three close strains of
Castrel and Selim (2) it is easy to conceive that his son Teddington

FIREWORKS.

GASLIGHT (10) (imp.)		KELPIE (1) (imp.)	
FACTORY GIRL.	SIR HERCULES. (2)	CHILD OF THE MIST.	WEATHERBIT. **(12)**

Dr. of Juniper (9) by *WHISKEY.* (2)

LAMPLIGHTER (4) { Merlin **(8)** by *CASTREL.* (2) / Dr. of Walton (7) by *SIR PETER.* **(3)**

Peri. ....

WHALEBONE (1) ...... { Waxy. (18) / Penelope.

Wanderer **(11)** { Gohanna. (24) / Dr. of Alexander. (13)

Taurina ....

St. Francis (18) by *ST. PATRICK.* (4) { Taurus. (21) / Dr. of Zingainee. (6)

Miss Letty by *PRIAM* (5) by Emilius (28); Dr. of Orville. **(8)**

Short Anchor **(12)** by Lottery (11); Dr. of Mulry (7) by Orville. **(8)**

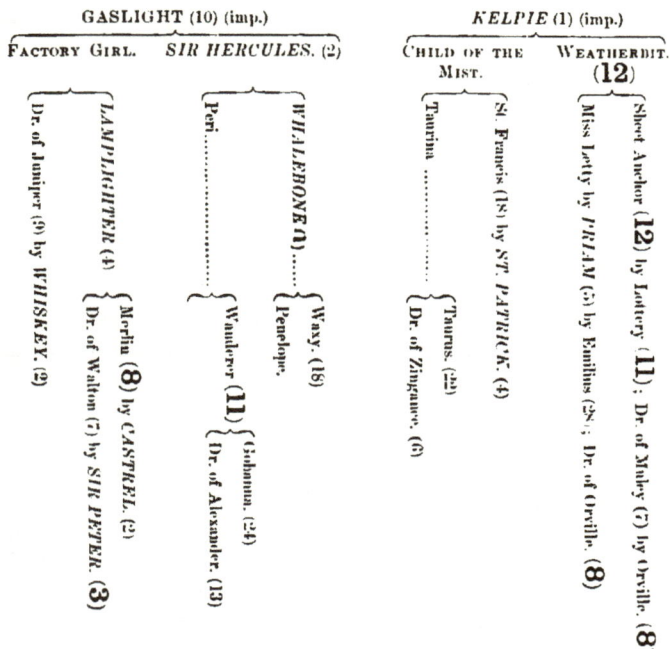

represented the 2 line perhaps better than any horse since Blacklock
and Don John. Then cross Teddington upon Don John and
Blacklock, and the family (2) is intensified to an extent hardly met
with in any pedigree in Stud Books. Again, the mating suited

Pero Gomez, inasmuch as he is *outbred* to the flashy strains of Castrel and Selim, and will be likely to succeed only with mares inbred to the brothers, as Adelaide was.

If the student will turn back to Lexington (page 121) he will be confronted with a repetition of this law of mating, which holds good in America, Australia, and everywhere else that the thoroughbred is raised for racing purposes. When tabulated with a mate Lexington has only one strain through Sumpter (4) of running blood, until at the sixth remove we find Sir Peter Teazle (**3**), and, as I have shown, he made an immense hit on Glencoe blood inbred to 1, 2, and **3**; also with Yorkshire, a horse of the 2 line. Lexington had no Castrel and Selim in his veins, another reason why the Glencoe blood made such a hit with him, giving the element of speed to his progeny.

In Australia a striking instance to confirm the above was Kelpie (imp.), whose best son was Fireworks (a great racehorse), and sire of Mr. Frank Reynolds' Goldsborough. Though Kelpie is in the No. 1 line, it does not count for much, because he is persistently bred away from it, and it plays therefore no great part in the influence on his progeny unless his mates are rich in that strain or the running lines generally, in which case it would respond to them more freely than an outside line.

The breeding of Malua (page 114) may be taken as bearing out this aspect of the question, always keeping in mind that No. 3 blood possesses the dual quality of running and sire tendencies, and seems to so readily adapt itself to its associations that it can hardly be misplaced in a pedigree, *i.e.*, within reasonable limits.

Another instance of a Weatherbit horse (Brown Bread) comes to my memory, and the dams of his two sons, Hilarious and Toastmaster, both good racehorses.

One might go on piling up instances *ad lib.* if space permitted. Other examples bred in this fashion are Venison and his sire Kingston, Adventurer, Teddington, Lord Clifden, Hermit, Pleni-

HILARIOUS.

HYGEIA. (2)   BROWN BREAD.

DR. OF.   *KNIGHT OF KARS.* (**3**)   DR. OF.   WEATHERBIT. (**12**)

- Dr. of Orlando (13) by Touchstone. (**14**)
- *ST. ALBANS* (2) by *STOCKWELL.* (**3**)
- Pocahontas by *GLENCOE.* (1)
- Nutwith (9) by Jerry. (15)
- Dr. of Birdcatcher (**11**) by *SIR HERCULES.* (2)
- West Australian (7) by *MELBOURNE.* (1)
- Miss Letty by Priam. (6)
- Sheet Anchor (**12**) by Lottery. (**11**)

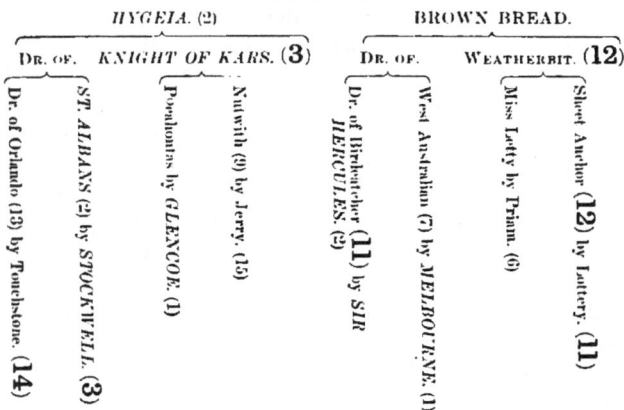

MAYORESS (Dam of **Toastmaster**).

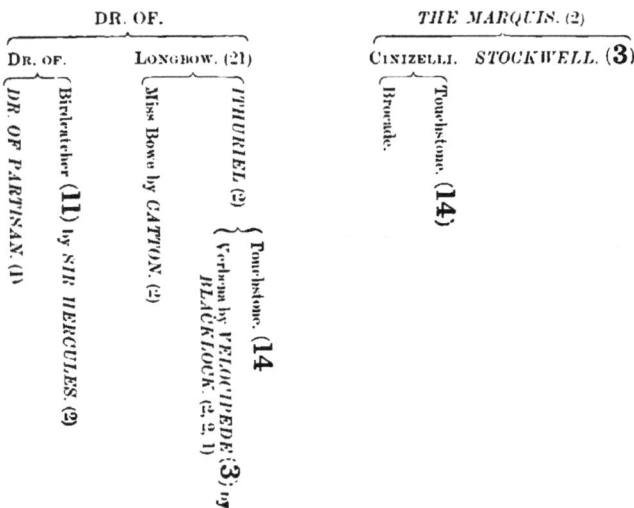

DR. OF.   *THE MARQUIS.* (2)

DR. OF.   LONGBOW. (21)   CINIZELLI.   *STOCKWELL.* (**3**)

- DR. OF PARTISAN. (1)
- Birdcatcher (**11**) by *SIR HERCULES.* (2)
- Miss Bowe by *CATTON.* (2)
- ITHURIEL. (2) { Touchstone. (**14** / Verbena by *VELOCIPEDE* (**3**) by *BLACKLOCK.* (2, 2, 1)
- Brocade.
- Touchstone. (**14**)

potentiary, Marsyas, Cambuscan, The Palmer, Macgregor 2000 (Guineas), Weatherbit, Priam, Blue Gown, &c. Students can examine these and other pedigrees, and see for themselves that it is very rare indeed to find any horse in the *first class* having *no* No. 1, 2, **3**, 4, or 5 on either side of pedigree table in the three top removes. Many instances may be met with in the course of investigations which are bred the other way; but they are not included in the class which have distinguished themselves on the turf. Again, scores have been born fulfilling this particular condition, and yet not in the first flight, because other conditions were wanting. Many a horse, having in his veins all the elements of a good sire, has wasted his sweetness in the desert of want of opportunity. As before remarked, where would Lexington have been if Glencoe and Yorkshire had not preceded him, and laid the foundations of his success?

CHAPTER IX.

HOW TO BREED GREAT STAKE HORSES (AND SIRES) BY RETURNING YOUR STALLION THE BEST STRAINS OF HIS DAM.

THIS is one of the most important rules to observe. It has been pretty generally recognised amongst stud masters that the best blood in sire should be nicked; but I do not know of any writer who has distinctly laid it down as a general law that the *best* blood of the stallion's *dam* should be nicked in preference to his sire's side of pedigree table. There is a saying as old as the hills, " he is the son of his mother," or "she is the daughter of her father." My observation has proved this to be a truism; but it is only necessary to point to the now generally accepted rule in physiology, that a brilliant son inherits his talents from his mother, and where the daughters of a family are more brilliant than the sons, they inherit from the father. If we start by accepting this, it follows as a natural result that in the science of horse-breeding the same rule applies. Therefore it appears only reasonable that, whatever *good quality* or strain of blood the mother possessed, and which gave her the power to produce a great son and sire, is precisely that strain we should look for in his mates.

Let us take Carbine for an illustration.

I have no doubt in my own mind that Musket owed his excellence to his second dam of the **3** line, Brown Bess, as she contained in her single person not only the main tap root of this splendid line, but close infusions of Blacklock (2), Whalebone (1), and Selim (2) as well. Built, therefore, as Musket was, no happier

CARBINE.

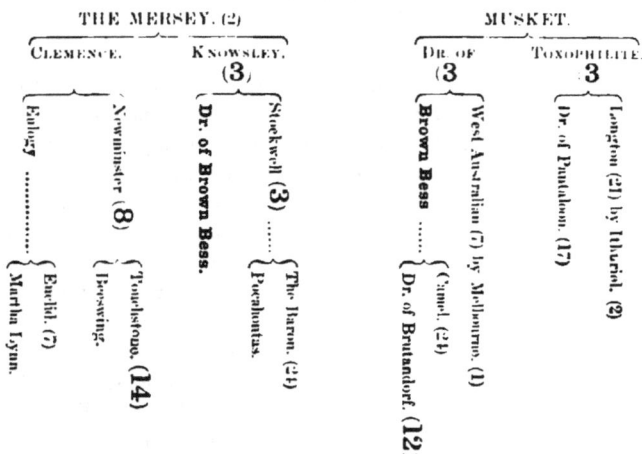

BARCALDINE.

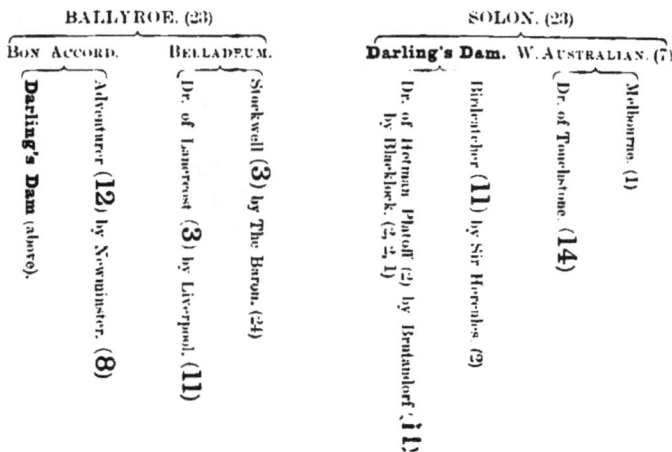

mate could be selected than The Mersey of the 2 line, who owed her existence to Knowsley (**3**) by Stockwell (**3**) from the identical

BENDIGO.

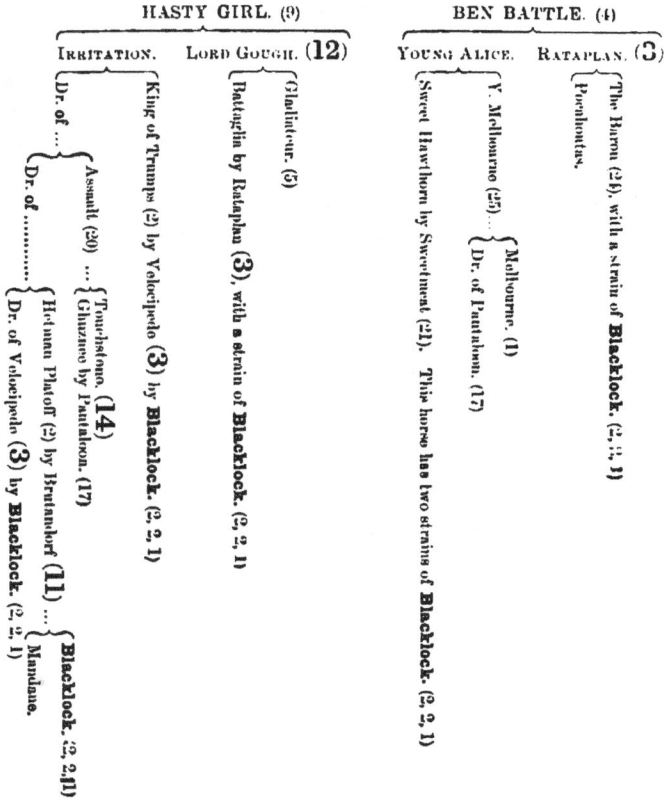

HASTY GIRL. (9)

BEN BATTLE. (4)

IRRITATION.   LORD GOUGH. (**12**)

YOUNG ALICE.   RATAPLAN. (**3**)

Dr. of ....

King of Trumps (2) by Velocipede (**3**) by Blacklock. (2, 2, 1)

Gladiateur. (5)

Battaglia by Rataplan (**3**), with a strain of Blacklock. (2, 2, 1)

Sweet Hawthorn by Sweetmeat (2t). This horse has two strains of Blacklock. (2, 2, 1)

Y. Melbourne (25)

Melbourne. (1)
Dr. of Pantaloon. (17)

Pocahontas.

The Baron (24), with a strain of Blacklock. (2, 2, 1)

Dr. of ....

Assault (26) ...

Tourbillon. (14)
Ghazuee by Pantaloon. (17)

Hetman Platoff (2) by Brutandorf (11) ...

Blacklock. (2, 2, 1)
Mandane.

Dr. of Velocipede (**3**) by Blacklock. (2, 2, 1)

Brown Bess above. This is a most scientific mating, and, at the same time, a most remarkable exposition of the rule I have just laid down. One swallow, however, does not make a summer, and I give a few more illustrations, as well as the names of many great horses bred in this fashion. Take Barcaldine and Bendigo. Both of these horses were in the first flight, and are both bred in this fashion.

Here is a startling instance, indeed, of the rule; and there is no doubt that but for the West Australian, Melbourne, Adventurer outcross, as well as the inbreeding of the 23 family to itself, such a close return of the same strains, Birdcatcher and Blacklock, must have ended in failure.

Few will dispute that Sweetmeat, with his dam incestuously bred to Blacklock, was the most potent element in Ben Battle; and surely never did a horse get so strong a return of his best strain, in the person of Hasty Girl, with four Blacklocks, and two through Velocipede.

In the year 1888, when the late Andrew Town, of Richmond, near Sydney, purchased Trenton, he wrote asking me to select twenty mares in his stud to mate with his new stallion. I looked through his pedigree carefully, and, finding that Australian Sir Hercules and Rous' Emigrant (imp.) were without doubt the best strains in his dam, I advised him to put all the mares in his stud with that strain, especially through Yattendon (who combined both), to Trenton. The result has been very satisfactory, as from the few Yattendon mares he produced Bliss and her brother Trenchant (a J. C. Derby) from Bridesmaid by Mattendon; Gaillardia, from Paresseuse by Yattendon; also Gerard, from Geraldine by Yattendon, &c. To outside Yattendon mares Trenton sired Lady Trenton, a first-class mare (Sydney Cup), from Black Swan by Yattendon; and Etra Weenie (dead heat for Oaks), from Nellie by Tim Whiffler (imp.), from Sappho by Australian Sir Hercules.

Chester (Australia) was out of a Stockwell mare. His sons, Carlyon, Cranbrook, and Camoola, are from dams with a close strain of Stockwell. His best son was Abercorn. His pedigree is given below. He was a worthy rival of Carbine, and many consider him to have been his equal in every respect.

Abercorn's dam certainly combines the blood of both sides of

ABERCORN.

CINNAMON. (**3**)

    BROWN DUCHESS.

- Clove .... Hybla by The Provost (4) by The Saddler. (**3**)
- Whalebone (**3**) ......
  - Sweetmeat (1) with **Blacklock** (2, 2, 1) twice.
  - Paraguay (imp.) by **Sir Hercules** (2) by Whalebone. (1)
  - Speculation (imp.)

    GOLDSBOROUGH. (13)

- Sylvia ....
  - Juliet (**11**) by Touchstone (**14**) by Camel (29) by Whalebone. (1)
  - Scipio. / Second dam Sister to Whalebone. (1)
- Fireworks (10) ......
  - Fisherman by Heron (19) by Bustard. (35)
  - Goodnight by **Sir Hercules** (2) by Whalebone. (1)
  - Kelpie (1) by Weatherbit (**18**) by Sheet Anchor. (**18**)

CHESTER. (**8**)

    LADY CHESTER.

- Austry .... Iælia (2) by Emilius. (29)
- Stockwell (**3**) ......
  - Harkaway by Son of Whisker. (1)
  - Pocahontas by Glencoe. (1)
  - The Baron (24) ...... { Birdcatcher by **Sir Hercules**. (2) / Dr. of { Economist by Whisker. (1) / Miss Pratt by **Blacklock**. (2)

    YATTENDON. (17)

- Cassandra .... Alice Grey by (imp.) Rous' Emigrant. (4, 1, 2)
- True (**12**) by Priam (6) by Emilius. (29)
- Sir Hercules (**3**) ...... Paraguay by Sir Hercules. (2)
- Cap-à-pie (5) by Colonel (**8**) ...... { Whisker. (1) / Dr. of Sultan. (**8**)

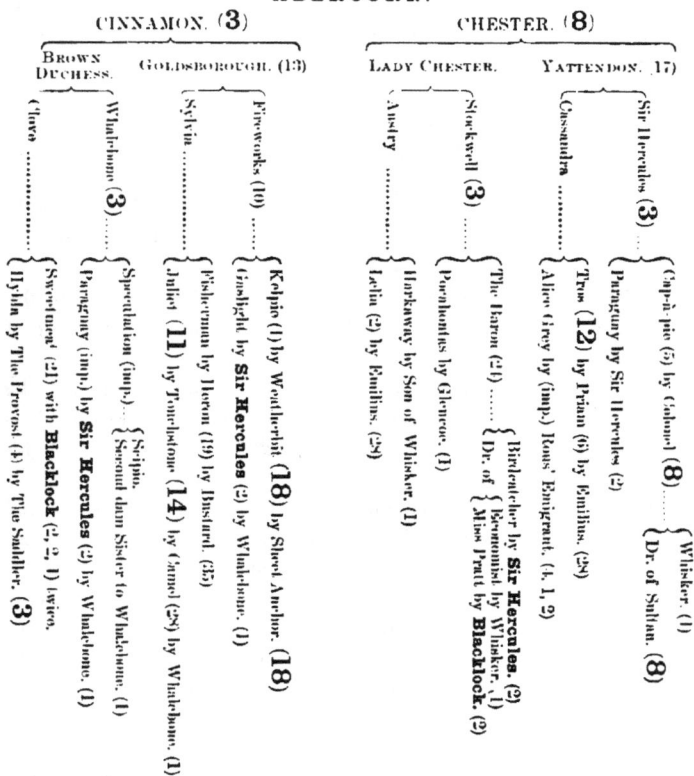

Chester's pedigree; but, seeing that the most potent strains in Cinnamon's pedigree are Blacklock and Sir Hercules, the same may be claimed for Stockwell, who is, moreover, from the same line **3**, as Cinnamon, so that it is a nicking of not only names, but families, as in Carbine. These few instances will suffice to show students how the nicking should be made.

In the dam of St. Albans (Bribery, by The Libel) we have The Libel from Pasquinade, sister to Touchstone; and St. Albans' best son, Springfield, is from Viridis by Marsyas, by Orlando by Touchstone.

Hermit's third dam is by Belshazzar, son of Blacklock; and Peter, his most brilliant son, is from Lady Masham, whose second dam is by Belshazzar.

Hightlyer's dam, Rachel, was by Blank, son of Godolphin Barb, from a Regulus (**12**) mare. His best son, Sir Peter Teazle, was out of Miss Cleveland by Regulus (**12**).

Sultan was from Bacchante by Ditto (brother to Walton by Sir Peter). His son, Bay Middleton (never beaten), was out of Cobweb by Phantom, son of Walton.

Lord Clifden's second dam, Volley, was by Voltaire by Blacklock; and his son, Wenlock (Leger), was from a Rataplan mare inbred to Sir Hercules and Blacklock, both No. 2 horses. Lord Clifden's dam was of the same line.

Parmesan's dam is very inbred to Whalebone, Whisker, and Wire. His son, Favonius (Derby), is from Zephyr (by King Tom), with *four* strains of Whalebone, Whisker, and Web.

The Derby winner Blue Gown's grandam Vexation was by Touchstone. His sire Beadsman is from Mendicant by Touchstone.

There is another phase of this kind of nicking bearing on the previous examples which is interesting and instructive, as widening the partiality some sires show for their maternal lines in preference to those from which their sires are descended. For the purpose of brevity, and because it will be useful to the student, I give the pedigree in a different form. This will show at a glance how the *figures* are nicking. The figure underlined is the sire's own line; the

NOTE.—The figure underlined is the sire's own line, the left-hand one that of his sire, and the right-hand figure his maternal grandsire.

Blair Athol by Stockwell	(3)	...	(10)	...	Dr. of (1) Melbourne	Silvio (Derby and Leger).
	(1) (11) Venison				Dr. of (11) Birdcatcher	
Silverhair by Kingston	(11)	...	(1)	...		
Blair Athol	(3)	...	(10)	...	(1)	Craig Millar (Leger).
Miss Roland by Fitz Roland	(1)	...	(1)	...	Dr. of (6) Hesperus	
Blair Athol	(3)	...	(10)	...	(1)	Prince Arthur (a great stayer).
Lady Betty by Trumpeter	(1)	...	(1)	...	Dr. of (6) Hesperus	
Marilyruong by Fisherman	(11)	...	(3)	...	Dr. of (3) Flying Dutchman......	Richmond (Derby). Bosworth (Leger).
The Fawn by The Premier	(4)	...	(3)	...	Dr. of (2) Harkaway	
Marilyruong (above)	(11)	...	(3)	...	Dr. of (3) Melbourne	Hamlet (Derby) and Horatio (a good racehorse).
Rose of Denmark by Stockwell ...	(3)	...	(2)	...	Dr. of (1) Melbourne	
(Imp.) Panic by Alarm	(19)	...	(14)	...	Dr. of (1) Melbourne	Wellington (V.R.C.) Derby.
Fun Fron by Macaroni	(14)	...	(1)	...	Dr. of (14) Touchstone.........	
St. Simon by Galopin	(3)	...	(11)	...	Dr. of (3) King Tom	Memoir (Oaks and Leger). La Flèche (Oaks and Leger).
Quiver by Toxophilite	(3)	...	(3)	...	Dr. of (23) Y. Mel	
Isonomy by Sterling	(12)	...	(19)	...	Dr. of (3) Stockwell	Isinglass (2000 gs., Derby, and Leger, 1893).
Deadlock by Wenlock	(4)	...	(3)	...	Dr. of (2) Chevalier d'Industrie ... Dr. of (3) Flying Dutchman	
Son of Lord Clifden ...	(2)					
From Dr. of Ratniden	(3)					

Isonomy by Sterling .... (12) ... (19) — (3) Stockwell ....
St. Marguerite by Hermit .... (5) ... (4) — (3) Stockwell ....
}— Seabreeze (Oaks and Leger, 1888).

Galopin by Vedette .... (19) ... (3) — (3) Flying Dutchman.........
Mowerina by Scottish Chief ...... (12) ... (7) — (3) Stockwell ....
}— Donovan (Derby and Leger, 1889).

Galopin by Vedette .... (19) ... (3) — (3) Flying Dutchman ....
St. Angela by King Tom .... (3) ... (12) — (4) Ion ....
}— St. Simon (never beaten).

Hampton by Lord Clifden .... (2) ... (10) — (3) Kettledrum ....
 — (3) By Rataplan ....
}— Ayrshire (Derby, 1888).
Atalanta by Galopin .... (3) ... (8) — (4) Thormanby ....
Flying Duchess by The Flying Dutchman ...... (3) — (3) By Windhound ....

Rataplan by the Baron .... (24)

Hybla by The Provost .... (4) (3)
(by the Saddler)

(3) ... (1) Glencoe .... } Kettledrum (Derby).

(3) ... (3) Lanercost ....
(11) Liverpool.
(3) Tramp.

Chester by Yattendon (17) (8) (3) Stockwell .... } **Abercorn** (A.J.C. Derby and Leger, V.R.C. Leger, &c.)

Cinnamon by Goldsborough ...... (13) (3) (3) Whalebone (Aus.) ....

Chester (see above) .... (17) (8) (3) Stockwell .... } **Dreadnought** (V.R.C. Derby, St. Leger, A.J.C. Derby, and Champion, 3 miles.

(Imp.) Trafalgar by Blair Athol (10) (3) (3) Toxophilite ....

Chester .... (17) (8) (3) Stockwell .... } **Cranbrook** (Newmarket, 6 fur., 3 yrs. Set. 12lb, 1 min. 14½ sec.)

La Princess by Cathedral .. (8) (8) (13) (3) Stockwell ....

Chester .... (17) (8) (3) Stockwell .... } **Stromboli** (also Lava A.J.C. Oaks) (A.J.C. Derby and Sydney Cup, 2 miles, 3 yrs, 3d., 3 min. 31¼ sec.)

Etna by Marthyrnong .... (3) (3) + (1) (Imp.) Kingston ....
(from Flying Dutchman mare) (3) New Chan. sire of second dam

Chester .... (17) (8) (3) Stockwell .... } **Carlyon** (and Arno) (a high-class horse, winner of many races).

+ Moonstone by Blair Athol ...... (10) (3) (11) (14) Touchstone
Son of Stockwell ....

St. George (brother to Chester).. (17) (8) (3) Stockwell .... } **Loyalty** (a great racehorse and winner of N.Z. Derby).

Dr. of Apremont .... (3) (17) (19) Caulhausen ....

Chester (above) .... (17) (8) (3) Stockwell .... } **Camoola** (A.J.C. Derby and Leger, V.R.C. Derby and Champion, 3 miles).

Copra by Robinson Crusoe .... (13) (3) (9) (1) Nutbourne ....
(from a Stockwell mare)

Stockwell by The Baron	(31)		
Harkest by Lanercost	(3)	(1) Glencoe ⎫ Cailee On Leger, 1841).
		(22) Gladiator ⎬
		(1) By Partison ⎭
Stockwell by The Baron	(31)	Dr. of (1) Glencoe ⎫ Blair Athol (Derby and Leger).
Blink Bonny by Melbourne	(1)	Dr. of (31) Gladiator ⎬
		(1) Partison ⎭
Stockwell (above)	(31)	(1) ⎫ Lord Lyon (2000 Guineas,
Paradigm by Paragone	(2)	(8) Red-hank ⎬ Derby, and Leger).
Whitelock by Hambletonian		Achievement (Leger).
Dr. of Coriander		(2) Phenomenon ⎫ Blacklock (a great runner).
		(13) Highflyer ⎭
(Imp.) Jim Whiffler by Van Galen	(7)	Dr. of (4) Ugly Buck ⎫ Briseis (V.R.C. Derby and
Musidora by The Premier	(4)	Dr. of (12) Gratis ⎬ Melbourne Cup at 3 yrs.).
Son of Torrboy		
(There was in this case no other nick to speak of except the figures 1 . The Premier was by Torrboy, also).
The Peer by Melbourne	(1)	Dr. of (14) Touchstone ⎫ Darebin (V.R.C. Derby and
Larline by Traducer	(20)	Dr. of (3) King Tom ⎬ Sydney Cup.
Son of The Libel	(14)	
Sterling by Oxford	(12)	Dr. of (3) Flatcatcher ⎫ Ismony.
Isola Bella by Stockwell	(3)	Dr. of (12) Ethelbert ⎬
Hesperian by Beadsman	(13)	Dr. of (2) Cowl ⎫ Bonnclere.
Bonny Bell by Voltigeur	(2)	Dr. of (22) Gladiator ⎬
Springfield by St. Albans	(2)	Dr. of (12) Marsyas ⎫ Goldfield.
Crucible by Hesperian	(3)	Dr. of (3) Camerino ⎬
Maley Moloch by Maliy	(6)	(4) Dick Andrews ⎫ Alice Hawthorn.
		By Jno Andrews ⎬
Helicon by Lottery	(11)	Dr. of (8) Cervantes
Lord Lyon by Stockwell	3	Dr. of (2) Paragone ⎫ Placida (Oaks).
Fleta by Pelion	(1)	Dr. of (13) Orlando ⎬
Lord Lyon (above)	3	Dr. of (12) Marsyas ⎫ Minting.
Mint Sauce by Young Melbourne / M-Bourne	(22) (1)	

left hand one, that of his sire, and the right hand figure, his maternal grandsire.

This is a curious confirmation of the rule I am endeavouring to illustrate. Lord Clifden is the sire of Wenlock, who is from a Rataplan (3) mare. Deadlock's first dam is by Chevalier d'Industrie (2), and her second dam by the Flying Dutchman of the same family as herself, so that she was bred three times to this useful family, and therefore eminently suited as a mate for Isonomy, bred away, as we have seen, from running figures in most of his top lines. Seabreeze, another good race mare by Isonomy, is bred somewhat on the same principle, and with close return to Stockwell.

This compares in many respects with Ayrshire, both creditable specimens of English high class horses. I thought Atalanta the best looking mare I saw in England in 1883. At the breaking up of the partnership between the late Lord Rosslyn and Mr. Dan Cooper Atalanta was bought in for a trifle by Lord Rosslyn, who had just purchased her dam. Few could have foreseen what a brilliant future was being treasured up for her, else I fancy there would have been more spirited bidding. Kettledrum, the only Derby winner by Rataplan, was bred by a return of figures.

In the above cases of Chester and his brother there is a startling regularity in their marked preference for the figure **3**, nor can this be the outcome of mere chance. It is unquestionably (as in Blair Athol) the result of a natural law which demands that the best blood or line of dam shall be returned to a stallion through his mates.

It would be tedious to repeat the pedigrees of the many hundreds of excellent racehorses bred in this fashion. Enough has been shown to draw the attention of stud masters to this important phase of mating. As a fact, they have been all along unconsciously (in most cases) nicking the figures while carrying out experiments in the nicking of individuals, such as Touchstone, Birdcatcher, and Blacklock. That this nicking of figures is destined to play an important part in future breeding operations I feel assured, because there is *less* danger of sacrificing temper and staying power in the practice of inbreeding to figures than under the old plan of inbreeding to individuals. The exceptions to this nicking of the stallion's dam's blood (and family figure) only serve to prove the rule. Where a stallion is bred like Sir Modred (page 128), flashy on sire's side and stout on dam's, it would be courting defeat to return the flashy blood, *i.e.*, if one desired to breed great stake horses and sires. Horses of the Herod and Matchem lines especially are only able to perpetuate themselves in *male* line through their stout Eclipse blood. Consequently it is the Blacklock and Touchstone (Whalebone) which should be given to him (Sir Modred) through mares by such horses as St. Simon or by horses with a double strain of Stockwell, as no stud can be built up successfully without Stockwell.

CHAPTER X.

HOW GREAT RACE FILLIES ARE MOSTLY BRED.

In last chapter I endeavoured to explain that the success attendant upon strongly returning the blood of stallion's dam arises from a natural law (see Starkweather on "Law of Sex"), which clearly shows that an unusually clever son inherits his ability from his mother. The natural inference therefore is that a daughter gets her intellectual powers from her father. We have only to look at the records of our own national history to find how rarely a great and clever father is followed by an equally clever son, or one who even approaches him in ability. We can count the instances to the contrary upon the fingers of one hand, beginning with the Pitts and ending, well—wherever you choose. On the other hand, we find the daughters of our departed statesmen and literary men constantly coming to the front as writers, editors, painters, musicians, philanthropists, and, indeed, any work which requires more than the average amount of brains and vital force. As with the human race, so with horses, in a measure. The cases are not exactly on all fours, of course, because in racehorses the quality in most request is not so much a matter of brains as vitality and muscular force. A careful inspection of hundreds of pedigrees has convinced me that not only do some sires beget a larger number of excellent fillies than colts, but also that these fillies are mainly the result of nicking the blood of *right-hand side* of stallion's tables.

Later on I will deal with the reasons why one horse sires mostly good fillies and few good colts, Adventurer to wit. Isonomy is pretty evenly divided in this respect, but Petrarch has a decided

Hermit by Newminster .... (8) ⎱ ... (6) ... (18) Tadmor .... ⎱ Thebais (Oaks).
By Touchstone .... (14) ⎰
Devotion by Stockwell............. (3) ... (4) ... (14) Touchstone......................... St. Marguerite.

Adventurer by Newminster ...... (8) ... (12) ... (28) Emilius .... ⎱ Wheel of Fortune (Oaks, nick
By Touchstone .... (14) ... of Touchstone).
Queen Bertha by Kingston......... (12) ... (1) ...⎰ (2) Surplice .... ⎰
⎱ (14) By Touchstone ....

Melbourne by Humphrey Clinker (8) ... (1) Dr. of (8) Cervantes .... ⎱ Cuvam (nick of Sorcerer
Grandson of Sorcerer ... (6) four removes).
Madame Pelerine by Velocipede (3) ... (26) ... ⎱ Baline......................... ⎰
⎱ (1) By Whalebone ....
⎰ (6) From Dr. of Sorcerer

Adventurer by Newminster ...... (8) ... (12) ... (28) Emilius................... ⎱ Isl Gul (a crack two-year-old).
By Touchstone .... (14) ...
Cantiniere by Stockwell .... (3) ... (2) ... (13) Orlando.................... ⎰
(14) By Touchstone ....

Dutch Skater by Flying Dutch-
man .... (3) ... (5) ... (22) Gladiator .... ⎱ Dutch Oven (Leger, 1882).
Cantiniere by Stockwell .... (3) ... (2) ... (13) Orlando

(Strong nick (the brothers Castrel and Selim, and a return of the best figure No. 3 in sire.)

M 2

tendency to throw better fillies than colts. Of course, a great deal depends upon the mares. If they nick the running or effeminate strains in the sire it will be likely to result in breeding good fillies, but this will be more assured if, as before said, the *best* blood of your stallion's *sire* is nicked as well as *his figure*. I have seen so many remarkable instances confirming this that I cannot doubt, in my own mind, the correctness of this theory, if it is looked at on general principles and with a due regard to surroundings.

Rêve d'Or (Oaks) is bred by a nick of her sire, Hampton's Melbourne and Touchstone blood in Lord Clifden, her third dam being a West Australian mare. This is another strong example, as West Australian is by Melbourne from a Touchstone mare.

This example of Jannette fits both the nicking of figures theory and the one under consideration, but the return to Touchstone is so close and strong that it may be reckoned as having more influence than the figure mating. In any case it does not weaken the contention, because the theory of producing high class fillies is based as much upon the nicking of *individual* names in sire's table as upon the bringing together of figures. The other phase of this interesting question of sex law referred to developed itself during a long series of investigations on this subject, viz., the tendency of some sires to produce good fillies only, and *vice versâ*. The bare fact has been known to breeders and trainers to their cost long enough ago to set many men engaged in raising thoroughbreds wondering why it is so, and where the remedy is to come from? That a practical method will some day be discovered to control the law of sex is quite within the range of probabilities. In the meantime we must content ourselves with seeking for the reason why the fillies of one stallion are so superior to his colts. Personally, I have for many years been so satisfied about the cause that I have had the confidence to predict beforehand how a racehorse was likely to act when put to stud work. I cannot do better than cite a case in point. While on a visit to Newmarket (England) in 1882, I carried a letter of introduction to

Longbow by Ithuriel .... (2) } (14) ... (21) ... Dr. of (2) Cæton.............. } Feu de Joie (Oaks).

By Touchstone .... (14)

Jeu d'Esprit by Flatcatcher ...... (3) } (14) ... (7) ... (28) Emilius ....

By Touchstone .... (14)

Teddner by The Libel .... (14) ... (20) ... (13) Ellis............. A wonderfully fine mare.

From Sister to Touchstone

Dr. of King Tom.................... (3) ... (14) ... (3) Flying Dutchman....... Lurline (dam of Darebin).

(14) Dr. of Touchstone.

Lord Clifden by Newminster...... (8) } (14) ... (2) ... (1) Melbourne ....

By Touchstone .... (14)

Chevisaunce by Stockwell .... (3) ... (1) ... (2) Paragone .... Jannette (Oaks and Leger).

(14) By Touchstone ..

Captain Machell, who can corroborate my statement if this happens to come under his notice. He very kindly showed me over his own stud, and we then crossed to the late Lord Calthorpe's stables to see Petrarch. When the horse was led out for inspection Captain Machell observed, " You are now looking at the best racehorse of his day in England. What do you think of his prospects as a sire?" My answer was, " He will get more good fillies than colts if one may judge by his pedigree." It goes without saying that this remark was received with a very incredulous smile, in which the owner of the horse joined, and I feel quite sure I was put down as "another pedigree crank." "The long result of time," however, has proved that I was fairly correct in my prediction. Petrarch has since sired two Oaks winners, " Busybody " and " Miss Jummy," and a St. Leger winner, " Throstle," against only *one* high class colt, " The Bard," who ran second to Ormonde for the Derby. It was rather a bad piece of luck to run against such a wonder, but the fact remains that the *only classic* winners by Petrarch are *fillies*. His pedigree when looked into closely will show a strong inbreeding on both sides to the effeminate strains of Herod and Matchem, and through Herod's flashiest representatives, Castrel and Selim. Laura, his dam, was by Orlando, a horse that I before remarked had three close strains of Selim and Castrel and one of Whalebone. Laura's first dam was by Alarm (by Venison from Dr. of Defence, son of Whalebone and a Rubens mare), of the Herod line, and Laura's second dam was by Whalebone. In this connection the double Whalebone would lose its proverbial stoutness and become effeminate. This, then, was the mare that was mated with Lord Clifden, a horse of the 2 line, and the dam of Lord Clifden was "The Slave" by Melbourne (1) (of the effeminate Matchem male line), and Newminster, sire of Lord Clifden, was out of Beeswing by Dr. Syntax, also of the (male) Matchem line. The only real stoutness in the pedigree was Banter and Voltaire, the maternal great-grandsire of Lord Clifden. As a proof that these *stoutest* strains of Petrarch were the proper ones to nick, his daughter Busybody was from Spinaway by Macaroni, with two strains of Blacklock and one through Voltaire, also one of Banter close. It is also worthy of note that in this filly's pedigree it is Petrarch's *sire's* blood (Voltaire) which is nicked most strongly, Blacklock being more intense than any other strain, especially through the incestuously bred Lollipop, dam of Sweetmeat. Sweetmeat himself was a great filly getter, mainly, I take it, through the *stoutness* of *his dam*, in comparison with his sire Gladiator. Such horses always have a tendency to sire good fillies. In Petrarch's case there was a general effeminacy all through the pedigree, as distinguished from Sweetmeat. Horses bred like the latter will only sire *good* males when they get a strong return of Eclipse through their mates; Parmesan to wit, a son of Sweetmeat from Gruyere by Verulam by Lottery (Tramp), from Wire by Waxy. Parmesan's second dam was by Touchstone, and in all his top main lines goes to Eclipse, so that Parmesan's dam was the kind of mare exactly suited to a horse like Sweetmeat of the Herod line. Stud masters cannot have this point too often impressed upon them, viz., that the only chance of keeping the *male lines* of Herod and Matchem from dying out is to mate horses of these two lines to mares *very much inbred* to Eclipse through his best branches —Stockwell, Sterling, and Galopin. I have shown how this was successfully carried out in Darebin's case (page 131), the result being the Australian Peer, a horse very nearly equal to Abercorn and Carbine, both worthy representatives of Eclipse in male line. Sweetmeat sired two Oaks winners in Mincemeat and Mincepie.

Adventurer is another horse whose fillies have raced better than the colts. A close look into his pedigree shows him to be very stoutly bred on dam's side. To start with, he comes from same female line as Eclipse (**12**), and *his* branch would naturally enough amalgamate more freely with any other main branches of Eclipse coming into the connection. Take Adventurer's third dam, the Orville (**8**) mare, she would have a far stronger infusion of Eclipse *in* her veins than if by Orville, from, say, the 7 or 9 lines. Consequently when crossed by Partisan, whose dam was by Pot-8-os a son of Eclipse, the stoutness would be still further intensified The filly from this union was mated with Emilius (by Orville), and so we may safely infer that Palma, the dam of Adventurer, was stouter bred than Newminster, who carried in his veins a blending of the Matchem line (through Dr. of Syntax) with effeminate Camel, whose dam was by Selim, second dam by Sir Peter. This would account clearly enough for the goodness of Adventurer's fillies— Apology, Wheel of Fortune, and Bal Gal.

In Australia (imp.) Kelpie was conspicuous for the badness of his fillies, as compared to his colts. His breeding is given at page 217. His sire Weatherbit was from the **12** line (same as Eclipse), and his grandsire Sheet Anchor from same, so that, looking at Weatherbit's pedigree from any point of view, it is perhaps one of the stoutest in the Stud Book of his day. Kelpie's dam, Child of the Mist, is, on the contrary, an effeminately bred mare with no close **12** or inbreeding to Eclipse, or any of the sire lines in her figures for some five or six removes. Therefore Kelpie was bred on reverse lines to Adventurer and Sweetmeat, and, according to the views I have given expression to, his colts ought to have been superior to his fillies, as they undoubtedly were.

Priam has always been cited as a remarkable instance of a horse siring three Oaks winners in four years with scarce any good colts. His dam Cressida was in the 6 family, also her sister Eleanor (first filly to win the Derby) and Young Giantess, dam of Sorcerer (sire of Sorcery, Oaks). Again, Priam was closely inbred to Whiskey of the 2 line, distinguished for its large number of Oaks winners (fifteen). The above conditions are of themselves sufficiently strong to point to him as a sire of good fillies if further proof were not at hand. Pedigree on next page.

I have alongside of me some old memoranda, made while investigating this matter many years back, which shows that

Priam's dam carried in her veins (8) eight strains of Godolphin Barb, (11) eleven of Darley Arabian, and (3) three of Byerly Turk's. His sire Emilius had 21 G., 23 D., 9 B.

The combined Godolphin and Byerly in Cressida only equalled in volume the Darley, showing how very stoutly bred she was. In Emilius the combined Godolphin and Byerly were as 30 to 23 of Darley—a large predominance. It is quite clear that Priam was very much *stouter bred on dam's side*, and therefore should, by my theory, produce superior fillies.

Emilius himself furnishes a very apt illustration of the other

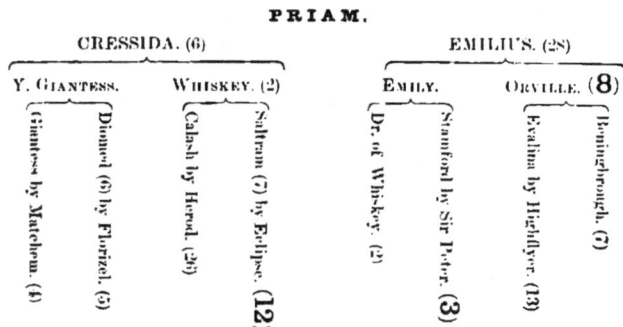

PRIAM.

CRESSIDA. (6)		EMILIUS. (28)	
Y. GIANTESS.	WHISKEY. (2)	EMILY.	ORVILLE. (8)
Giantess by Matchem. (4) — Dismal (6) by Florizel. (3)	Calash by Herod. (26) — Saltram (7) by Eclipse. (12)	Dr. of Whiskey. (2) — Stamford by Sir Peter. (3)	Evalina by Highflyer. (13) — Beningbrough. (7)

side of the question. His figures are—Emilius by Orville (8)—28 from Emily (30) by Stamford. Orville's dam coming from a good sire line (the same as Marske, sire of Eclipse) would be an admirable *stem* upon which to graft the strain of Eclipse (8, 12, 11) through Beningbrough. In addition to this, Emilius strains in male line to Eclipse and through dam to Herod, and is altogether much more stoutly bred on his sire's side. He sired two Derby winners, Priam and Plenipotentiary, against one Oaks winner, Oxygen. Nevertheless, from the *total* quantity of Godolphin and Byerly in his veins, 30 as against 23 Darley, his blood has been very valuable through his mares, and may be classed as good pliable blood, like that of Stockwell and Yattendon.

Priam, deficient in sire figures, forms no exception to the rule that they should be returned to him (also No. 2) in his mares. His Oaks winner, Miss Letty, dam of Weatherbit, was from the (**12**) family—from an Orville (**8**) mare. Industry, another Oaks winner, comes from No. 2 line, her dam, Arachne by Filho da Puta (**12**), grandson of Sir Peter (**3**) ; Crucifix (Oaks) came from the No. 2 line, with a strain of Y. Marske (**12**) by Marske (**8**).

King Tom is another case in point, for while his half brother Stockwell has founded several male branches to represent him, King Tom's sons have yet to demonstrate that they possess the power of male transmission. A look into King Tom's pedigree will show that his dam Pocahontas was infinitely stouter bred than his sire Harkaway, in whose veins coursed more strains of the Godolphin Barb than any horse (perhaps) in the Stud Book, comprising the *same number* of *generations* in his family tree. There is no question that King Tom's fillies were, taking them all round, better than his colts. Against one Derby winner in Kingcraft, a very moderate horse, or he would never have succumbed to Hawthornden in the Leger, he sired three Oaks winners, Tormentor, Hippia, and Hannah, the latter a Leger winner as well, besides her contemporary and stable companion, Corisande, winner of the Cesarewitch. If he had never done more than sire St. Angela, the dam of St. Simon, his fame was assured for all time. In addition to the above, there are the dams of Royal Hampton, Post Restante, and, in Australia, Miss Giraffe, dam of Neckersgat, whose son Portsea ran the three miles (1894) in 5min. 23½sec.

The above results prove that I am justified in claiming him as bred to get better fillies than colts ; in contrast to such a horse as Newminster, sired by Touchstone (**14**), his dam Beeswing by Dr. Syntax, a scion of the God. Barb, so that his pedigree was built on opposite lines to King Tom.

Isonomy got some very good fillies (notably Seabreeze, Oaks and Leger, 1888), but he shows a preponderance of good colts. I have already pointed out that he is an unusually stoutly bred horse on his dam's side. Over ten years ago, when I saw him presiding at Lady Emily Peel's choice stud of mares, I was disposed to think this very stoutness would be a bar to success at stud, though even then of opinion he would leave good sons behind him to carry on the line, in consequence of his strong inbreeding to sire families on both sides. At that time I was strongly imbued with the idea that the greater stoutness (*i.e.*, Eclipse inbreeding) *must* necessarily be on the sire's side of pedigree table ; but I have had reason to modify my views since then, as recorded elsewhere.

A look through Isonomy's pedigree again will show in his sire, Sterling, strains of Melbourne, Flatcatcher, and Bay Middleton—as against Stockwell on top of Faugh-a-Ballagh—Prime Warden and stout Sir Hercules on side of dam, all three branches of Eclipse male line. It would be false reasoning to ignore the part the dam of a good filly plays in determining her sex and class, and I have already pointed out that the running lines (1, 2, **3** and 4) have a marked tendency to produce good fillies, notably 4, from which Seabreeze springs.

So strong is this feminine potency, that St. Simon has sired Memoir and La Flèche from the **3** line. St. Simon's pedigree (page 75), however, is such an evenly balanced one, that it would be more difficult to predict which way he would act, than in decided cases like Adventurer, Sweetmeat, &c. Yet his close inbreeding to the figure **3**, always effeminate when bred to itself, might well have foreshadowed his tendency to beget high-class fillies.

Probably the greatest race mares ever saddled in America were Miss Woodford and Firenze, and their pedigrees are a singular justification of the rule of breeding good fillies. These two valuable mares are the property of Mr. J. B. Haggin, Rancho del Paso Stud.

In this, as in the previous examples of good fillies, it is the Blacklock strains on *sire's* side of Billet's pedigree which is so strongly nicked. There is also a double cross of the No. 2 line, as Billet's sire and dam are both in this line, as well as Blacklock

MISS WOODFORD.

FANCY JANE. +   BILLET. (2) (imp.)

(three times) and Sir Hercules twice.   Though a short pedigree mare, Miss Woodford should be valuable at stud.

Firenze is bred on similar lines.   Her sire Glenelg got a strong return of his two most potent strains, Birdcatcher and

Blacklock. In many respects her dam's (Florida) pedigree resembles that of Miss Woodford's dam.

This is a pedigree which readers may study with considerable profit. It will be seen that in the first three (top) removes there

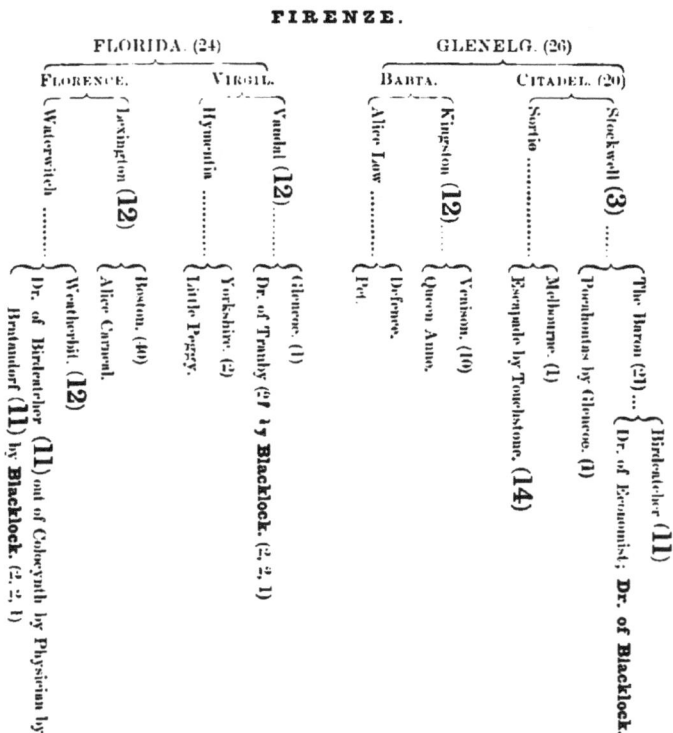

FIRENZE.

FLORIDA. (24) GLENELG. (26)

FLORENCE. VIRGIL. BABTA. CITADEL. (20)

Stockwell (3) ...... { The Baron (2?) ... { Birdcatcher (11)
{ Dr. of Economist; **Dr. of Blacklock.**
{ Pocahontas by Glencoe. (1)

Sortie ...... { Melbourne. (1)
{ Escapade by Touchstone. **(14)**

Kingston (12) ...... { Venison. (10)
{ Queen Anne.

Alice Law ...... { Defence.
{ Pet.

Vandal (12) ...... { Glencoe. (1)
{ Dr. of Tranby (2? 1 by **Blacklock.** (2, 2, 1)

Hymenia ...... { Yorkshire. (2)
{ Little Peggy.

Lexington (12) ...... { Boston. (40)
{ Alice Carneal.

Waterwitch ...... { Weatherbit. (12)
{ Dr. of Birdcatcher (11) out of Colocynth by Physician by
Brinckhoff (11) by **Blacklock.** (2, 2, 1)

is an absence of running blood. We only have one figure **3** (Stockwell). In such cases the inbreeding lower down *must of necessity* be to the *pure* figures to counteract the sire and outside lines.   In Gladiateur the reverse conditions existed, and he would have been a failure on the turf without the inbreeding to *sire* figures.   In Firenze the required inbreeding came through the best strains in stud book, Blacklock and Sir Hercules, and the *right* hand side of sires pedigree table was nicked.

CHAPTER XI.

PHENOMENAL RACEHORSES.

I TAKE it the ambition of every breeder of racehorses is to produce something phenomenal, in the turf acceptation of that expression. Many of the so-called phenomenal performers, from and including, Flying Childers, and down to Ormonde, owe their extraordinary powers, without doubt, to experiments in *close* breeding. In most cases these experiments were grave blunders, in view of results expected, because experience has shown us that any individual horse, bred for instance like the third dam of Flying Childers, could not have been anything better than a third class sprinter. I have no turf records of the doings of Lollipop, dam of Sweetmeat, but it is safe to say that she was only a sprinter, even if she raced in any shape. Yet in both these cases the breeders, no doubt, expected to get splendid results; or were they mere experiments to see how closely horses could be bred without deterioration ? *We* of the present day, however, are not so much concerned with their motives as with the curious effect of such abnormal inbreeding upon the racehorses of past and present days, for it is very evident that incestuous breeding to the best strains of blood (as in Lollipop's case) has the effect of concentrating a larger proportion of vital force in the veins of one individual than under ordinary circumstances would fall to its share, though that increased vitality may not be capable of utilisation until the next and succeeding generations.

The records of Childers' performances are shrouded somewhat in the haze of tradition, and it is asking far too much, to expect us to swallow the assertion that he was "timed to have run 82½ft. in a second of time," or nearly a mile in a minute. Yet he undoubtedly showed his heels to all contemporary racehorses and must have done something very wonderful to have evoked so much "tall talk." His pedigree shows incestuous breeding in his dam.

It will be seen by this pedigree that Spanker was bred to his own dam, who produced a filly which was put to the Leeds

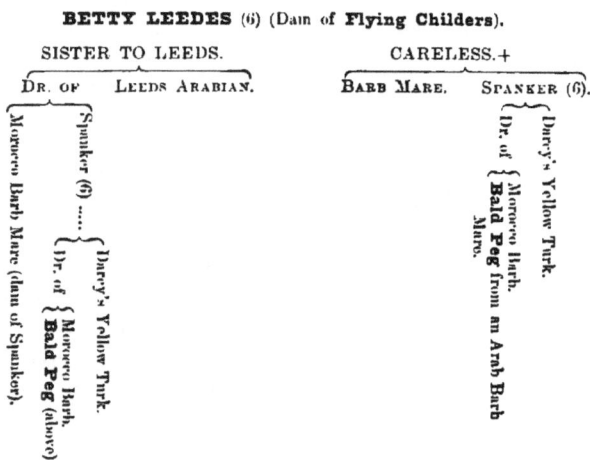

BETTY LEEDES (6) (Dam of **Flying Childers**).

SISTER TO LEEDS.		CARELESS.+	
DR. OF	LEEDS ARABIAN.	BABB MARE.	SPANKER (6).

Morocco Barb Mare (dam of Spanker).

Spanker (6) ...... { Darcy's Yellow Turk. / Dr. of { Morocco Barb. / **Bald Peg** (above).

Dr. of { Morocco Barb. / **Bald Peg** from an Arab Barb Mare.

Darcy's Yellow Turk.

Arabian. The result of this cross again was a filly (sister to Leeds), and she, in turn, was mated with Careless, a son of Spanker, thus renewing and intensifying the Spanker blood. Betty Leeds, the outcome of this curious combination, was fortunately mated with the Darley Arabian—not only a complete outcross, but the best Eastern male ever introduced into the English stud, if he is to be judged by the doings of his descendants in male line. It is a matter for regret that Betty Leeds did not also throw a daughter, because in that case we might possibly have seen the progeny of this daughter crossed with Marske (**8**), and this would in all probability have given us another male line of Eclipse, besides producing a phenomenal racehorse. The excellence of Herod and Eclipse was due, in a great measure, to this piece of incestuous breeding, especially in Herod's case, where the name of Flying Childers (bred as shown) occurs once through his dam, by Blaze, son of Flying Childers, and twice again, through Y. Bald Peg and Jigg's dam, so that the inbreeding is doubly repeated or nearly so. This is quite sufficient to account for Herod's racing powers, and also for the goodness of his daughters, especially crossed with Eclipse rich in-sire blood. Indeed, no two horses were ever better suited to each other, the bulk of the obligation laying with Herod perhaps.

Gladiateur is generally acknowledged to be the most phenomenal animal ever seen on a racecourse since the days of Childers and Eclipse. His pedigree differs in construction very slightly from those of most of the extraordinary racehorses, but there are some peculiarities in it not generally found, and I wish to draw especial attention to them, because it so distinctly points to the necessity of working by *figures*. I do not remember ever reading, amongst the many treatises and articles upon breeding racehorses, any attempt to explain either the failure of Gladiateur at stud work or where he got his extraordinary powers of racing. As a fact, the figures afford the only feasible explanation, because he was bred on quite orthodox sire conditions, gauged by any of the old theories. His main lines ran mostly to Eclipse, and his dam was from the Herod line.

The great want (as before stated) in this pedigree was *sire blood* in *top* lines. I have also previously mentioned that no horse of modern days, so far as I have discovered, has proved a high-class racehorse with an absence of sire figures in the three top removes. In this respect Gladiateur is no exception, for Sheet Anchor comes

N

GLADIATEUR.

MISS GLADIATOR. (5)   MONARQUE. (19)

TAFFRAIL.   GLADIATOR. (22)   POETESS.   THE EMPEROR. (5)

Dr. of ......

Sheet Anchor (12)

Partisan (1) ... {
Pauline ...... {

Ada ......

Royal Oak (3) ...... {

Design ...... {

Dr. of ......

Revellor (19) ...... {

Whalebone (1) ...... {

Defence (5) ...... {

Defence ...... {

Reveller (19)

Walton (?) by Sir Peter. (3)
Parasol by Pot-8-os by Eclipse. (12, 8, 11)
Moses (5) by Seymour (1) or Whalebone.
Quadrille.

Cotton (2) by Golumpus.
Dr. of Sandbeck. (19)
Whisker. (1)
Anna Bella.

Tramp (3) by Dick Andrews (grandson of Eclipse).
Defence dam of Defence (above).

Cafton (2) by Golumpus.

Shuttle (2!) { Y. Marske (12) by Marske. (8, 11)
Dr. of ...... { Vauxhall Snap Mare. (1

Drone.
Confessinn ...... { Y. Marske (12) by Marske. (8, 11)
{ Tuberose (above).

Little Folly (3) by Highland Fling.
Connie (25) ...... { Surveyor.
{ Dr. of Sir Peter. (3)

Bennington (7) by King Fergus by Eclipse.
Dr. of Tandem from Tuberose.

Wavy (18) { Pot-8os (38) by Eclipse.
{ Maria by Herod.
Penelope ...... { Trumpator.
{ Prunella.

Rubens (2) by Buzzard.

Morgiana (1) ...... {
Dr. of ...... {

Tartary (11) ......

Lottery (11) ...... {

Morgiana 9 ...... {

Dr. of ......

Airdrossan ...... {

Dr. of ...... {

Y. Marske (12) (above) by Marske. (8, 11)

Maley (7) { Orville (8) by Eclipse.
{ Dr. of Whiskey by Eclipse.
Mandane ...... { Surveyor (above).
{ Dr. of Woodpecker.

Tramp (3) by D.A. by J.A. by Eclipse.
Mandane ...... { Pot-8os by Eclipse.
{ Dr. of Woodpecker.

Whalebone (1) by Wavy to Eclipse.
Dr. of Orville.

John Bull.
Miss Whip... { Volunteer.
{ Dr. of Evergreen. (3)

Shuttle (2!) by Y. Marske (12) by Marske (8) by Eclipse.
Buzzard (3) by Woodpecker.
Dr. of King Fergus (6) by Eclipse.

in the third remove, and though his is the only sire figure (on top),
he **is** strongly inbred to sire blood for three generations, finally
ending in a mass of Eclipse at the back of his pedigree, and it will
be readily understood that very few horses in the stud book could
have supplied Sheet Anchor's place, and with such good effect, to a
horse bred away from sire families like Monarque. The Emperor
was produced by an *inbreeding* to Defiance through the family (the
best running one outside of 4). His *third* dam Defiance was also
the dam of his sire Defence—or, in plainer phraseology, Defiance's
grand-daughter was incestuously mated with her own uncle,
Defence. This close inbreeding to Defiance (5) was followed up by
mating The Emperor to Poetess by Royal Oak, also of the 5 line.
Monarque, the result of this union, was then crossed upon Miss
Gladiator of the same 5 family. But as all this continued inbreeding
was to a *non-sire* line (5), it must be assumed by the light of the
figure key that even the presence of Sheet Anchor (**12**) in the third
remove was hardly equal to the task of counteracting the anti-sire
influence of No. 5. We must look elsewhere for the solution of
Gladiateur's racing qualities. It will be remembered that in the
pedigrees given of Peter, Bendigo, Ormonde, Barcaldine, and
Carbine (and later on I shall give Domino) that the causes of their
excellence as racehorses lay in the close inbreeding to *running blood*,
to wit, *Blacklock* (2) at *bottom* of pedigree on both sides. But in
these cases there was a sufficiency of sire blood in top removes. And
to have further inbred to back strains coming from sire families
would have brought about certain failure, because they had sufficient
in the first three removes. Gladiateur's sire and dam were built on
totally opposite lines, and, as a consequence, the inbreeding back in
their pedigrees must of necessity be, to horses of *strong sire* figures,
to counteract the 5 influence. The actual state of affairs, revealed
by a further examination of the pedigrees precisely what has been
foreshadowed. Monarque's *third* dam Anna Bella (by Shuttle) was
the outcome of a union of Shuttle (son of **Young Marske** (12)

with a Drone mare, daughter of Comtessina by **Y. Marske (12)**, in other terms a mating of uncle with niece.   Young Marske **(12)** was by Marske **(8)** by Squirt **(11)**, identically the same figures as Eclipse, than which no greater compliment could be paid to his stout sire breeding.   So much for Monarque.   When we turn to the left-hand side of pedigree table we find Miss Gladiator's fourth dam was a daughter of the same Shuttle by Y. Marske **(12)** by Marske **(8)** by Squirt **(11)**, thus disclosing a nick of the elements most required at about the distance usually found in extraordinary race-horses.

It may sound somewhat premature to bracket Domino, the sensational two-year-old of America in 1893, amongst phenomenal horses, yet his two-year-old running under heavy weights, and the suspicion of a "leg," will mark 1893 as "*Domino's* year" for all time. His pedigree is very similar to the great cracks of the world, and deserves recording.

Edith, from a Glencoe mare, was put to her cousin Lecompte, also from a Glencoe mare, Reel.   The result, a daughter, was then mated with another of Reel's sons, War Dance, and produced Lizzie G., her sire War Dance being a son of Lexington as well. Lizzie G., the result of this incestuous union, was mated with Enquirer, a son of Leamington and Lida by Lexington (above). This double cross of Lexington and a strain of Leamington acted as a judicious outcross to the previous intense inbreeding to Glencoe, and the outcome of this union, Maimie Grey, should have had a fine turn of speed herself.   For such an inbred mare the correct thing was to mate her with an *outbred* horse, leaving only a dash of her strongest and best blood to act as a connecting link.

It would be difficult to find a more outbred horse than Hymyar, and in consequence he will always do best with a *strong* return to his stout Blacklock, Birdcatcher, and Glencoe blood, as in this case.

If I have not made this clear before, it cannot be too strongly

DOMINO.

MAIMIE GREY. (27)   HIMYAR. (2)

LIZZIE G. (37)   ENQUIRER. +   HIRA.   ALARM. 15

Eclipse (D) (imp.) ...... { Orlando (13) ...... { Touchstone. (14)
{ Vulture.
{ Gaze ...... { Bay Middleton (1) by Sultan. (8)
{ Flycatcher by Dr. of Colwell.

Maud (imp.) .... { Stockwell (3) ... { The Baron by Birdcatcher. (11)
{ Pocahontas by Glencoe.
{ Dr. of ...... { Lanercost (3) by Liverpool. (11)
{ Sister to Hornsea by Velocipede (3) by Blacklock

Lexington (12) ... { Boston (40) by Timoleon + by Sir Archy. (41)
{ Alice Carneal by Sarpedon. (41)

Higera ...... { Ambassador ...... { Plenipotentiary (6) by Emilius.
{ Dr. of Whisker. (1)
{ Flight ...... { Leviathan by Muley. (7)
{ Dr. of Sir Charles (12) by Sir Archy.

Leamington (14) ... { Faugh-a-Ballagh (11) by Sir Hercules (2) by Whalebone. (1)
{ Dr. of ...... { Pantaloon (17) by Castrel. (2)
{ Dr. of Blacklock (2) by Whitelock. (1)

Lida ...... { Lexington (12) by Boston. (40)
{ (Am.) Eclipse.
{ Lize ...... { Gabriella (3) .... { Sir Archy. (11)
{ Calypso, with a lot of close inbreeding at bottom of pedigree to Fearnought.

War Dance (27) ... { Lexington (12) by Boston. (40)
{ Reel by Glencoe (1) ... { Sultan (8) by Selim. (2)
{ Dr. of Tramp. (3)

Dr. of ...... { Lecompte (57) ... { Boston. (40)
{ Reel by Glencoe (1) .... { Sultan (8) by Selim. (2)
{ Dr. of Tramp. (3)
{ Edith ...... { Sovereign by Emilius.
{ Judith by Glencoe (1) ...... { Sultan (8) by Selim (2) by Buzzard. (3)
{ Dr. of Tramp. (3)

impressed upon stud masters that an *outbred* sire should always be mated with mares *inbred* closely to his *best* strains, and *vice versâ*. I have endeavoured to prove in Chapter VIII. that the vitality of the racehorse is due to the infusions of the running families 1, 2, (3), 4, and 5 ; also that these families are not effective when bred to one another, but require to be grafted on to the coarser and more masculine stems of the sire or *outside* families. In the case in point there is a persistent return to No. 27, as both Lecompte and War Dance are offshoots of Maimie Grey's parent stem (27), but this strong inbreeding to 27 alone must have proved a failure but for the influence of Glencoe. The "peerless" Boston (sire of Lexington) was probably one of the greatest racing phenomenons of early American days. He started in forty-five races, running first in forty, and of these thirty were four-mile heats, and nine three-mile heats.

His pedigree, like most extraordinary racehorses, was curiously inbred at bottom of sire and dam pedigree, and resembles that of Gladiateur in this respect. His fifth dam by Kitty Fisher was by imported Fearnought (a son of Regulus 11), from imported Kitty Fisher by Cade, son of Godolphin Barb.

Y. Kitty Fisher was mated with Symme's Wildair, a son of imported Fearnought (by Regulus) from a daughter of imported Jolly Roger, from imported Kitty Fisher (above) by Cade. This breeding was incestuous, as may be seen by the tabulation. For the rest of Boston's pedigree, see Lexington, page 121.

It will be noticed also that Clockfast was from a Regulus mare, and another strain of Regulus comes in through Alderman (the sire of Boston's second dam), a son of Pot-8-os, from a Regulus mare. Timoleon, sire of Boston, had for his *second* dam a daughter of the identical Symme's Wildair who figures in the above tabulation of Boston's dam ; so that the inbreeding to Fearnought was more intense and effective, because it came through the same source, *i.e.*, Kitty Fisher, and of itself might have been sufficient to produce a good racehorse, *being so close to* the God. Barb. But the inbreeding was continued still further through Timoleon's dam, a daughter of Saltram (7) by Eclipse, son of Marske, and Spiletta, by Regulus (the sire of Fearnought), and two more strains of Regulus are found back in the pedigree. Here, again, as in Gladiateur and Emperor of Norfolk (page 178), it will be found that there was a dearth of sire blood on top; consequently the inbreeding to Regulus (11) was of far

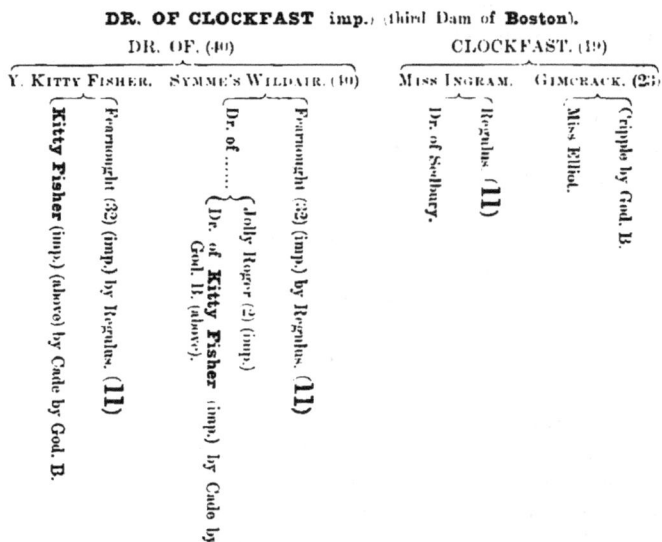

DR. OF CLOCKFAST imp.) (third Dam of **Boston**).

DR. OF. (40)   CLOCKFAST. (19)

Y. KITTY FISHER.   SYMME'S WILDAIR. (40)   MISS INGRAM.   GIMCRACK. (23)

- Kitty Fisher (imp.) (above) by Cade by God. B.
- Fearnought (32) (imp.) by Regulus, (11)
- Dr. of ...... { Jolly Roger (2) (imp.) / Dr. of **Kitty Fisher** (imp.) God. B. (above).
- Fearnought (32) (imp.) by Regulus, (11) / Dr. of **Kitty Fisher** (imp.) by Cade by
- Dr. of Sedbury.
- Regulus (11)
- Miss Elliot.
- Cripple by God. B.

more importance than under ordinary circumstances. In another way this pedigree illustrates what I have in a previous chapter laid down as the correct method of mating, viz., to examine closely the *dam's side* of your stallion's pedigree table, and having discovered the best and most potent strain (in this case Regulus), then mate him with mares inbred closely to the same blood. Though an undoubtedly great racehorse, Boston was very deficient in sire blood in his top

removes, and when tabulated with a mate, only one appears until
Eclipse (**12**) is reached in the fourth remove. To sire a son likely
to carry on the line, it was imperative that he should get mates
in sire lines, and in view of Eclipse (**12**) being his stoutest and

CALYPSO + (fourth dam of **Enquirer**).

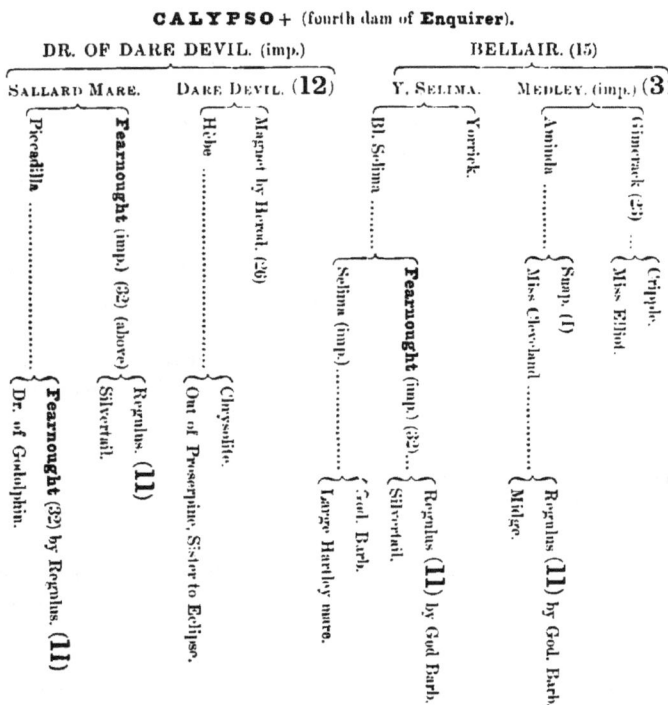

DR. OF DARE DEVIL. (imp.)   BELLAIR. (15)

best strain, it was to be expected that his greatest son Lexington
should owe his existence to Alice Carneal of the (**12**) line.

Though not in the category of " world-beaters," Enquirer was
both a high class racehorse and good sire, and it will not be out

of place to insert a portion of his dam's pedigree alongside of that of Boston's just given, because there is a great similarity in the back breeding. Enquirer was by imported Leamington (page 96) from Lida by Lexington, from Lize by American Eclipse **3**), from Sabiella by Sir Archy, from Calypso by Bellair, and thence to an American mare.

If we turn to Lexington's pedigree (page 121), and note the incestuous inbreeding to Fearnought in Boston, which is continued and strengthened by Maria, fourth dam of Lexington, also very inbred to Fearnought, with a strain of Muley as well; it will be realised that Enquirer's dam Lida was a typical inbred American pedigree, and well suited for an *outcross* to a stoutly-bred horse of the male Eclipse line, like Leamington.

Few will deny that Bendigo is entitled to take rank amongst racing phenomenons, nor does his pedigree differ a whit from the rule which evidently prevails in the production of such animals, except that here the inbreeding to Rataplan is closer than is usually found in great stayers. Against this are splendid outcrosses of Y. Melbourne, Gladiator, and Pantaloon.

The fourth dam of Bendigo, Newton Lass, was produced by a mating of cousins, eighth son and eighth daughter of Blacklock. Her daughter, Patience, was bred to King of Trumps, also an eighth son of Blacklock, thus intensifying the inbreeding to Blacklock; and Hasty Girl got yet another Blacklock strain through Rataplan. The second dam of Ben Battle was by Sweetmeat, whose dam was incestuously bred to Blacklock.

Without doubt Salvator may be classed as the best all-round American racehorse of late times. In regard to intense inbreeding to certain strains, his dam, Salina, forms no exception to the great examples I have drawn from in this chapter. His pedigree will be found at p. 99. Salina's ninth dam was by Fearnought (son of Regulus), her eighth dam by Highflyer (son of Highflyer), seventh dam by Mebzar, son of (imp.) Medley (**3**) from Kitty Fisher (a daughter of the (imp.) Kitty Fisher that figures so largely in the pedigrees of Boston and Lexington), and Kitty Fisher was by

BENDIGO.

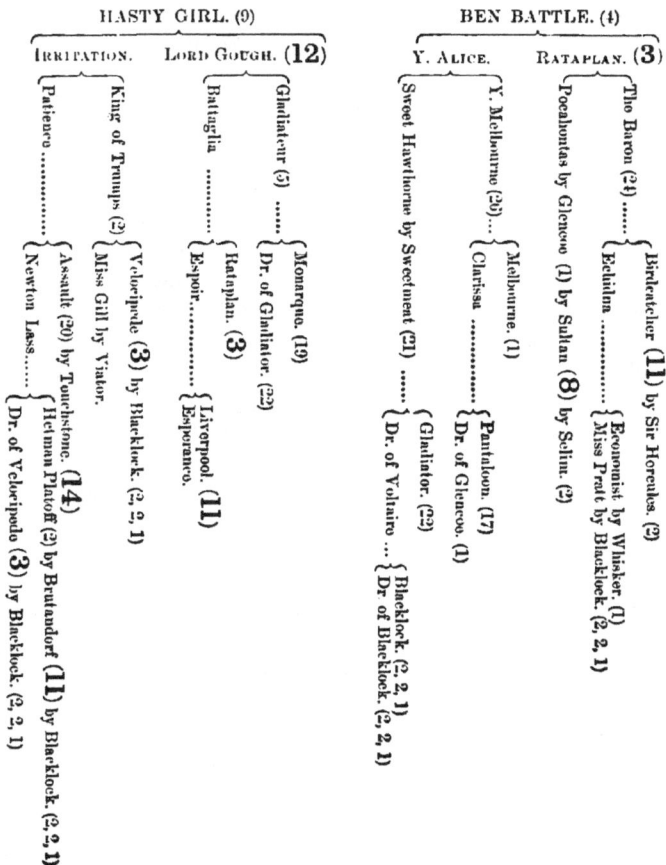

HASTY GIRL. (9)

IRRITATION.   LORD GOUGH. (**12**)

BEN BATTLE. (4)

Y. ALICE.   RATAPLAN. (**3**)

The Baron (24) ...... { Birdcatcher (**11**) by Sir Hercules. (2)
                    { Echidna .... { Economist by Whisker. (1)
                                  { Miss Pratt by Blacklock. (2, 2, 1)

Pocahontas by Glencoe (1) by Sultan (**8**) by Selim. (2)

Y. Melbourne (26)... { Melbourne. (1)
                      { Clarissa .... { Pantaloon. (17)
                                  { Dr. of Glencoe. (1)

Sweet Hawthorne by Sweetmeat (21) ...... { Gladiator. (22)
                                    { Dr. of Voltaire ... { Blacklock. (2, 2, 1)
                                                         { Dr. of Blacklock. (2, 2, 1)

Gladiateur (2) ...... { Monarque. (19)
                      { Dr. of Gladiator. (22)

Battaglia .... { Rataplan. (**3**)
                    { Espoir............ { Liverpool. (**11**)
                              { Esperance.

King of Trumps (2) { Velocipede (**3**) by Blacklock. (2, 2, 1)
                      { Miss Gill by Viator.

Patience .... { Assault (20) by Touchstone. (**14**)
                    { Newton Lass...... { Hetman Platoff (2) by Brutandorf (**11**) by Blacklock. (2, 2, 1)
                                { Dr. of Velocipede (**3**) by Blacklock. (2, 2, 1)

Symme's Wildair, a son of (imp.) Fearnought, and grandson of (imp.) Kitty Fisher. This shows Melzar to have been incestuously bred to (imp.) Kitty Fisher. Again, Salina's sixth dam, Lady Grey, was by Robin Grey, whose dam was by Grey Diomed, a son of (imp.) Medley (**3**) above. This combination gives a lot of curious inbreeding in Salina's sixth, seventh, and ninth dams to Fearnought and his son, Symme's Wildair; also Medley, with an incestuous inbreeding to (imp.) Kitty Fisher through Melzar. On the top of this come (through the fifth, fourth, third, and second dams of Salina) respective strains of Orphan, by Ball's Florizel (a son of Diomed), Trumpeter. Tranby (son of Blacklock, 2) Trustee (son of Catton (2) and Whisker 1), and finally Glencoe (1). Salina herself was by Lexington, whose *third* dam was the identical Lady Grey who figures as the sixth dam of Salina, thus repeating all the inbreeding noted above ; and Boston (sire of Lexington), we have seen, was in his own person *intensely* inbred to Symme's Wildair and his sire Fearnought, his fourth dam also incestuously bred to Fearnought and Kitty Fisher (imp.). In the whole course of my researches I have not come across anything so remarkably inbred as this, and it may be taken as being even more intense than a casual glance would convey, seeing that Lightsome (the dam of Salina) and Lexington share a common descent from the old Montagu mare (**12**). This was quite as it should have been, because neither Lightsome nor Lexington, apart from this, carried much *sire* blood in their veins. True they were in direct descent from a good sire family (**12**), and this explains why, as before told, the "Levity family" has been so consistently successful in America, where there was so *little sire* blood in the *old* pedigrees. The fact that more good *sires* spring from this family than any other in America is a splendid vindication of the soundness of the figure system and selection of sire families, which were decided upon many years before I saw an American pedigree. To return to Salina. As already noted, she may be classed as an extraordinary inbred mare to the old

American strains of blood, and for that reason required a mate of *opposite* breeding, yet bearing in his veins some connecting link common to both.   Luckily she was mated with Prince Charlie (imp.), whose dam, Eastern Princess, as well as her sire, Sesostris, traced in direct descent from the same old Montagu mare.   In addition to this powerful medium, there was a nick of Glencoe at three and five removes.   Salvator may well be said to owe his greatness to the palpable blunders of inbreeding committed by some early American stud masters, who evidently only looked for immediate results, never contemplating the subsequent good effects.   I give here the breeding of Dr. Hasbrouck, the champion miler of America. His dam, Sweetbriar, furnishes another example of inbred dams. We have just seen how, in the case of Salvator's dam, there was an extraordinary amount of inbreeding to Fearnought and Kitty Fisher (imp.).   In this respect Sweetbriar runs her very closely. She is by Virgil, a son of Vandal, from Impudence by Lexington. Now, seeing that Vandal's fourth dam, Lady Grey, is the third dam of Lexington, we get a repetition of the same intense inbreeding to Fearnought and his son, Symme's Wildair, and (imp.) Kitty Fisher. There is also in Lexington a considerable inbreeding to Diomed, and this is intensified by the Vandal strain, as that horse's third dam is by Orphan, the result of a union of a son and daughter of Diomed. Truly the early American stud masters were much given to close breeding experiments, for we find Virgil's third dam, Peggy Smith, by Cook's Whip, mated with Cripple, whose dam, Grecian Princess, was also by Cook's Whip; and, further, Cook's Whip was out of Speckleback, a daughter of Randolph's Celar (son of Mede's Celar), from Speckleback, by Mede's Celar.

Curiously enough, in the whole of Sweetbriar's pedigree there is only one strain of the speedy brothers Castrel and Selim, through Glencoe, and therefore it is not to be wondered at, as I before remarked, that she hit well with a horse like Sir Modred, descended in male line from Castrel and inbred to the brothers Selim and

Castrel, and bearing also in his veins a strain of Blacklock, to nick with the Blacklock which Sweetbriar inherits through Vandal's dam.

Morello, now 4 years, has been placed by good judges amongst the list of America's best racehorses of any day. And more than one good judge of racing consider him the very best, though I do not share that opinion. He is by Eolus from Cerise by Mocassin, a son of Macaroni. His pedigree quite bears out the rule in such cases, and may be studied with profit.

This pedigree shows a considerable inbreeding to the celebrated (imp.) Cub mare who figures as the progenitor of so many illustrious American horses. This Cub mare, in turn, traces back to the Layton Barb mare, No. 4, one of the best running lines. If mating scions of the same family tends to reproduce the present stock, then must Miss Obstinate have been endowed with all the characteristics of the 4 line, because her sire, Sumpter (by Sir Archy, by Diomed) claimed the Cub mare as his fourth dam, the same Cub mare being her *seventh* dam. Further, Miss Obstinate's dam was by Tiger, whose fourth dam was the same Cub mare. Miss Obstinate's daughter, Mary Morris, was by Medoc, a grandson of Diomed. Sumpter (above) was also a son of Sir Archy by Diomed. Coupling this with the fact that Fanny Washington (dam of Eolus) was inbred to Sir Archy (11) at three removes, we have a repitition of the conditions which produced Gladiateur, Boston, &c., only in this instance the inbreeding to Sir Archy was accompanied and strengthened by the curious inbreeding to No. 4 already noticed, as well as *four strains* of Blacklock, one of Sir Hercules, and four of Whalebone and Whisker. Morello is not too well supplied with sire strains in his top removes, and will require a strong return to them in his mates to overcome all his non-sire element.

Foxhall may well claim to be placed amongst America's greatest racehorses, if not at the very top. He was the only horse up to that

MORELLO.

CERISE. (1)   EOLUS. (6)

LIZZIE LUCAS.   MOCCASSIN. (imp.) (13)   FANNY WASHINGTON.*   LEAMINGTON (imp.) (14)

Fangho-Ballagh (11) by Sir Hercules. (2)

Dr. of .... { Pantaloon (17) by Castrel. (2)
                 { Daphne by Laurel (21) by Blacklock. (2, 2, 1)

Trustee (7) ... { Catton. (2)
           { Dr. of Whisker. (1)

Revenue { Dr. of Sir Charles by Sir Archy (11) by Diomed.

Sarah Washington ... { Zinganee by Sir Archy (11) by Diomed.
                  { Stella.

Macaroni (14) { Sweetmeat (2) ... { Gladiator (22) by Partisan. (1)
                             { Dr. of ... { Voltaire (12) by Blacklock. (2, 2, 1)
                                            { Dr. of Blacklock. (2, 2, 1)
             { Dr. of Pantaloon (17) (above).

Madam Strauss .... { King Tom (3) { Harkaway. (2)
                                 { Dr. of Glencoe.
                                 { Melbourne. (1)
                  Jetty Treffz ... { Dr. of ... { Lord Mayor by Pantaloon. (17)
                                        { Dr. of Voltaire (12) by son of Blacklock. (2, 2, 1)

Australian (imp.) (11) { West Aus. (7) { Melbourne. (1)
                                   { Dr. of Touchstone (14) by grandson of Whalebone. (1)
                           Emilia. .... { Y. Emilius.
                                   { Dr. of Whisker. (1)

Eagless .... { Grey Eagle by Woodpecker.
                         { Mary Morris by Mother by American Eclipse by Duroc by Diomed.

Fifth dam Miss Obstinate by Sumpter (1) (son of Sir Archy), whose fourth dam was Cerise's twelfth dam.
Sixth dam Jenny Slamerkin by Tiger (1), whose fourth dam was Cerise's twelfth dam, the imp. Cub mare.

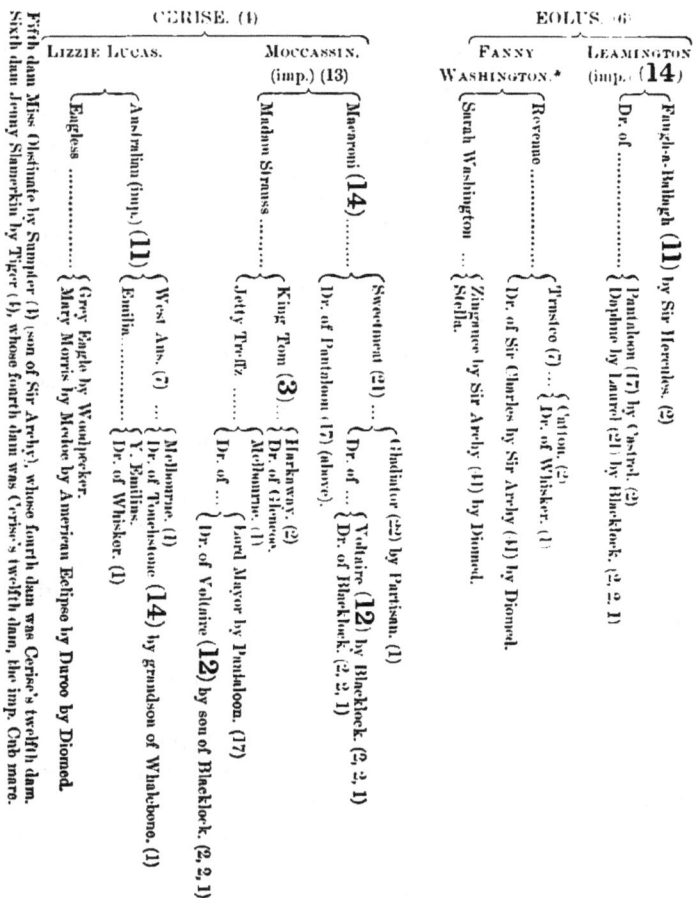

* Inbred to Sir Archy at three removes.

year, bar Rosebery, that had won the great double of Cesarewitch and Cambridgeshire, and he carried 7st. 12lb. and 9st. respectively. In the latter race that good horse, Tristan, same age (3 yrs.) was beaten with only 7st. 9lb. up, and this alone shows what a wonderful horse Foxhall was on that day. If the reader will turn to page 109 he will find that Capitola, the first dam of King Alfonso, was almost a full sister in blood to Mollie Jackson, the third dam of his son Foxhall. These matrons were both by Vandal from Margrave mares, and, seeing that Vandal was out of a mare by Tranby, son of Blacklock, we have another strong reminder of the immense value of this blood, which figures in the pedigrees of most of the modern racehorses, and, more than all the arguments I can bring forward, establishes the truth of the figure theory, because there is no horse in the stud book so inbred to the three great running families, 1, 2, and 4. Foxhall's pedigree bears a striking resemblance in one respect to another racing wonder, Barcaldine, inasmuch as the *first* dams of both sires are almost full sisters in blood to the *third* dams of their respective mates. It should be noted that in Foxhall's case the inbreeding to Vandal **(12)** was highly necessary, in conjunction with such non-sire figures as 9 and 15, and inbreeding to Margrave (2) and Blacklock (2). Foxhall will mate best with mares by Isonomy, St. Simon, or Sterling, from the good running lines, as his only chance of getting racehorses is from mares combining sire and running strains.

Ormonde's pedigree may be taken as another instance of intense inbreeding in dam's pedigree, in this case to Blacklock and 2 generally :

It would not be easy to discover in the whole range of the stud books **a** pedigree so inbred to 1, 2, 4 (and **3**) as that of Lily Agnes. It includes three strains of Blacklock, with *incestuous* inbreeding in the case of Lollipop intensified by the additional strain of Blacklock, as well as numerous other strains of No. 2. And, just as in Domino's dam, all this purity of the bottom section of the pedigree is grafted upon an outside but rapidly improving strain (16). And it will be

ORMONDE.

LILY AGNES.* (16)		BEND OR. (1)	
POLLY AGNES.	MACARONI.† (14)	ROUGE ROSE.	DONCASTER. (5).

Stockwell (3) ... { The Baron (24) ... { Birdcatcher (11) by Sir Hercules (2) by Whalebone. (1)
{ Echidna .... { Economist by Whisker. (1)
{ Pocahontas by Glencoe by Sutton. { Dr. of Blacklock (2, 2, 1)

Marigold .... { Teddington (2) ... { Orlando (13) by Touchstone. (14)
{ Miss Twickenham.
{ Dr. of .... { Ratan.
{ Dr. of Melbourne.

Thormanby (4) ... { Windhound (3) ... { Pantaloon (17) by Castrel. (2)
{ Dr. of Touchstone. (14)
{ Alice Hawthorn... { Muley Moloch. (6)
{ Rebecca by Lottery. (11)

Ellen Horne ...... { Red Shank.
{ Delhi by Plenipotentiary. (6).

Macaroni† (14) ... { Sweetmeat (21) ... { Gladiator (22) ... { Partisan. (1)
{ Pauline.
{ Lollipop .... { Volaire (18) by Blacklock (2) by Whitelock. (2, 1)
{ Belinda by Blacklock (2) by Whitelock. (2, 1)

Dr. of .... { Pantaloon (17) ... { Castrel (2) by Buzzard (3) by Woodpecker. (1)
{ Idalia by Peruvian by Sir Peter. (3)
{ Banter .... { Master Henry (3) by Orville. (8)
{ Boadicea.

Polly Agnes ... { The Cure (21) ... { Physician (6) by Brutandorf (11) by Blacklock (2) by Whitelock (2) by Hambletonian. (1)
{ Morsel by Mulatto (5) by Catton. (2)

{ Miss Agnes ...... { Birdcatcher (11) by Sir Hercules (2) by Whalebone. (1)
{ Agnes .... { Clarion (6) by Catton (2) or Sultan. (1)
{ Annette ... { Priam (6) ... { Emilius. (28)
{ Dr. of Winkey. (2)
{ Dr. of Don John‡ (2) by Waverley (2) by Whalebone. 1)

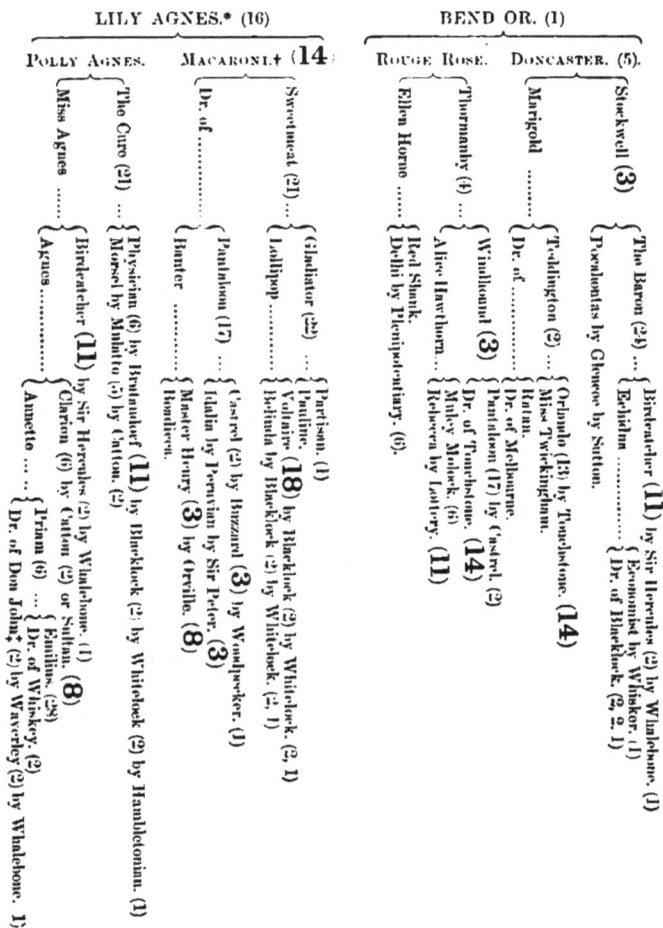

* Won Prince of Wales's Stakes and seventeen races.   † Derby, 2000 Guineas.
‡ See previous notes as to this error of " Don John " for " Don Juan," which I have thought it best not to correct in the text.—W. A.

noticeable that the resemblance does not end here, but, as in Maimie Grey, we can find none of the running figures 1, 2, **3**, or 4 in the *four top* removes. To carry the similarity still further, we find the sire, Bend Or (like Himyar), directly from a running family, and the running families (1 and **3**) strongly represented in the first, *second*, and *third* removes. The foregoing examples of Flying Childers, Domino, Gladiateur, and Ormonde, and in a lesser degree Herod and Eclipse, quite justify me in claiming for the figure key that it affords a practical and satisfactory elucidation of the causes of phenomenal excellence in racehorses. It is no news to English, American, and Australian breeders to be told that the best strains in the stud book are Eclipse, Herod, Matchem, Sir Peter, Whalebone, Sir Hercules, Blacklock, Glencoe, Touchstone, Birdcatcher, Stockwell, Isonomy, Galopin, and others of nearly equal merit. The veriest tyro finds unmistakable evidence of it at every page of the " Racing Calendar." The want has always been, for some clearly defined *reasons*, *why* these horses were so great, and such reasons founded on sound physiological principles as laid down by such great masters as Darwin, Spencer, and others in their treatises on the laws of heredity and the " survival of the fittest." So strongly has this law been working in the English stud, that, as previously mentioned, out of 2800 odd mares in the 13th edition of the Stud Book, about 1000 are descendants in female line of the four renowned mares which form the tap roots of what I have designated the running families proper, 1, 2, **3**, and 4. Many of the lines have died out to the extent of only having four or five representatives. I have not taken the trouble to go through the last vol. (XVI.), but it may be taken for granted that 1, 2, **3**, and 4, have forged still further ahead.

CHAPTER XII.

THE BREEDING OF SPRINTERS.

THERE is so great a similarity between most of the pedigrees of phenomenal horses and sprinters, that one may well be forced to the conclusion that no horse can achieve fame nowadays unless he be possessed of a great burst of speed. Provided he is equipped with this reserve force, it only requires, in most cases, good temper, constitution, and high training to enable him to stay over long courses, and make any post a winning post. A careful review of the pedigrees of the great two-year-olds, or sprinting wonders, will disclose the fact that there is either some considerable inbreeding in the dam or sire, or else there is a *close* nick of some common ancestor on both sides of pedigree. For all-round purposes I prefer the inbreeding to be in the *dam* of the youngster, because she will be more likely to throw racehorses to various sires. If the reader will turn to Domino's pedigree (page 181), he will see that his 2nd dam is intensely inbred to Glencoe ; and, as I have shown, Domino gets his great vitality from these repeated infusions of No. 1 blood admirably outcrossed by three strains of Lexington, which latter would of themselves have been powerless but for the vitality imparted to them by the inbreeding to Glencoe. Dr. Hasbrouck and Salvator are both (as shown) from inbred dams. As a contrast to these, turn to the breeding of such horses as Carbine, Barcaldine, &c. The latter's dam, Ballyroe, is fairly inbred to Birdcatcher at three and four removes ; but the intensity of the inbreeding which produced Barcaldine comes from the nick of Darling's dam on *both sides* of pedigree at two and three removes Galopin was a very brilliant two and three year old, and scarcely ever suffered defeat. He is the result of a nick of Voltaire at three removes on either side. In Australia, a remarkably speedy colt (Strathmore) won all his important two-year-old races, if I mistake not ; also the V.R.C. Derby and Leger three years. His dam Ouida was by Yattendon, whose second dam, Alice Grey, was by (imp.) Rous's Emigrant (4). Ouida second dam was young Gulnare by Gohanna, a brother to Alice Grey. Ouida's first dam was by Little John (3), a son of Problem by Theorem (1), and her third dam was also by Theorem. As this inbreeding was to the running lines 1, **3** and **4**, Ouida was possessed of great vitality, which she transmitted to her son Strathmore. "Stromboli," afterwards taken over by me to America, had the misfortune to run against this colt, and played second fiddle to him on more than one occasion. Nevertheless, Stromboli has shown a fine turn of speed on several occasions as well as staying, and won A.J.C. Derby and Sydney Cup, two miles in 3min. 31¼sec. His third dam, Lilla, was by New Chum **3**, a son of one of our good race mares, Industry by Theorem (1), and Lilla was from Eva, by Y. Marquis, a son of Little John, whose dam Problem (also by Theorem) was a full sister to Industry. It is worth noting that these two rivals, Strathmore and Stromboli, are bred on very similar lines, and they both have a strain of Yattendon as well. Though none of us are confiding enough to believe that Flying Childers "ran a mile in a minute," there is no doubt he was possessed of phenomenal speed, and we have seen elsewhere how incestuously bred his dam was. Peter (Middle Park Plate) was probably faster than any horse he was ever pitted against, and his dam was inbred to the figure 2 through Blacklock, Selim, &c., and the same applies to the dams of Ormonde, Bendigo, Australian Peer, and Lamp-lighter (Am.). Lucky Dog, by Darebin from Lou Lanier, showed a great turn of speed as a two-year-old last season. He is a full brother to Kildeer, an American record breaker, and bids fair to place some good stakes to the credit of his owner, Mr. Simeon G. Reid —

a clever enthusiast in pedigree, who is building up a valuable stud
of racehorses in Southern California.   Lou Lanier is by Lever (a son
of Lexington and Levity from Vandal's dam).   I have already
shown how inbred both Lexington and Vandal were to (imp.)
Kitty Fisher.   But, as before remarked, this inbreeding is not to
running blood, nor would it have produced good results unless
co-mingled with infusions of Glencoe (1), Whisker (1), and Blacklock (2).   In Lou Lanier we have this same happy blending,
because her second dam Re-Union was produced by crossing Union,
a son of Glencoe, with Gallopade, jun., a daughter of Glencoe,
step-brother and sister.   It is clear therefore that to get great
speed there must be close inbreeding either on dam's side alone, or
by a nick of the same blood on both sides of pedigree, as in the case
of Galopin.   Speed may also be produced by breeding from an
inbred sire like Galopin, as witness Donovan out of the by no means
remarkably inbred mare Mowerina, bred to Touchstone at three and
four removes, with three strong outcrosses of Melbourne, Pantaloon,
and Bay Middleton—so that we may reasonably attribute Donovan's
wonderful speed to his inbred sire.   Wisdom is another example of
an inbred sire throwing speedy stock (see Surefoot and Sir Hugo,
winner of 2000 Guineas and Derby respectively).   The foregoing
will suffice to show that intense inbreeding and great speed are
synonymous, nor can we hope to obtain high speed where the
conditions are otherwise.

CHAPTER XIII.

THE THEORY OF SATURATION; OR INFLUENCE OF SIRE UPON DAM.

HAVING pointed out in the foregoing chapters how successful sires and dams are bred, and explained whence comes the great potency necessary to produce phenomenal racehorses, I now propose, with some diffidence, to deal with a physiological aspect of the question, which is one of the most important factors in racehorse breeding. However much pedigree students may differ as to the causes which produce good or bad effects in the various breeding problems submitted yearly by breeders for their consideration, I believe I am correct in saying that we are quite agreed upon one point, viz., that all our theories and systems are more or less powerless in the face of the unpleasant fact that two full brothers are rarely equal in racing powers. During my long course of study, I have been so constantly met by this query from sceptics in breeding, that I was forced into a careful inquiry as to the reasons why one brother should be so immeasurably superior to his immediate successor or predecessor, bred and reared under apparently precisely similar conditions. The result of these inquiries I now lay before my readers, who may judge for themselves. In 1889 I wrote a letter to the *Melbourne Australian* embodying my views, and calling the attention of breeders to this bugbear in the path of stud masters. Both in that paper and the *Sydney Pastoralist* the subject was pretty well threshed out, and, curiously enough, the same subject was at the same time (as I found after) being ventilated at Cape Colony in a very able manner by Mr. Hutcheon, V.S. Some few years previous I had consulted an eminent physiologist in Australia as to the possible effects of repeated bearing by a mare to same sire, and whether there was any actual communication between fœtus and dam. And while disposed to take the orthodox scientific view that there was *no actual* exchange, except from dam to fœtus, he was so so shaken in his ideas by the examples I gave him, that it encouraged me to investigate it still further, and I was fortunate in having at my disposal the experience of Mr. H. C. White, of Havilah—a successful horse, cattle, and sheep breeder in New South Wales. Feeling that I had good backing, it urged me, in the interests of breeders, to write as mentioned (to the *Australasian* and *Pastoralist*) ventilating the theory I had formed on the subject. Briefly put, it means that, with each mating and bearing the dam absorbs some of the nature or actual circulation of the yet unborn foal, until she eventually becomes as it were saturated with the sire's nature or *blood*, as the case may be. I very naturally cited the authentic case of the mare bred to a zebra, her subsequent offspring by a blood stallion showing unmistakable signs of the zebra taint, nor was this lost until after a second and third crossing with a blood stallion. Of course, in *cross* breeding of this kind the traces of the first bearing to zebra would be plainly observed in subsequent progeny. Not so in *line* breeding, *i.e.*, thoroughbred to his kind. Yet it is evidently working in the latter instance, though not so visible, and rarely looked for. Many writers have attributed the zebra appearance in the blood foals to the effects of imagination, but I cannot think imagination could play so marked a part, and believe the results were brought about by the mare having absorbed from the living, breathing, young hybrid she bore some of his circulation and nature. I have seen, both in horses and cattle, so many instances where the *subsequent* progeny from same sire and dam more closely resembled the sire than the first born, that I feel convinced it could only occur through the dam's powers of absorption. What is applicable to animal nature, will also apply to human, and in the masses around us most persons have far better opportunities of studying natural laws than in stock breeding. While the controversy alluded to was going on, I received many congratulatory letters from stock breeders of more than average intelligence, whose names I would gladly give but for obvious reasons. One sent me the following case in human beings : " A light reddish haired, blue-eyed man, married to a half-caste (a cross of white man and aboriginal) woman, has three girls. The first bears unmistakable evidence of the black blood, her hair and eyes dark brown. The second might be placed amongst a lot of Anglo-Saxon girls, and, unless attention was drawn to her, she would pass as of pure white origin. The third daughter, now about seven or eight years old, has *light flaxen* hair and blue eyes, and where her skin is not exposed to sun is *remarkably* white." This was the substance of my friend's communication. I have tried in vain to satisfactorily connect this remarkable case with the imagination theory, or that propounded by J. H. Saunders, of Chicago (whose exceedingly able and interesting work on horse breeding was only recently put into my hands for perusal), who, after quoting Darwin, McGillivray, Professor James Law, and other authorities, thus sums up his own views: " How then can we avoid the conclusion that the impregnated ovum impresses its own characters on the mass of the decidua, and through this on the maternal mucous membrane, and that this in its turn impresses its characters on the membrane and embryo of the next succeeding conception." This theory is probably founded upon the assumption that there is no actual communication by veins or bloodvessels between the fœtus and the mother. Quoting from the same authority, in a treatise by Professor James Law, we find this paragraph : " McGillivray advances the theory that the elements from the blood of the fœtus, absorbed into that of the mother, contaminates her blood, and reduces her to a cross, thus rendering her for ever after incapable of producing a pure bred offspring. Not that he supposes the blood of the fœtus, as such, to circulate within the veins of the mother, but that fine particles from the blood of the offspring pass through the intervening layers of cells, and thus reach the maternal blood and reproduce themselves. But the whole theory is assumption. We know that the placenta, or after-birth, by which the fœtus is connected with the mother, serves the purpose of both stomach and lungs. From the glands in the wall of the womb a milk-like liquid is constantly secreted, which being absorbed by the fœtal vessels branching in the placenta, is carried into the blood of the young animal and serves to nourish it, just as the milk from the udder does after birth. Again, from the blood of the offspring circulating in the placenta, carbonic acid is given off and taken into the maternal blood, while oxygen supplied by the blood of the dam is taken up by the blood of the fœtus. So far these membranes fulfil the functions of stomach and lungs to the young animal. But we have no proof of living particles of blood of the fœtus entering the circulation of the mother, unless we accept as such the very phenomenon we are endeavouring to find an explanation for ; and this would only be admissible if no other or more reasonable explanation could be found." Further on he says: "The gradual extinction of the influence of the first male in successive pregnancies by other males is scarcely what would be expected, if the blood was charged with gemmules from the first capable of reproducing themselves, and especially prone to rapid increase and development in connection with the development of offspring. Again, similar elements must be introduced into the maternal blood when the vital fluid has been transfused into her veins from those of another person or beast, and the ovules then in course of development in her ovaries must be 'affected and hybridized,' if such blood is not exactly identical in composition with her own. But though transfusion of blood into the female system is not uncommon, and though that blood has been repeatedly taken from a person of a widely different race, no complaint has ever been made that the children have been thereby affected." I have quoted Professor Law at length, as the foregoing gives a clear and lucid explanation of the accepted theory on this subject, and shows how the fœtus is situated in regard to the mother. With all due deference, a non-professional view of the situation would lead one to the conclusion that if there is sufficient connection between fœtus and mother to maintain and nourish the former, it would surely be capable of *reciprocal* action. Indeed, I believe I am correct in saying that the majority of practical physiologists have accepted the absorption theory. We know what absorption does in the extraction of the elements of blood from the food while passing through the intestines, and though the channels are so minute as to almost defy detection, it would be absurd to deny their existence, because the individual eats and lives, and is strengthened and benefited by this elaborate process of digestion. Not being a professional man, it may seem presumptuous for me to air my views upon the theory of the generation and subsequent development of the yet unborn animal. Speaking for stud masters, we are more interested in the *results* than the process, but I wish to know from professional physiologists why it is that in the case cited the third daughter bears such a marked resemblance to her white father? My own view is that during the process of development of the first child, the mother received infusions of its blood by some channels still unknown to science, and thus absorbed into her system, through the medium of the unborn child, a proportion of the alien white blood of the sire. Having once established a tenure, this alien blood would naturally be strengthened in volume and invigorated by each subsequent child-bearing finally culminating in the curious phenomenon described by my friend. It is admitted by all writers on the subject that the sire undoubtedly *does* impress his influence (by means not yet ascertained) upon the dam after the first conception to him, and also that this influence (or taint) *is transmitted* by dam to her subsequent offspring by a different sire.   Granted! then why should this influence cease with the *first* conception, as many contend?

Also I would draw attention to the fact, that with the exception (so far as I know) of Mr. Hutcheon, V.S., Cape Town, South Africa, who wrote on this subject about the same time as myself (1889) none of the writers, including those previously mentioned, have attempted to give an explanation of *why* two full brothers are rarely of equal merit.   Their writings have been mostly directed to an elucidation of the *process* of development, rather than the effect upon the racing qualities of the progeny, even admitting that a thoroughbred mare, to a certain mating of her own class, produced a good racehorse, and by reason of the *effects of imagination* threw to the same embraces a piebald as her next foal, the elements brought into the combination being exactly similar, the piebald should be equally as good, or better than his predecessor; but such is not the case, nor will our scepticism allow us to believe that the mere "impress of the impregnated ovum upon the mass of the decidua," is sufficient to account for the *extreme* difference in merit which is so constantly seen between full brothers.   The words *full brothers* are used advisedly, because experience will have shown most stud masters that the combination which produces a good male is generally quite unfavourable for the production of an equally good female—Lord Lyon and his sister, Achievement, being one of the few exceptions to this rule.   To an unprejudiced mind, such evidence as that given, based upon the human case, can lead one to no other conclusion than this—that the sire influence is *accumulative.*   Admit this, and the stud master's troubles as regards the strange dissimilarity in the racing merits of full brothers is satisfactorily solved, and, consequently, more than half remedied. But one example is not sufficient to prove a case.   The following particulars were at the time (1889) sent me by a friend from a different part of the country.   He says: " I have read your letters with considerable pleasure, because I have always taken an interest in physiological subjects, and the example you give of the effects of white cross on the half-caste explains what has been for years a mystery to me in the case of a family I have lived near for twenty years. 'The father is a tall, raw-boned, light-haired, fine specimen of a man; the wife, with dark blood in her veins, small, dark, and with very small, well-shaped hands and feet. The children number eight of both sexes. The elder ones are small and dark haired like the mother, getting taller, bigger framed, and lighter haired as they come down the line to the youngest boy, as tall and heavy as his father was when he first married, and inheriting his flaxen hair and blue eyes.'"

Professor Law endeavours to make a point by the remark, "But though transfusion of blood into the female system is not uncommon, and though that blood has been repeatedly taken from a person of widely different race, no complaint has ever been made that the children have thereby been affected." It entirely depends upon what is meant by widely different races. If Russian, Chinese, Esquimaux, &c., it is quite on the cards that any transfusion from, say, a Chinese, even if it did affect the offspring of a dark-haired woman, would not be noticed because never suspected, and therefore never looked for. Then, again, the foreign blood in the woman's veins would not be likely to show strongly, if at all, in the offspring, unless she were mated with a male having a Chinese strain of blood. This point might be settled by transfusing from a liver-coloured spaniel to a small terrier (fox), and maiden fox terrier, and then breed the two terriers to one another. I tried to induce a friend in Sydney some years ago to carry out this experiment, but, though a breeder of terriers, he was either not sufficiently interested in the subject, or else did not care to chance tainting his high priced dogs. I cannot think otherwise than that the progeny would show unmistakable signs of spaniel appearance and colour.

Taking a consensus of the stud book reveals the fact that there are very few cases of full brothers being of fairly equal merit where the dam had been successively bred to same sire, and after producing a *good* racehorse to the *first* conception. Such an one is that of Whalebone and Whisker (both Derby winners), by Waxy from Penelope. In this case there was an interval of five years, the mare having meanwhile produced Web, Woful, Wilful, and Wire, all by Waxy, and all good performers. Though I may be incorrect in saying that Whisker was an inferior racehorse to Whalebone, showing that the repeated bearing to Waxy had over saturated Penelope, later on I will show why this mating withstood the evil effects of saturation so long. To use a homely illustration, the stud master's effort to produce a racehorse may be compared to the making of a plum pudding. The plums represent the Stockwell strains he is endeavouring to *nick* on both sides of tabulated pedigree, say at three or four removes. If the nick comes off the *first* time, the *exact* quantity of plums has been brought into the composition, and the result is a great racehorse, or an excellent pudding. If I am correct in supposing that saturation has taken place in the dam, she clearly contains *more Stockwell* element in her system than *before* the conception, or at any rate the Stockwell influence or nature of the male having encountered in the female (through the medium of the fœtus), its own affinities, has left the dam's system strengthened and more potent in Stockwell nature than she was before. We again breed the mare to same sire. This time she absorbs still more of the Stockwell nature, but the second result, sad to say, is far inferior to the first. In other words, there are *too many plums* in the pudding this time ; it is a failure, and will be worse with each successive mating.

We have a notable case in Australia of the first foal (Richmond) of Maribyrnong and The Fawn (given at page 118) proving a very high-class racehorse. The second foal by same sire - Richmond Belle, I think—was never trained. The third foal, Bosworth (a Leger winner), to same mating, though a good racehorse, was not within

12lb. or a stone of his elder brother, and so on down the line they continued to deteriorate. Buyers came up smiling every year, and gave from a thousand to fifteen hundred guineas for the youngsters, but few paid for the oats they consumed in training. The English stud books teem with such cases, notably West Australian, a great horse, and his succeeding brothers and sisters. Marley Hill, Aurifex, Victoria, and Go-ahead, all vastly inferior as racehorses. If we turn to Isonomy's dam, Isola Bella, we find her throwing to Sterling a high-class animal in Isonomy, and subsequently and successively to same sire The Pyx, Fernandez, Isola Madre, Privilege, &c.— of very unequal merit to the first named. But the theory of saturation would amount to nothing if it did not in some cases also work in the *opposite* direction, and improve the chances of the *later* progeny. This was the case in Australia with the dams of Carbine, Commotion, Le Grand, and Grand Flaneur, all uncommonly good animals, and in each case third and fourth foals to same mating—clearly showing that in the first conception the nick was not close enough, but became stronger with successive matings. As if to prove my contention still further, in each case the apex of success having been at last reached, the process of deterioration set in, and the *immediate* followers to these great horses were far *inferior* as racehorses. Nor does it require very deep research to find the solution of the apparent riddle, if the theory is admitted to be feasible. For instance, in the case of Penelope, she was bred right away from stout Eclipse to The Godolphin and Byerly Turk. Her sire, Trumpator, was a male descendant of The Godolphin, and his dam Brunette was from Dove by Matchless, son of The God. B. Penelope's dam, Prunella, was by Highflyer, a son of Herod, from a mare by Blank, son of God. B. from sister to Southby Regulus, son of God. B. Penelope's second dam was by Snap from Julia, by Blank—God. B. This combination gives four very close strains of Godolphin Barb, grafted on to the effeminate No. 1 line. Any tyro would decide that Penelope required mating with a *close* descendant

of the *stout* Eclipse, and in a fortunate moment Waxy was selected
as her mate.   The very first foal, Whalebone, only fifteen hands and
half an inch, was a brilliant racehorse.   As a three-year-old he won
the rich Newmarket Stakes and Derby, and several matches,
and performed well up to six years old.   He was altogether a
higher class racehorse than any of his brothers or sisters except
Whisker, though it may easily be imagined that the succeeding
ones from such a mating, and such a splendid running line
as No. 1, would hold their own and more, against the racehorses
of the day not so fortunate in their lineage.   In Isola Bella's
case the conditions were reversed.   I have pointed out how
very stoutly she was bred, rather more so than her mate Sterling,
notwithstanding that he was the product of a *double* cross of
Eclipse's own family (No. 12).   Happily his first mating with
Isola Bella produced Isonomy, therefore it would not be at all
probable under the conditions of saturation that the succeeding
progeny by same sire could be so good as the first.   In Penelope's
case there was the want of stoutness to correct.   In Isola Bella the
stoutness would be *intensified* by each bearing, and hence throw the
proper natural conditions which must exist out of gear.   A case
very much in line with that of Penelope is the Alexander mare, dam
of that wonderful consecutive quartet Castrel, Selim, Bronze (Oaks),
and Rubens, all by Buzzard.   They are descended in female line
from Burton's Barb mare of the No. 2 line.   They play such an
important part in pedigrees that I append a tabulation.

   "The Druid" has described Woodpecker as a coarse, gross, lop-
eared horse, who only made a good hit with Buzzard's dam, Acto (3),
and this was as it should be, seeing that he had no sire blood in his
veins.   It may be presumed that Buzzard was, like the majority of
Woodpecker's stock, coarse and lusty, and therefore well suited to a
weed like the Alexander mare, who went a-begging for £25, and was
finally given away by the Duke of Queensberry to his surgeon.   We
hear nothing as to the merits of her first foal by Buzzard, Piccadilly,

foaled in 1800, but she turned over a new leaf with the New Year.
and threw the magnificent chestnut, Castrel, sixteen hands high, and
with "great quality," and, but for his roaring, there were few better
on the turf, says "The Druid." Her next foal, Selim, was also considerably on the leg, and the same writer adds : "He was *full of*

CASTREL, SELIM, and RUBENS.

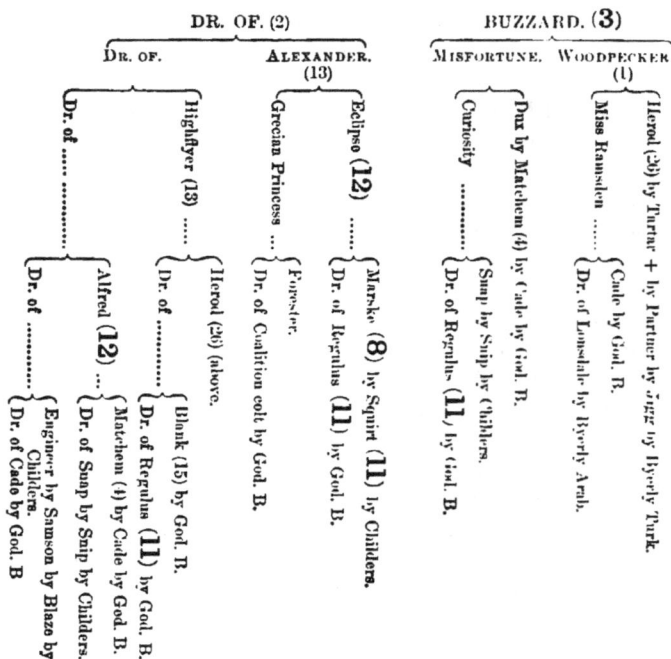

DR. OF. (2)		BUZZARD. (3)	
Dr. of.	Alexander. (13)	Misfortune.	Woodpecker (1)

Dr. of ....
{ Engineer by Samson by Blaze by Childers.
{ Dr. of Cade by God. B

Alfred (12) ...
{ Matchem (4) by Cade by God. B.
{ Dr. of Snap by Snip by Childers.

Highflyer (13) ......
{ Herod (28) (above.
Dr. of ....
{ Blank (15) by God. B.
{ Dr. of Regulus (11) by God. B.

Grecian Princess ...
{ Forester.
{ Dr. of Coalition colt by God. B.

Eclipse (12) ......
{ Marske (8) by Squirt (11) by Childers.
{ Dr. of Regulus (11) by God. B.

Curiosity ....
{ Snap by Snip by Childers.
{ Dr. of Regulus (11) by God. B.

Dux by Matchem (4) by Cade by God. B.

Miss Ramsden ....
{ Cade by God. B.
{ Dr. of Lonsdale by Byerly Arab.

Herod (28) by Tartar + by Partner by Jigg by Byerly Turk.

quality, and so majestic that no one would have suspected him to be
the workman he was at all distances." His picture and performances
are given in that excellent work, "Portraits of Celebrated Racehorses." The apex of success in this meeting would appear to have

been reached with this third effort, Selim, as neither Bronze (Oaks
nor Rubens were so high class, though the latter was phenomenally
fast over short courses. Viewed from any light, however, the
pedigree is so good in the combination of the superior running lines
of (1), (2) and **3**). as well as the physical conditions, that the worst
of the four may well have been better than the great majority of the
horses of the day, as in the case of Whalebone and his brothers and
sisters. In the work I have alluded to the portraits of the three
brothers are given, and it is worthy of note that, whereas Castrel and
Selim are described as "full of quality," and light-fleshed horses.
Rubens, the *sixth* consecutive bearing to the coarse, fleshy Buzzard,
was modelled exactly on similar lines. He is described as "a heavy-
topped, fleshy horse, standing sixteen hands high, and with a flash
of speed like lightning." The results in this case are hardly to be
accounted for, except on the presumption that the stoutly-bred but
weedy, delicate mother continued with each foal-bearing to imbibe
more of the coarse, fleshy, healthy, but non-staying nature of
Buzzard. In fact, it is almost a parallel case with the one cited in
the previous chapter— the case of the delicate wife and the robust,
healthy husband. I am aware that scores of cases might be brought
forward to show, apparently, contrary results, but they could in no
wise alter the facts which are recorded in the preceding pages, and it
must always be borne in mind that the failure of health of either
parent will arrest the working of the natural law such as I am
endeavouring to elucidate by the examples given. In the human
race, for instance, where a family consists of four or five consecutive
daughters, and then a son, inquiry will generally elicit the fact that,
the year previous to the birth of the latter, the husband had some
severe illness or mental overwork, resulting in a break in the natural
law previously working harmoniously.

If I were breeding racehorses, and hit off a highly successful
nick the first time, I should *at once outcross* the dam to some
distinctly opposite character of blood, but containing one of the best

strains of the previous sire. In the case of Isola Bella, she should have been once or twice mated to such a horse as Petrarch so soon as Isonomy had developed his powers and declared his goodness. Petrarch was not strong in sire strains, and his breeding was decidedly effeminate, so that he would almost to a certainty have made a great hit with this mare, to the benefit of all concerned. Two high-class racehorses within the last ten years or so in Australia were full brothers—Navigator and Trident, by Robinson Crusoe, from Cocoanut (imp.) by Nutbourne. When Navigator was a yearling, he was a very small fellow, and it is presumed his breeder, Mr. De Mestre, was induced to change the venue to a big stallion on the farm called Piscator, Cocoanut having in the meanwhile thrown a filly foal, sister to Navigator. Small though he was, Navigator was a brilliant two and three year old, so very naturally back went the mare to Robinson Crusoe, with the splendid result of producing Trident, a *bigger* and *better* horse than his full brother. The second foal by Robinson Crusoe, the filly (Copra), was an inferior race mare, but afterwards proved a right good dam, her son Camoola winning the A.J.C. and V.R.C. Derbies and A.J.C. Leger, showing that saturation had probably been at work, but was checked by the accidental putting of Cocoanut to Piscator. The Piscator mating produced a handsome, well-grown horse (Coir) of only second class. Cocoanut herself was a big, stary, delicate-looking mare, and I cannot help thinking that she was constitutionally strengthened and invigorated by bearing to big, lusty, healthy-looking Piscator, and imparted some of this imbibed vigour to the succeeding foal, Trident, a much finer individual than his full brother, Navigator. My friend, Mr. H. C. White, to whom I have more than once referred, is the owner of a very high quality *delicate*-looking mare called Avaline, by (imp.) Yelverton (son of Gemma de Vergy and Deceptive by Venison from a Defence mare—all quality strains). Mr. White was not satisfied with the stock she threw by a blood horse, so decided to breed hackneys from her, and crossed her with an English hackney

stallion, Flying Shales (imp.). Repenting afterwards, he bred her
to (imp.) Grandmaster, and got a wonderful sprinter under big
weights from the latter union, the renowned "Bungebah," a big,
thick-fleshed chestnut, with straight hind legs, coarse hair, and tufts
at his fetlocks, and altogether showing unmistakable signs of having
hackney blood in his veins. His breeder and I have often exchanged
ideas on this matter, and my convictions about saturation were very
much strengthened by this and other instances given me by Mr.
White, who has been largely engaged all his life in breeding cattle,
sheep, and horses, and has had exceptional opportunities of observing
these curious effects of continued breeding to one sire. He believes
with me that a delicate-constituted thoroughbred mare may be
actually benefited by being bred to a healthy hackney stallion. Who
can say with certainty that the original English mares at the *roots*
of the *sire* families are quite free from the taint of a cross of
Cleveland blood bays, with their magnificent shoulders, round
barrels, and lengthy quarters. The good shoulders of our modern
high-class racehorses certainly do not come from the Arabs and
Barbs. They are undoubtedly the heritage of the early English
breed, whatever they were, and some writers suppose them to have
been the *destrier quar*, strong enough to carry a knight in full armour,
and nothing short of a Flemish or a Cleveland bay could have been
equal to this feat. The government of Australia in the early days
of Colonial occupation bred some high-class troop horses and elegant
gentlemen's hackneys from an Arab sire Satellite and half-bred
Cleveland bay and blood mares. I have been told by an old
colonist and good judge that many of these Government police
horses were capable of winning steeplechases in those days, and were
high couraged, enduring roadsters.

I must not be understood as advocating the crossing of our blood
stock, for racing purposes, with Clevelands or hackney *sires*. I
should be the first to consider this a retrogressive policy, and not to
be considered even, unless under the exceptional circumstances

alluded to in Bungebah's case ; and even then I should for preference select a lusty, healthy thoroughbred by long odds. The case was cited merely for the purpose of showing that the taint of the hackney stallion was clearly visible in the subsequent blood cross—and undoubtedly proved an important factor in deciding Bungebah's non-staying powers. I have in the course of the last seven or eight years seen such unmistakable proofs both in humans and animals of the effects of saturation, that I cannot do otherwise than hope it will soon be considered an established fact in physiology. One of my strongest opponents in the controversy mentioned at the beginning of this chapter paid me the compliment three years afterwards of saying that he " was quite a convert to the theory," as he never went through a thoroughbred stud without seeing evidences of it at every turn. It is very noticeable in cattle also. At the Royal Agricultural Show in Sydney, a few years ago, a well-known breeder took me over to the yards to see three pens of Shorthorn heifers, a non-competitive exhibit of four weanlings, four year-lings, and four two-year-olds, all heifers and got by the same bull. These heifers were from a small select stud herd of cows, and a fresh strain of blood had been introduced about four or five years previous in the person of a very light roan bull *inbred* to some *white* stock. The younger progeny showed such decided evidence of the effects of saturation that I had no difficulty in deciding that the bull was much lighter in colour than the cows from the fact that the two-year-olds were darkish roans, the yearlings considerably lighter in colour, and the weanlings nearly white or very pale roan. When I mentioned the result of my deductions, the breeder confirmed it by saying that the only objection he had to the bull was his tendency to throw light-coloured progeny, inclining to white, also that all the mothers of these heifers had been bearing calves to the bull for at least three years in succession. If it can be clearly demonstrated that each conception leaves, during its development, an addition to the previous or first influence, then indeed are the possibilities immense of working this important factor in the direction of raising high-class animals of all kinds.   The stud master may with truth say, " If this theory is correct, a mare may not be all she is represented to be ! "   In other words, " the Hermit mare I am about to purchase to breed to St. Simon contains, according to your theory, a strong admixture of the blood of Sterling, because she has been bred four times consecutively to the latter sire."   This is precisely what would be the result of such continuous inbreeding, if I am correct in my suppositions, and I am convinced that breeders cannot be too careful, when selecting mares, to ascertain what sires they have been bred to previously.   For my own part, if I had a *first-class sire*, I would prefer to buy maidens, for the simple reason that there is no influence as yet in force.   Of course, to carry the argument to its logical conclusion, the very maiden filly I am buying for her Petrarch blood may be in effect partly Galopin, seeing that the latter horse was bred to her mother for five or six successive years before crossing her to Petrarch. Granted that it is so, I minimise the evil considerably by selecting only maiden mates for my stallion.   The saturation theory accounts in the only satisfactory way for the many hundreds and thousands of (racehorse) breeding failures, which have been ushered into the world under the most flattering conditions as regards high lineage and performances of both sire and dam, the close following up of known successful nicks, climate and health conditions, and subsequent rearing, and training, &c.   But perhaps the most ludicrous (if it were only more harmless) feature in connection with breeding, is the confident style in which a pure amateur will sail into this intricate and really scientific business of raising racehorses.   If a patient went to the same man complaining of severe illness, and asked for advice, he would naturally enough say, " Go to a physician, I am not a professional man, nor do I understand the first principles of medicine."   Yet he undertakes with confidence an occupation which demands a deep knowledge of natural laws, a close intimacy with the stud books, and a cultivated as well as a natural eye for symmetry and character reading in the equine race. However, out of evil good occasionally results, and perhaps, if it were not for the stupid blunders of amateurs in putting daughters to their sires and brothers to sisters and half-sisters, clearly in the hope of producing something extraordinary, we should not have had the materials at hand to breed such phenomenal racehorses as Flying Childers and Gladiateur.

I cannot close this subject of saturation without giving still further examples of the working of natural laws in this direction as evidenced by the practice of the late Lord Falmouth, who rarely ever mated his mares more than twice consecutively to same sire, showing without doubt that he considered the practice of continuity, a bar to the brilliant success he attained as a breeder of racehorses. If we turn to page 360, vol. xiii. of English General Stud Book and take the illustrious Queen Bertha as an example, it will be seen that from 1866 to 1877—ten years—she was mated with five different sires, producing in the following order

QUEEN BERTHA.

Bred by Lord Falmouth in 1860, got by Kingston ; her dam Flax by Surplice (by Touchstone) out of Odessa by Sultan, &c.

1867.—B. f. Gertrude by Saunterer.
1869.—B. c. Queen's Messenger by Trumpeter.
1870.—Ch. c. Paladin by Fitz Roland.
1871.—B. f. Blanchefleur by Saunterer.
1872.—B. f. Spinaway by Macaroni.
1873.—B. f. Fame by Trumpeter.
1874.—Ch. c. Queen's Herald by Trumpeter.
1876. B. f. Wheel of Fortune by Adventurer.
(In 1868 had dead foal, and was barren in 1875.)

I am strongly of opinion that, if the mating to Saunterer had been continued for a couple of seasons after Gertrude was foaled, the result would have been still more successful seeing that this sire brought into the connection a strain of Birdcatcher and Velocipede. Whereas Trumpeter and Fitz Roland were both from the same line (No. 1) as Queen Bertha, and, besides, were very inbred to flashy Castrel and Selim through Orlando—rather unsuitable blood for a mare bred as she was. The consequence was that, when again submitted to the embraces of Saunterer, she had been weakened by saturation with effeminate strains of the two intermediate stallions, and the issue, Blanchefleur, was a far inferior race mare to her full (?) sister Gertrude. In an opposite direction was Macaroni benefited by following Saunterer's Birdcatcher and Blacklock influence, two strains of blood that he always was partial to, as witness Ormonde's dam. If the reader will turn to page 143, where I have treated of Adventurer's partiality for pure blood, *i.e.*, 1, 2, and 4, he will the more easily understand why this sire scored a splendid success like Wheel of Fortune from a mare saturated as Queen Bertha was by two successive coverings of a No. 1 horse like Trumpeter, also full of the brothers Castrel and Selim (2).

In Australia, at the stud of Mr. Frank Reynolds, of Tocal, near Sydney, was another case in point, Melody by The Barb from Mermaid by (imp.) Fisherman.

MELODY.

1879.—Ch. c. Trumpet Major by Goldsborough.
1880.—Ch. f. Music by Goldsborough.
1881.—Ch. c. The Broker by Goldsborough.
1882.—Ch. f. Melodious by Goldsborough.
1883.—Ch. c. Minstrel Boy by The Drummer (imp.).
1884.—B. f. Leidertafel by The Drummer (imp.).
1885.—Melos (a first-class racehorse) by Goldsborough.

It is interesting to watch the developments in this example. The first of the Goldsboroughs to show any good form was The Broker, amongst his best being the Adelaide St. Leger; but he was never more than a second or third class horse when compared with his full brother Melos (A.J.C. Derby and Leger), who was unfortunate in meeting Carbine and Abercorn at their very best, yet despite this he ran some desperate races against them, and once defeated both in a champion race (three miles) at Flemington, Victoria.

How is this superior excellence to be reasonably accounted for except by the theory of saturation? Previous to the advent of Melos upon the scene, his dam was bred for two successive years to The Drummer (son of Rataplan), a No. 1 horse, and choke full of the strains that Goldsborough has scored most of his successes from, as witness his son, Arsenal (winner of Melbourne Cup), from a Blinkhoolie Rataplan mare. I also give below the case of Cocoanut before alluded to.

Cocoanut was by Nutbourne from Miss Vivian, by Rattle out of Subterfuge, by Sir Hercules. Robinson Crusoe was by Angler from Chrysolite, by Stockwell from Juliet, by Touchstone.

COCOANUT.

1874.—B. c. James I. by King o' Scots.
1875.—Br. f. Queen o' Scots by King o' Scots.
1876.—B. c. (dead) by King o' Scots.
1877.—Br. f. The Shell by the Marquis or Angler.
1878.—Br. f. Kernal by Angler.
1879.—Br. c. **Navigator** (D. and L.) by Robinson Crusoe (1) son of Angler)
1880.—Ch. f. Copra by Robinson Crusoe 1 son of Angler).
1881.—Br. c. Coir by Piscator (Angler or The Marquis).
1882.—Ch. c. **Trident** (D. and L.) by Robinson Crusoe.

The change from Robinson Crusoe to Piscator for a season resulted in producing Trident, a better individual and racehorse than Navigator. Both Navigator and Trident were classic winners and high-class horses. Copra was delicate in constitution and far inferior race mare to her brothers, nor was Coir a success. There are two or three well-known cases in America of dams throwing a succession of racehorses to same sire, of course varying in degrees of excellence. I find that, wherever this excellence has been *continuous* to same sire, as in Penelope and the Alexander mare (dam of Castrel, &c.), and the other examples I am about to give, the breeding (and conformation) of sire and dam *always* shows a *marked contrast*. If the theory of saturation is admitted, this peculiarity explains why the absorption is beneficial in some cases and the reverse in others. I have shown elsewhere how Penelope, by her close inbreeding to the God. Barb (and Herod), was able to absorb repeated infusions of

Eclipse, through Waxy, without any such baneful effects as occurred in the case of Isola Bella. This is only another phase of the working of that natural law which demands that opposites shall be mated if continued success is expected. It is easy to comprehend that sire and dam, bred on *very similar* lines, may produce a good animal to, say, a first mating, but it follows just as naturally that the *balance* which existed through those very conditions of similarity is more easily disturbed than when *contrasts* are mated. The first may be compared with a well-adjusted pair of scales—*i.e.*, the stout and soft strains are fairly distributed through the pedigrees of both. We will suppose also that Isonomy occurs on both sides of pedigree, and represents the stoutness. If after the first foal the dam has absorbed more Isonomy blood than she originally possessed, she will *outweigh* the sire in the potency of Eclipse, and the balance will not only be disturbed, but such disturbance will be accentuated with each successive mating, as in the case of Richmond's dam (page 118.) Now, in a case of mating *opposites* like Penelope and Waxy, the mare, being very inbred and potent, was able to absorb repeated infusions with impunity. The following American case is in line with that of Penelope as regards contrast between sire and dam. Perhaps the most remarkable mare in the States is Marion, a veritable mine of wealth in successful sons and daughters. She has produced the following in the order given, all racehorses, and in three instances—viz., Emperor of Norfolk, Czar, and El Rio Rey—very high-class ones :

MARION.

1878.—Duke of Norfolk by Norfolk (a good racehorse).
1879.—Duchess of Norfolk by Norfolk (also a very good mare).
1881.—Prince of Norfolk by Norfolk (was a fairly good horse).
1883.—King of Norfolk by Norfolk (was a fairly good horse).
1884.—Vera by Norfolk (was only fairly good).
1885.—Emperor of Norfolk (D.) by Norfolk (a first-class, and won a Derby).
1886.—Czar (D.) by Norfolk (never beaten; won Californian Derby, 2min. 36sec.).
1887.—El Rio Rey by Norfolk (unbeaten; said to be the best of lot ; burst hoof, and only ran as two-year-old).
1888.—Rey del Reyes by Norfolk (only second class).
1889.—Yo Tambien by Joe Hooker (a first class mare).

Six out of the above list were good racehorses. The apex seems to have been reached with the Emperor of Norfolk (winner of American Derby and other races). The two succeeding colts, Czar

EMPEROR OF NORFOLK.

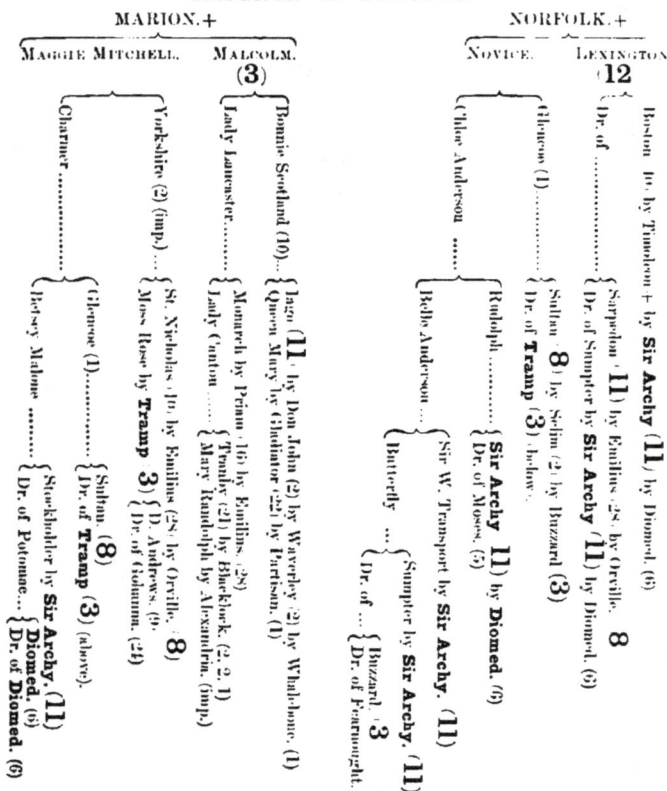

MARION.+   NORFOLK.+

MAGGIE MITCHELL.   MALCOLM. **(3)**   NOVICE.   LEXINGTON **12**

NORFOLK side:

- Boston (10) by Timoleon + by **Sir Archy (11)** by Diomed. (6)
- Dr. of ...... { Sarpedon (11) by Emilius (28) by Orville. **8**
  Dr. of Sumpter by **Sir Archy (11)** by Diomed. (6)
- Glencoe (1) ...... { Sultan 8) by Selim (2) by Buzzard (3)
  Dr. of **Tramp (3)** below.
- Chloe Anderson ......
- Randolph .... { **Sir Archy 11)** by Diomed. (6)
  Dr. of Moses. (5)
- Belle Anderson ... { Sir W. Transport by **Sir Archy. (11)**
- Butterfly ... { Sumpter by **Sir Archy. (11)**
  Dr. of ... { Buzzard. **3**
  Dr. of Fearnought.

MARION side:

- Bonnie Scotland (10)... { Iago (11) by Don John (2) by Waverley (2) by Whalebone. (1)
  Queen Mary by Gladiator (2) by Partisan. (1)
- Lady Lancaster......... { Monarch by Priam (16) by Emilius. (28)
  Lady Canton ...... { Tranby (2) by Blacklock. (2, 2, 1)
  Mary Randolph by Alexander. (imp)
- Yorkshire (2) (imp.) ... { St. Nicholas (10) by Emilius (28) by Orville. 8)
  Moss Rose by **Tramp 3)** { D. Andrews. (9
  Dr. of Giohanna. (24)
- Glencoe (1)............. { Sultan (8)
  Dr. of **Tramp (3)** (above).
- Betsey Malone .... { Stockholder by **Sir Archy. (11)**
  Diomed. (6)
  Dr. of Potomac... { Dr. of **Diomed. (6)**
- Chariner ......

and El Rio Rey, were remarkably speedy, but did not meet the same class as the Emperor. Rey del Reyes was quite second class.

Marion was very much stouter bred than Norfolk. Most of her
main lines strained to Eclipse, and she was inbred at bottom of
pedigree to Tramp, one of the stoutest bred horses of his day.
Norfolk, on the other hand, is bred quite to Herod. His second and
third dams were incestuously inbred to Sir Archy, with a strong
inbreeding to same horse through Lexington ; so that he was bred
like most of the great racehorses ; nor was he ever beaten. This
Sir Archy inbreeding was, in more than one sense, an advantage, as
it strengthened the sire as well as the Herod influence ; and, as we
have seen all through the piece how that male line has only sur-
vived by mating with mares inbred strongly to Eclipse, nothing
could have been more fortunate than the mating of Norfolk and
Marion. This wide *contrast* in strains also permitted the union to
be repeated very *often* without breaking the sequence of success.
The pedigree is a real object lesson, inasmuch as it combines *several*
phases of breeding which I have been endeavouring to make plain
It fits the phenomenal clause, as there is an incestuous breeding at
bottom of sires' pedigree, with a *return to same* blood, Sir Archy **(11)**
and Diomed (incest again) at bottom of dam. Also there is hardly
enough sire blood in three top removes, and it was right that the
inbreeding below should be to Tramp **(3)** and Sir Archy **(11)**. The
back pedigree of Marion runs out obscurely, but Mr. Joseph Carne
Simpson, of San Francisco, who bred the mare, assured me that she
traces to an imported mare, and on this point I feel sure that he is
right, because there is no one more reliable, intelligent, or enthusiastic
on breeding in America than this gentleman.

Idalia, imported to New Zealand, threw several high-class racehorses to successive covers of Traducer (imp.). The first son,
Betrayer (Derby), was a small, but good racehorse. Sir Modred, the
next foal, was one of the handsomest horses that ever looked through a
bridle, and a splendid racehorse. He won a Derby (New Zealand)
and Sydney Metropolitan in the hollowest fashion—simply galloped
over his opponents. Another son, Cheviot, won a New Zealand

SIR MODRED.

IDALIA. (17)   TRADUCER. (20)

DULCIBELLA.   CAMBUSCAN. (19)   ARETHUSA.   THE LIBEL. (16)

Priestess ......

Voltigeur (2)

Newminster (8)

The Arrow ......

Pantaloon (17) ...... {Castrel (2) by Buzzard. (3) / **Idalia** by Peruvian (27) by **Sir Peter.** (3) by Highflyer. (13)

Pasquinade ...... {Camel (24) ...... {Whalebone. (1) / Dr. of ...... {Selim. (2) / Dr. of **Sir Peter.** (3)

Banter by Master Henry. (3)

Elis (13) ...... {Olympia by Sir Oliver (13) by **Sir Peter.** (3)

Langar (7) ...... {Selim (2) by Buzzard. (3) / Dr. of Walton (7) by **Sir Peter.** (3)

Languid ...... {Coin (8) ...... {Pantowiz (8) ... {Sir Paul (8) by **Sir Peter.** (3) / Dr. of Highflyer. (13) / Dr. of Trumpator. (3)

Lydia by Paulton by **Sir Peter.** (3)

Touchstone (14) {Camel ...... {Whalebone. (1) / Dr. of ...... {Selim. (2) / Dr. of **Sir Peter.** (3)

Banter by Master Henry. (3)

Beeswing ...... {Dr. Syntax. (57) / Dr. of Ardrossan. (2)

Slane (25) ...... {Royal Oak. (5) / Dr. of Orville. (8)

Southdown by Defence (5) by Whalebone. (1)

Voltaire (12) ... {Blacklock (2) by Whitelock. (2) / Dr. of Phantom (6), W. by **Sir Peter.** (3)

Martha Lynn ...... {Mulatto (5) by Catton. (2) / Dr. of Orville. (8)

The Doctor (1) .. {Dr. Syntax. (57) / Dr. of Lottery (11) by Tramp. (3)

The Biddy ...

Beau (1) by Humphrey Clinker (8) {Comus ... {Sorcerer. / Dr. of **Sir Peter.** (3) / Dr. of Clinker (3) by **Sir Peter.** (3)

Idalia ...... {Peruvian (27) by **Sir Peter.** (3) / Meteor by Eclipse. (12) / Dr. of Highflyer. (13)

Meteora ...

N.B.—Humphrey Clinker (above) was produced by the mating of cousins grandson and granddaughter of Sir Peter. (3)

Derby, and sired, in America, Rey el Santa Anita, the Derby winner
of 1894. The other two brothers, Idalium and July, were both
winners. Idalia's third dam, The Biddy, was very inbred to Sir Peter
(and his sire, Highflyer), and Traducer likewise; consequently Sir
Modred was bred after the fashion of other phenomenal racehorses.

Traducer (for his time) probably combined more strains of Sir
Peter and Herod than any sire that ever left the shores of England.
He goes direct to Herod in ten top main lines and six of them
through Sir Peter. His mate, Idalia (imp.), on the contrary, is
bred to Eclipse in nearly all her top lines, with Sir Peter underneath
these good mares The Biddy and Idalia (the dam of Pantaloon),
whose name consequently shows at the top and bottom of this
pedigree of Sir Modred. The Biddy was the second dam of Regalia,
the Oaks winner. It would take too much space to give one-tenth
of the instances in the stud books of England, America, and
Australia, bearing upon this important feature of breeding. Stud
masters and pedigree students will find, after prosecuting their
studies in this direction, that I am mainly correct in asserting
that this *sustained excellence* of a sequence of three or more brothers
or sisters by same sire is only found where the mating of opposites
takes place. In nearly every case where the pedigrees of sire and
dam are fairly even as regards strength of Eclipse and Herod or
Matchem—only one, or at the most *two*, high-class racehorses may be
produced from same sire or dam without a change of stallion. Briefly
summarised, it would appear that the unborn foal leaves some of the
sire influence, probably through blood circulation, in the constitution
of the mother, also that such influence increases with each successive
bearing to same sire, until she becomes saturated, sooner or later.
That where there is a very wide divergence in the nature of the
strains comprised in the pedigree of sire and dam—in other words,
where *opposites* are mated—the mating may be continued for a much
longer period without bad results, even though the first mating has
produced a high-class racehorse.

In other cases, for instance, where the pedigree of sire and dam is evenly balanced, and the stud master has mated them for the express purpose of nicking the strongest and most potent strain in either pedigree, such as Stockwell or Blacklock, and it produces a first class racehorse the first attempt, he should at once change to a stallion whose strain of blood would be considered the best outcross for Stockwell and Blacklock. After one or two matings with such outcross, the original sire should be again used. Wherever such a course has been pursued, either by accident or design, the result has generally been beneficial; whereas, repeated matings without such outcross mostly result in failures, the exception being as given above; or where it is found that the first attempt of a mating like that just described produces a good-looking individual, but not a high-class racehorse, then the same stallion should be used until the result sought for is obtained, as in the examples of Carbine, Commotion, Stromboli (third foal, and undoubtedly the best), Le Grand, &c., all third and fourth and best foals of their respective dams.

CHAPTER XIV.

INBRED DAMS AND OUTBRED SIRES.

A CAREFUL comparison of the pedigree tables of great sires of the
world cannot fail to reveal that the majority are not *inbred* as we use
the term. Count Lehndorff, in " Horse Breeding Recollections,"
has furnished a very useful table of most of the great English sires,
which shows that the majority of high-class stallions range from
four to six removes before any common ancestor is found on either
side of table; but these facts must strike any close observer of
pedigree, and were noted many years ago by Mr. Reynolds and
myself. For those who have not seen the work in question I give a
few examples, taking The Miner as a better known case than most
of close breeding to show how I compute the degrees of relationship.

THE MINER.

MANGANESE (4) (First remove).		RATAPLAN (3) (First remove).
		THE BARON (2) (Second remove).
MOONBEAM Second remove).	BIRDCATCHER (11) (Second remove).	BIRDCATCHER (11) (Third remove).

Here we have Birdcatcher at two and three removes. The
Miner was just as pronounced a failure at the stud as his sisters
Mandragora and Mineral were great successes. Orest and Knight of
St. George come under the same degree of inbreeding. Wisdom
(sire of Surefoot and Sir Hugo) is even more closely bred, being
by Blinkhoolie (son of Rataplan) from Aline by Stockwell, brother
to Rataplan, but these two strains appear to stand closer inbreeding
to one another than any modern ones. Some of those with
inbreeding at one degree further away, or three removes, such as

Galopin (inbred to Voltaire at three removes), Partisan (inbred to Highflyer at three), Petrarch (Touchstone at three), and The Baron (Whalebone and Whisker at three), are about the best in a short list. Count Lehndorff has included Priam, but without justification, as he is inbred to Whiskey at two and four removes, and experience leads me to the conclusion that this is not so detrimental to racing excellence as three removes.

In the list of stallions inbred at three and four removes are Vedette (Blacklock, three and four), Orlando (to Castrel and Selim), Isonomy (Birdcatcher, three and four) Weatherbit (to Orville, once at three and twice at four removes), Lexington (Sir Archy, three and four), King Tom (to Whisker and Web at three and four), The Flying Dutchman (to Selim at three and four), Emilius (to Highflyer at three and four), Tramp (to Eclipse at three and four), Windhound (to Peruvian, three and four), and many others, including Blacklock (Highflyer, three and four).

Outside of this come Sultan (Highflyer and Eclipse at four), Pantaloon (Highflyer and Eclipse at four), Lanercost (Gohanna at four), Wild Dayrell (Selim at four), Flatcatcher (Waxy at four), Cambuscan (Whalebone at four), The Palmer (Priam at four). Sir Hercules (Eclipse at four (twice) and at five once), Touchstone Eclipse four and five), Harkaway (Pot-8-os at four and five), Voltigeur (Hambletonian four and five), Saunterer (Waxy four and five), Plenipotentiary (Highflyer at four (once), and four times at the fifth remove). Here is a case in which this stallion (Plenipotentiary) was actually more inbred to Highflyer than Emilius, with two strains of Highflyer at three and four. Venison was also inbred to Highflyer at four removes. Sterling Whalebone at four and five), Kingston (Sir Peter at four and five), Stockwell (inbred to Whalebone, Whisker, and Web at four removes), Macaroni (to Castrel and Selim at three and five). Blair Athol (to Whalebone twice and Whisker once at five removes). St. Albans (to Castrel and Selim at four once and five twice, also

Whalebone at five removes), Favonius (to Wire at the fourth,
Whisker (thrice), and Whalebone at five), Hermit (to Sultan at four
and five removes, and Whalebone at four and six), Lord Clifden
(bred to Orville at five and six), Yattendon (Partisan at four),
Chester (Whisker and Whalebone four times at five, and twice at
six ; also Orville at five and six, and Sultan at five), Musket (Touchstone at four), Carbine (Touchstone at three and five), Spendthrift
(Emilius four and five), Leamington (Sir Peter at five), Sir Modred
(Idalia at four and five), St. Simon (Blacklock twice at five, once at
six), Iroquois (Whalebone and Whisker at four and five removes),
Orme (Pocahontas at four and five), Ormonde (Birdcatcher at four
and five), Common (Touchstone four and five), Springfield (Camel at
five), Peter (Belshazzar at four and five).

The foregoing examples tend to show that the great sires are as
a rule either only moderately inbred or else outbred. At the same
time it must be conceded that, amongst the closely bred ones, *i.e.*,
in the relationship of cousins, there are a few really high-class
animals, such as Galopin, Wisdom, Partisan, Petrarch ; nor must
we forget to make allowance for the fact that modern breeders as
a rule have been averse to close breeding, and there would in
consequence be fewer colts to choose from. Until proved to the
contrary, however, it may be taken for granted that the outbred
ones are the best sires. The tendency of inbred sires is to get
sprinting stock rather than stayers, and for this reason they will
probably become more fashionable in these degenerate days of
short races. While outbred sires take the palm in point of stud
value, the opposite would appear to rule as regards dams. The
pages of the stud book teem with examples to prove this, and the
many cases I have given in the course of this treatise will help to
confirm it. Is there any valid reason why this should be so? In
seeking for the solution of any apparent departure from the general
workings of nature, we must study those natural laws bearing upon
the subject, and trace their results where animals are left to natural

selection. Most, if not all, gregarious animals breed incestuously, and it therefore follows that the females of the herd must become more inbred than the males. Take the case of a wild stallion with a harem of females, and presuming that he retains his vigour and mastery over the herd until at least fifteen years old, it goes without saying that he will, on nearing that age, be cohabiting with his daughters, granddaughters, and great-granddaughters. Consequently while *he* stands still as regards his strains of blood, his mates are bound to get more and more inbred. Later on a younger male, of possibly the same herd, will deprive him of the leadership, and though the usurper be equally as inbred as most of his mates, the same process of inbreeding will commence again and yet again, nor will it be interrupted until excursions into neighbouring herds import fresh strains of blood into the harem, and to some extent arrest the process. It would appear as though nature has so constructed the female that she can, better than the male, withstand the effects of inbreeding, and if I am correct in supposing that the mere fact of bearing repeatedly to same sire causes her to become inbred to him, it would certainly follow that, unless some such law of compensation were in force, the younger members of a large family (from same sire and dam) would rapidly deteriorate. I have already shown, when dealing with the law of saturation, that where the pedigrees of sire and dam are *very similar* such is really the result, but when differing widely as to strains of blood, the consecutive matings either improve with frequency, or, at any rate, may be continued with impunity up to a certain point. This would explain why in the human race there is no apparent evil effect on the younger members of a large family, because there is rarely any *inbreeding* in the pedigree tables. And we may take it for granted that deterioration in the offspring of cousins will certainly increase with each conception, unless the male is physically and intellectually much the *superior* of the female, and in that case the younger children should be superior to the elder

Q

Back in the seventies I held an interest in a thoroughbred stud. My partner, without consulting with me, mated a mare (Preserve) with Yattendon. When informed of it, I ventured an opinion that the progeny would be too inbred to race, but, if a filly, would be almost certain to be a good brood mare. And a filly it proved to be (Persephone), a very handsome bay, but a dreadful failure as a race mare. She has, however, done well at the stud of Mr. Tom

PERSEPHONE (Aus.).

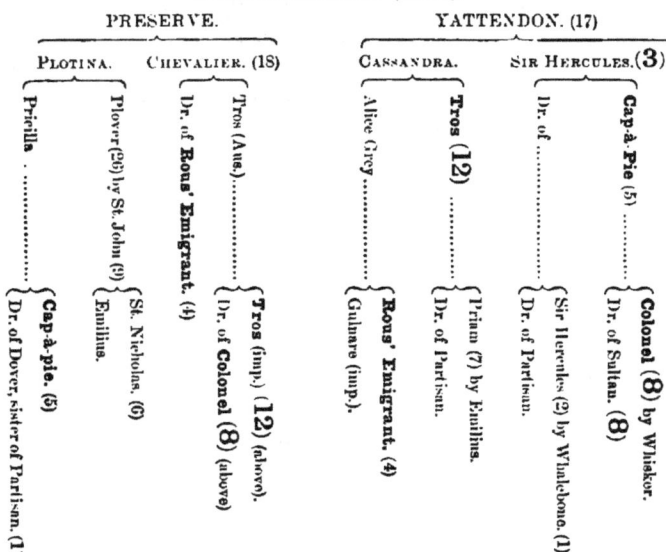

PRESERVE.		YATTENDON. (17)	
PLOTINA.	CHEVALIER. (18)	CASSANDRA.	SIR HERCULES. (3)

Priscilla .... { Cap-à-pie. (5) / Dr. of Dover, sister of Partisan. (1)

Plover (26) by St. John (9) { St. Nicholas. (6) / Emilius.

Dr. of Rous' Emigrant. (4) { Dr. of Colonel (8) (above).

Tros (Aus.) .... { Tros (imp.) (12) (above).

Tros (12) .... { Priam (7) by Emilius. / Dr. of Partisan.

Alice Grey .... { Rous' Emigrant. (4) / Gulnare (imp.).

Dr. of .... { Sir Hercules (2) by Whalebone. (1) / Dr. of Partisan.

Cap-à-pie (5) .... { Colonel (8) by Whisker. / Dr. of Sultan. (8)

Cook (N.S.W.), and is the dam of a very speedy mare (Vespasia) by (imp.) Vespasian, a fine outcross for her inbred dam, whose breeding is given above.

The strains of blood in both sire and dam were very similar, and *within four removes* on both sides we find repeated the names of Cap-à-pie, and his sire The Colonel, also (imp.), Tros (imp.), Rous's

Emigrant, and at some distance further away Partisan (four times), Emilius, Whisker, and Whalebone. But we have only to turn again to the many instances I have given of successful inbred dams, such as Vulture (the dam of Orlando), closely inbred to Selim and Castrel; the dam of Flying Childers; the dam of Highflyer (inbred to God. Barb); and the dam of Whalebone and his brothers, inbred to same strain. From these examples it would appear that the conditions required to produce successful sires and dams are widely different, if not quite opposite, and the only reasonable solution of the problem is the possibility of the existence of some natural law of compensation amongst all gregarious animals which checks the inevitable and rapid deterioration which would otherwise take place under incestuous breeding.

CHAPTER XV.

STUD FARM AND MANAGEMENT OF SAME.

A BOOK of this nature would be incomplete without some remarks relative to the selection and general management of a thoroughbred stud farm. It has been my privilege always to be more or less associated with blood stock, and in my travels I have inspected many of the great stud farms of England, America, Australia, and New Zealand. Upon the choice of location of farm a great deal of the future success or non-success hinges. It has been generally recognised that limestone formation is the most suitable for supplying bone and vigour to stock. As this is not always available, the next best alternative is to choose for your location, if possible, rich bottoms or river flats running back into undulating ridges. The main heads of nearly any given river are almost sure to traverse belts of limestone country, and the periodical overflows of the river supply to the soil lime, as well as other constituents, which are likely under less favourable conditions to be exhausted by overstocking over a long course of years. It is a mistake, however, to suppose that large bone cannot be obtained without a considerable amount of limestone in the soil. Much of the weediness and small bone met with in thoroughbreds is due to inbreeding to quality blood like Sweetmeat and Kingston, and avoiding Melbourne, Stockwell, Toxophilite, West Australian, &c. A return to Melbourne will do more in one cross to restore the bone to a desired size than a decade of breeding on limestone soil without such aid.

In respect of location, I know few places to compare to Rancho del Paso, the immense horse-breeding stud farm of Mr. J. B. Haggin (of New York), presided over by Mr. John Mackay. The part devoted to blood stock is mostly situated upon the rich "bottoms" of the American River (a branch of the Sacramento), and these flats are generally green with alfalfa (lucerne) most of the year, affording excellent pasture for mares and foals. The farm consists of innumerable small paddocks (with lanes between), ranging from two and three acres to twenty, fifty, and a hundred acres each. The smaller ones are used for isolating individuals, kickers, or hospital cases, and the largest for dry and breeding mares. At convenient distances there are immense sheds, with twenty to forty loose boxes in each, in which the mares and foals are housed at night, and after weaning occupied by the youngsters, which are turned loose in paddocks by batches during the day, and allowed to scamper about and run mimic races, and many an early beginner may be spotted by watching these spins. With freedom, exercise, and open air the colt hardens his legs and constitution, and grows muscle instead of beef and fat. This custom is also pursued upon Australian stud farms, where climatic conditions allow of the young stock being turned into paddocks during the day, both winter and summer. The future of the racehorse is so considerably influenced by the treatment he gets after weaning (and for that matter before), that too much stress cannot be laid upon this important point, otherwise the skill of mating sire and dam will be rendered valueless. While I am a great advocate for green and succulent food for the mother, and especially when she is suckling the colt, I would certainly discountenance it for the weaning, except medicinally to keep him in good health. The present abnormal conditions of racing two-year-olds demand that the youngster should be treated *abnormally*. Instead of being allowed to develop under natural conditions and green pastures, it is imperative that he should be matured by the aid of such stimulating dry foods as will tend to produce a rapid development of both bone and muscle, and fit him for the task of carrying as a two-year-old eight and nine stone over six and seven furlongs at a higher rate of speed than he will probably ever afterwards attain. This early development cannot be achieved by boiled barley or wheat and green food, which tend to produce beef and fat, soft bone, and a minimum of muscle. Yet at many of the stud farms I have visited this latter is the treatment adopted, and owners wonder why their stock do not come to the front. In the attempt to rid his colt of this useless and superfluous fat and beef, the trainer, unless exceptionally careful and patient, is almost certain to break down the youngster. While in England in 1883 I was shown over the farm of a big breeder, and remarked to the stud groom upon the obesity of the yearlings. Most of them actually had heavy crests of fat. His remark was, " I think it is a great mistake to fatten them up this way, but the master will have it so, and what am I to do ? " These colts and fillies had little or no exercise at large in paddocks, and I was told afterwards that a large percentage broke down in their first preparation. Every stud farm should have a kite-shaped track about three-quarters of a mile in length in connection with the youngster's department, with the neck of the kite opening into a round paddock of say an acre at least. A dozen youngsters could be turned into this just before feeding time, and allowed to have a spin round the track and back to water and feed. This would ensure every colt getting a fair amount of exercise. The prospect of the feed would act as a stimulant and cause considerable emulation amongst them. The track could be kept in order in winter by a coating of tan, and if properly graded need seldom be too wet to use. To prevent any possibility of the youngsters being injured, boots should be placed upon the hind legs and ankles. Colts treated like this, instead of coming to the sale ring, as they mostly do, fat inside and out, would be half trained for their early engagements, and worth double the money to racing men and trainers. Mr. William Kent, in his gossip about Lord George Bentinck, informs us that this giant amongst racing men rarely ever engaged a youngster without getting a trial out of him, and I venture to predict that, under such treatment as I have sketched out, the stud master would be able to get a very excellent line as to the capabilities of his colts and fillies.

While the colts are running with the mothers, and during the covering season, a handy man should be allowed to go through them every day and halter and handle each foal. This plan is in vogue at the immense horse-breeding farm (containing over 1000 head) of my old friend, Mr. Thomas Cook, of Turanville, near Sydney, N.S.W. There is little or no risk in carrying it out. He has an exceptionally patient old groom, who rarely engages in a struggle with even the highest-couraged colt, and almost before the colt is aware of it has him used to the halter and walking about with an old piece of bagging thrown across his back. A few repetitions of this treatment take away all nervousness from the foal, and establish a confidence between the animal and the man which lasts generally through life. Most of the bad-tempered and roguish animals on the race track have been brought to this state by impatient or brutal treatment when young. The strongest mental characteristic of the horse is memory. He never forgets good or ill treatment, or, if taken only once over a new and strange route, will remember for years the exact spot he turned off the beaten path, even though there is no track or evidence to guide him except his own wonderful instinct. I have lived quite half of my life on horseback, and know the habits of horses as well as most men, and often have I had occasion to regret the loss of temper which has caused me to spur a good horse for a slight stumble or shy. Unless a considerable amount of self-control is exercised under such circumstances, he will very soon become a confirmed shyer or a dangerous stumbler, always dreading the spur at the slightest trip, and, to try and avoid same, dashing away at a tangent. How many a race has been lost by severe and unnecessary punishment of a good, game, horse, doing his very utmost to win. The whip and spur are unmercifully applied, and, even if he succeeds in winning the race, the horse has in five cases out of ten been so cowed and discouraged by the treatment that his heart sinks at the first application of the whip ever after, and if he is of a timid disposition a swerve will be the only response. If vicious, he will simply lay back his ears and stop racing—at the very moment of victory, perhaps, had he been kindly nursed instead of being whipped and spurred. Dear eccentric old Dr. West (of New South Wales racing memory) once shouted out at the top of his voice when an old jockey came with a wet sail and did a youthful opponent upon the post by a head, under the sharp castigation of whip and spur, "Ninety-nine times out of a hundred a jockey should never be allowed to carry a whip; but, by God, this is the exception!" and the worthy old doctor was very near the truth, for more races are lost than won by whips.

In the successful manipulation of a stud farm, one of the most important elements of success is proper exercise of the stallions. In a state of nature, and, indeed, in captivity up to his retirement from the race track, no animal takes so much voluntary or forced exercise as the horse. Yet, in too many instances, directly he is relegated to stud work, he undergoes an entire change of life and habits. Many a score of once successful racehorses have I seen doomed to pass the remainder of their days either craning their necks in a vain endeavour to look out of an eight feet high window or sadly wearing away their existence before the narrow bars which give them a fleeting glimpse of green pastures such as they often scampered over in the unrestraint of youthful spirits; and at most, in the way of exercise, a monotonous promenade round a yard thirty feet in diameter, with solid boarded walls ten feet high, and not even a peep at the world around them. Is it a wonder that they get maddened by the outside clatter of hoofs, eloquently appealing to them of the more fortunate freedom of their fellows, and finally end by savaging their grooms? How one's sympathy does go out to the stalled stallion, or the chained hound howling at his kennel door. Sad sights both! and quite uncalled for, if owners were less blind to their own true interests, or gifted with more humanity. As a general rule it will be found that, if the usual walking exercise of the racehorse is not interrupted (because of the transfer from post to paddock) the health and temper of the animal will not suffer. So dearly do stallions value their daily exercise, that I have known them, when deprived of it by continued wet weather or other causes, take to pawing and kicking at the walls of their loose boxes, until taken out as usual. One of the gentlest tempered stallions I know, Clieveden (brother to Chester), taken by me to America in 1893, never fails to begin mildly rapping at the side of his box after a few days' neglect. It is hard to conceive any treatment more pernicious than to so suddenly change the habits of the most active of all the domestic animals? And it is bound to bring about vicious habits, loss of health, muscle, and temper, and increased liability to catch colds, or to suffer from constipation and a score of other ills, which tend to reduce the value of the animal, and often bring about his early death, and certainly render him comparatively useless in the desired transmission of those splendid racing qualities which led to his purchase. As a proof of the value of exercise, I have been told by reliable men that stallions which travel round a district to their mares get a higher average of foals than home stallions.

CHAPTER XVI.

ON THE LAW OF SEX.

IN the preceding chapter I touched upon the necessity of exercise for the stallion, and in connection with this there crops up an interesting phase in horse-breeding which is known to most stud masters. This is the tendency of some horses to sire more fillies than colts, and *vice versâ*.

I have treated at some length elsewhere as to how *high-class* fillies are bred, but I now refer more to the working of the law of sex. It has been pretty clearly laid down and fairly proved by the American writer, Starkweather, in his work on "The Law of Sex," that the strongest parent (in human beings) physically and intellectually decides the sex of the progeny, and fixes it *opposite* to his or her own, as the case may be. Many years ago, in Australia, long before Starkweather's book was published, my attention was drawn (away in the early sixties) to a case (in horses) so decided in its results, that every racing man in the district was fully alive to the absurdity of attempting to race any of the fillies by (imp.) Kelpie. What made this fact so marked was the superior excellence of his colts over all the racehorses of the same district. It was no uncommon occurrence for several years to see the placed horses in important events all by Kelpie, yet I do not remember ever to have seen or heard of one of his fillies winning a race during the same time. The horse was then the property of the late Mr. George Wyndham, and stood at Bukulla on the MacIntyre river, New South Wales. His harem contained some of the most highly-bred mares of that day in Australia, and, as proof of this, the progeny won all over Queensland and on the Sydney race-tracks. Amongst the prominent ones were Croyden (winner of Metropolitan), from a Wyndham mare; Kingfisher (twice winner of Sydney Cup), by Kelpie from one of the Bukulla mares; Circassian (Sydney Cup); Trump Card, by Kelpie, Caroola, and other first-class animals. The pasture before sheep were introduced on to the grand horse and cattle run was of an excellent description, and it was the custom to cover late so as to have the foals drop when the spring was well advanced, and young grass plentiful for milk supply. It will be gathered from the foregoing that the mares were not only highly bred (mostly containing strains of Cap-à-pie by Colonel, son of Whisker; also Whisker (imp.) by Whisker; and Prover by St. John (imp.), son of St. Nicholas, son of Emilius), but were living under very healthy conditions. Not so the stallion Kelpie. The only exercise he got was in a yard about forty by fifty feet; and during wet weather this was very muddy and sticky, being of volcanic formation. His feed during the year was dry hay, with grain, and, if the spring was early, green cut barley to commence the season on. Frequently, when the spring rains failed, he had no green stuff. Here we find the conditions of living and health quite the reverse to those under which the mares existed, and, by the theory of Starkweather, the mares being *physically superior* to the horse, would throw a decided preponderance of colts over fillies. As a fact, that was what really did occur. Very few fillies in comparison to colts were born, and these few were quite useless for racing purposes. Now, mark what happened when the conditions were reversed. Kelpie was purchased from the Bukulla stud by Mr. T. H. Smith, of Gordon Brook, Clarence River. Few stud masters are more fully alive to the advantage of treating his stallions to plenty of exercise and comfortable stabling. But his ranch is not so favourably situated as Bukulla in the matter of soil and pasture, and, as he bred for racing purposes, the mares were covered in the early spring, and before they had recovered from the effects of wintering in a moist climate. In fact, the conditions existing at Bukulla were exactly reversed, and the results likewise. Kelpie now commenced to sire a fair proportion of fillies, and some of them of quite good racing form, notably Thyra (won £1000 Handicap at Glen Innes), Maud, Atalanta, Ariadne, The Nun, and many others. It is true that the mares were not so stoutly bred as Mr. Wyndham's, being mostly got by (imp.) Livingstone, (imp.) Magus (a son of Pyrrhus I.), Glaucus (Arab), (imp.) Pitsford (a son of Epirus), &c. This, however, only tended to confirm the fact that Kelpie was physically, and in potency of blood, as much superior in stoutness to the mares at Gordon Brook, as he was inferior in those respects to the mares at Bukulla.

From many years' observation of the working of the law of sex in human beings, I can thoroughly indorse Starkweather in his conclusions as quoted above. The dominant parent in mental and physical force will be invariably found at the head of a family in which the opposite sex to himself (or herself) predominates. I have seen so many examples that there remains no doubt in my own mind of the soundness of the theory. Exceptions will occur when the mental and physical characteristics are evenly balanced, or when, as frequently occurs, a check in health has disturbed the working of the law, and allowed the previously weaker vessel to become the stronger. If this position is tenable, there is no reason why a stud master should not utilise this knowledge for his own benefit by selecting for a sire in the habit of getting a preponderance of fillies, mares in sire lines and very much stouter bred than himself. In this respect St. Simon's tendency to get so many good fillies and so few good colts in comparison might be checked by choosing him such strains of blood as Isonomy, Weatherbit, Pero Gomez, Brown Bread.

A coloured portrait gallery of the celebrated horses of the past would be of immense importance to stud masters, as affording an indication of the particular ancestors the young stock have reverted to. In 1883 I made a fairly numerous collection of coloured engravings by Herring, sen., Hall, Aitkin, and others, and it was very curious to note the likeness of prominent Australian-bred horses to some of their progenitors. Many of them bore a far greater resemblance to ancestors at three and four removes away than to their own sires and dams. Mr. Frank Reynold's Goldsborough was pronounced to be a perfect countertype (but lighter in colour) of Touchstone, the sire of his (8) dam Juliet, whereas he bears no resemblance to Fisherman, the sire of his dam, nor to his own sire, Fireworks. Darebin, by the Peer (imp.) from Lurline by Traducer, is a big-boned brown horse, with slightly Roman nose, quite the type of his (8) sire, Melbourne. He sires very big-boned stock, and likes plenty of quality in his mares.

Grandmaster (imp.), by Gladiataur from Celerima, by Stockwell from Slander by Pantaloon, is a dark chestnut, with some white about him, and both in colour and shape is a living picture of old Pantaloon, while he in no way resembles his sire Gladiateur. English stud masters, who have such great opportunities of making these comparisons, will recognise the value to be gained by watching the colours of the youngsters. Mr. Joseph Osborne, in his valuable " Handbook to Breeders," has made a great point of this by giving the colours where practicable. My experience has lead me to the conclusion that where any given horse is very inbred to some prominent and potent ancestor, he will inherit, in a great measure, the colour, shape, and disposition of such ancestor. It would appear to be the aim and design of Nature to be constantly reproducing and lifting to the surface again the characteristics of past generations, thereby causing them to exist over and over again through their living representatives. How often (as in Isonomy' case) do we see the short back and powerful loins of Sir Hercules reproduced in his descendants.

THE ARAB AS AN OUTCROSS.

It has been frequently stated, and by good authorities in England, that the thoroughbreds of the country need some outcross from America and Australia, the most suitable countries from which to draw for new infusions of blood. In a comparatively limited space like England, there is necessarily a constant interchange of animals from one stud to another, through the medium of the annual sales of blood stock, and from this cause alone inbreeding is more marked than in other countries. The result of such inbreeding has unquestionably led to much unsoundness in both wind and limbs, and infirmity of temper, and a change of blood such as that suggested would do much towards remedying these evils. The extremely favourable conditions under which blood stock is reared in Australia, where the climate is so temperate, points to that country being the most desirable of the two for the purpose. At most of the Australian stud farms, the foals, after being dropped in a spacious loose box, and confined with the mother for a few days, are turned into small paddocks, and rarely housed at night until weaning time. After weaning, the foals run together in the daytime in lots of six to twelve, or according to the supply of paddocks, and are stabled at night during the winter and early spring months. As the summer advances these tactics are reversed, and the youngsters are kept in their loose boxes until the sun has lost its power, after which they are turned out for the night. This is done for two reasons, viz., to avoid the troublesome swarms of flies, and to keep their coats from getting sunburnt and stary. But in either case the colts get plenty of exercise, harden their bone and muscle, and develop into wiry legged, sound winded, healthy animals, well suited for crossing with their less favoured English contemporaries. Yet, after all, this change of *blood* would not be a very marked one, as an examination of the pedigrees of both breeds disclose precisely the same common ancestors at less than six, seven, or eight removes back. What

is really required is a *complete outcross*, and the only source from
which this can be derived is the Arab.   By using the latter,
there are several distinct advantages to be gained, amongst
which, density of bone, good feet, admirable temper, sound
constitution, and freedom from roaring are not the least.   In
advocating the use of the Arab, I do so with a proviso that only
the very best shaped and highest public performers be chosen.   I
may be considered a theorist, or something worse, when I assert that
in one remove from the first cross I believe the present speed and
staying power of the English racehorse would be restored, while
from that out the staying power would be increased materially.   As
a fact, this experiment has been tried with most satisfactory results
in Australia, and in proof of this I need only point to such brilliant
racehorses as Loup Garou, by Lord of Lmine (imp.) from Hebe, by
Majas (imp.) from Lallah Rookh by Satellite, an imported Arab
stallion.   Loup Garou won the Australian Jockey Club Derby at
Sydney, and the Victoria Racing Club Derby, Melbourne.   He was
a horse of nearly sixteen hands, with a terrific turn of speed.   Last
racing season (1893) the A.J.C. Derby was won by Trenchant (by
Trenton) from Bridesmaid, by Yattendon from Esperance by Glaucus,
an imported Arab.   Satellite and Glaucus were both excellent
performers in India, and many of the *first cross* Glaucus horses raced,
to wit, Peter Fin.   This is not unusual.   Folly, by Grandmaster
from Sweetlips by Shanghai, an imported Arab, was a very speedy
mare, and won many races in good company.   Esperance (**8** . dam of
Trenchant), by Glaucus (Arab), possessed a rare turn of speed, and
also won many races.   Banshee, by Glaucus, threw some excellent
racehorses, as the following list will show : Piora, a winner of the
(two-year-old Clarence River Produce Stakes ; Bulgimbar, a first-
class horse (by imp. Pitsford), beat the celebrated Barb in the
Maiden Stakes, one and a half miles, and won some big handicaps
under heavy weights ; Boquet, by Middlesex (imp.), a very speedy
filly ; Banaghar, by Kelpie (imp.), another of Banshee's sons,

distinguished himself as a racehorse. A superior horse to any of those mentioned with the Arab cross was Dagworth, by Yattendon from Nutent, by (imp.) Pitsford from Amber by Glaucus. Dagworth won the Hawkesbury Handicap, the Metropolitan, and ran a dead heat for the Randwick Plate (three miles) with Reprieve, the best horse of the day, also by Yattendon. But I think sufficient examples have been given to show plainly that the cross of Arab on to English mares in Australia has proved highly successful, and breeders in England need be under no apprehension that such a cross entails any loss of speed and stamina after the first cross has been overcome. To come nearer to our own doors, we had an instance, at last Goodwood meeting, of a second descendant from an Arab mare (imported by Mr. Wilfred Blunt, of Crabbet Park) winning a race in fair company. This animal, Alfragan, was bred and raced by Lord Bradford, and is by Chippendale from a mare by Bend Or out of Basilisk.

But we have only to turn back to Vol. I. of English Stud books to find scores of cases where horses once and twice removed from Eastern sires proved to be the champions of the day. Matchem was by Cade, son of Godolphin Barb; Eclipse was from Spiletta, by Regulus son of Godolphin Barb. Much *quicker* results will be got by using, as in Australia, Arab sires in preference to Arab mares, though the latter would impart a more permanent influence provided the best performed or highest caste ones only were used, and the descendants of some of the Crabbet Park importations should in every way fulfil requirements, if any breeders are disposed to follow Lord Bradford's example.

GOSSIP ABOUT MEN AND HORSES.

There are few truer sayings amongst racing men than the one so often used, "They gallop in all shapes." I remember seeing on a country course in New South Wales a race won by a gelding with a ridiculously deformed fore leg. He evidently had sustained a fracture of the knee as a colt, because the other leg was sound and well shaped. The injured member stood out at an angle from the knee joint, and while both knees "knocked" to such an extent that they were constantly raw, his fore feet must have been quite eighteen inches apart when the horse was standing still. He showed quite good selling plate form, and set one wondering what he might have accomplished with a decent pair of legs. How he managed to get along without being tripped up, or throwing some of his opponents, has always been a mystery to me. I never saw but three or four really high-class horses with bent (or "sickle-hocked") hind legs. One of these was The Barb, bred by John Lee, raced by old John Tait, and afterwards in the stud of Mr. Charles Reynolds. The Barb got many of his stock with this defect, but minus his own wonderful loins and quarters and short back, which enabled him to carry 10st. 9lb. to the front in a high-class field, in the Sydney Cup, two miles. The trouble of bent legs is, that they give too much sweep and length to the stride, and unless the loin and quarters are strong enough to perform this extra work, the animal tires, and the hind legs get left behind. This was for the first time forcibly demonstrated to me about thirty years ago at a country meeting in New England (N.S.W.). I walked round, with a clever judge of horses and racing, to see the horses saddled for the Maiden Plate, having previously backed a colt by (imp.) Pitsford. My friend remarked, "You'll drop your money over Pitsford, he's too crooked in the hind legs, and will tire going up the hill at back of course, and be beaten half a mile from home." I was not at all disposed to take this view, and stood him for the small stake I had risked. As the field raced to the crest of the slight rise, with Pitsford beginning to tail off, my friend rather unkindly remarked, " Look at him now, old chap, just as I told you! his hind legs have got away behind him for all the world like a duck "; and sure enough he hardly saved his distance, nor could he ever run a decent race over

R

a mile except in tip top condition, and in company, well ! not tip top. Maxim by Musket, bred in New Zealand, and sent to Del Paso stud in California, was another of the bent-legged sort, but he had some compensation in quarters and loins like a draught horse, and in such cases, given condition, the bent leg is a case of the big wheel v. the medium-sized one. But taking them all round, in condition and out of condition, heavy and light weight, my experience has shown me that the hind leg inclined to be straight, provided it does not interfere with the formation of back, with ample room and play for the tendon Achilles, is the most serviceable kind. It stands to reason that an animal with a straight leg, well under and somewhat forward of a plumb line dropped from the round bone, gallops *well forward* and conserves his strength for a longer period without tiring than his less fortunate brother with the bent leg.

Ormonde and Carbine (Aus.) are good examples of the highest form of galloping hind legs. My memory takes me back a good span to a race meeting in Armidale (N.S.W.), where " old grey Harkaway," bred by Wyndham Brothers, at Bukulla, won all the principal races under heavy weights. He was at this time sixteen years of age. When a colt, Mr. Wyndham made him a present to an old servant (Bowly), who trained him in rather a primitive fashion for some years, and won many races. Harkaway had a playful habit of bucking " old Bowly " off, when he began to get too bearing ; but in any case the old man was too much of a welter weight to put the finishing touches to his work, so he hit upon the novel plan of turning the old grey loose with a kangaroo (half-bred stag and greyhound) dog. I never was fortunate enough to see the performance, but it was said to be worth going a long distance to witness the two animals trying conclusions, and Bowly sitting on a log, with an old silver " turnip," taking time. The old horse developed huge carbuncles on his ankles, and was turned out for a few years spell, and finally brought to the Armidale Meeting, above mentioned, at sixteen years of age. So ridiculously broken down

did he appear to be, that I refused to back him at a previous meeting
(sixty miles distant) the week before, and lost more than I cared to
admit even to myself. I, however, profited by experience, and won
it all back, and more, at Armidale, where he romped home in front
of everything. He had the straightest hind legs I ever saw on a
racehorse.

I accompanied the district medico, Dr. West, to look at Harkaway
after the big handicap. The doctor was one of the dearest old sports
that ever drew breath, and a grand judge of a racehorse, but inclined
to be profane. After running his hand over the carbuncles he
observed with a mysterious shake of the head, " Do you know, I'll
be d——d if I don't think Cheeseborough was right after all ! "
" He used to say that they acted as *buttresses to the legs!* Yes, sir !
buttresses to the legs! "

Dr. West in his younger days nearly always had a very fair stable
of horses and won many races. As might be expected from such a
father, his elder boy " Johnny " took kindly to the pigskin, and
frequently rode in public for his father. The old boy himself was
so nervous that he could not even look on while the race was being
run, and generally plunged into one of the temporary booths on the
course, from which questionable coign of vantage he was informed
by some obliging friend how the race progressed. Needless to say
that these occasions were too suggestive of practical jokes to be
overlooked, and in answer to queries as to how Johnny was riding
Tromby in the three miles (where he had received orders to ride a
waiting race) he would be told that Johnny was " forcing the
pace," " leading them twenty lengths," &c. Then up would go
a running, fiery torrent of oaths, and in his frenzy he often
seized hold of a streaming wet towel, and dabbed it on top of his
head, probably to save himself from an apoplectic fit. With all
his eccentric ways, he was a kindly, clever, cultured man, loved by all
who enjoyed the privilege of his friendship, and listened to his witty
summing-up of men, women, and horses.

R 2

Some few years back, "Rapier," in his always pleasant and instructive circular notes, gave his own and outside impressions of what the special qualities were which made one horse so superior to his field on a muddy, slushy course. In countries like England and America (to a less extent Australia), where the rainfall is so heavy, there are ample opportunities of studying this feature of the game. Yet a few remarks from the experience of one who has seen racing in all three countries may throw some additional light upon the subject. This ability to go in mud is not necessarily because the animal is gamer than his field. In the V.R.C. Leger of 1893, Camoola (by Chester), a double Derby winner, was on a wet and slippery track disgracefully beaten by Culloden and others, and reeled in like a drunken man, very much distressed. His action is of the long, low, creeping sort. On the following Saturday, the course being dry and firm, he stripped for the champion race (three miles) against the Leger winner and two of the best stayers in Australia, Portsea and Admiral, and put them all down comfortably; showing that it was not lack of stamina that lost him the Leger, but inability to gallop in mud without slipping and floundering. I took Stromboli (a Derby winner), son of Chester, up to San Francisco, and leased his racing there. He was never beaten fairly on a dry track in good company, but the ordinary plater could give him weight over the muddy tracks. His action was particularly long, and his hoofs somewhat large and flat, so that he floundered about unmistakably. I had ample opportunities to study mud-larking at San Francisco, as the course was either a sea of sloppy mud or sticky clay about five months out of the six the racing lasted. The crack two-year-old of the meeting, Lucky Dog (by Darebin), owned by Mr. Simeon J. Reed, of Pasedina, won all his races, but it was muddy each time. He has since then been racing at Chicago on dry tracks with indifferent success. His shape and action are, in my opinion, exactly what is required. His hind leg is straight, and his action short, compact, and a little choppy; so that he drives his

rather small, deep hoofs well into the mud, and loses no ground
by slipping about. Wildwood (by Wildidle), with much the
same style of going and feet, was simply invincible in the
mud under big weights ; but he has also performed indifferently
about Chicago in dry weather. Many of the sprinters at San
Francisco could only win in the mud, yet ability to negotiate mud
is often allied with stoutness over long distances. I purchased,
back in the seventies, at Bukulla, a brown colt (by Kelpie),
afterwards named Cyclone. At Bukulla the horses ran at large in
huge paddocks, and when a mob of some fifty were driven at a smart
gallop past the house (mares, colts, and foals all mixed), I noticed a
brown colt leading them all through the mud, and galloping with
apparent ease. Mr. Reginald Wyndham, to my inquiry, replied,
"that is Clifton Lass's, Kelpie colt." When we walked into the
large yard the horses were reeking with the sweat of a four mile
spin through the black mud. As we stood, some twenty yards off,
looking at them, the brown colt, though *unbroken*, deliberately
walked up and made a playful grab at my friend's beard, then
scampered back to the mob. These two incidents so convinced me
of the colt's gameness, that I bought him in preference to several
much finer looking horses: Indeed, he was such a weed that I got
chaffed considerably by friends, one good judge offering " to eat
his hat, if that weed ever proved a racehorse." He developed into
the best weight-for-age horse in New England at one, two, or three
miles. His hoofs were deep and small, and his action somewhat
high, with straight hind legs, and I never saw his equal in mud. In
a three mile handicap, at Armidale, he was weighted with 9st. 7lb. ;
Tommy Dodd, also by Kelpie (winner of three Maiden Plates), a
year younger, 8st. 6lb. Mr. J. J. R. Gibson, the owner of the latter,
was prepared to lay my partner (D. S. Anderson) and me tempting
odds that his horse would beat Cyclone, but in view of his condition
and recent consecutive victories, we declined. At dinner, the night
before the big race, heavy rain set in, and never was sound more

welcome to the confederacy. Before we separated for the night, the owner of Tommy Dodd was baited into laying me £30 to £10 that he was not distanced. We asked one of the stewards to go to the distance post, and sure enough Tommy Dodd and another horse failed to save their distance. Cyclone won the race comfortably, though he was by far the smallest horse in a field of twelve, and carried a stone more weight than anything.

A racehorse's disposition and temper may be read in his face as plainly as that of a human being, and very much on the same lines. Just as we see a Roman-nosed man of the Duke of Wellington type carrying war into the enemy's camp, or challenging discussion, so will the Roman-nosed horse be disposed to fight for his head, and in some cases pull like a demon. I like to see it in steeplechasers, because it means courage, and instead of shirking his jumps the Roman-nosed horse takes a firm grip of the bit, and will not be pulled off the obstacle. His countertype is the large-eyed, dished-nosed horse, with a prominent bump between the eyes. This customer is mostly sensitive and shifty, and his large eyes help to magnify the size of the jump, so that he is prepared to baulk at any moment. A thick, short-rounded, muscular neck is generally the indication of a stayer, either as a racehorse, hunter, or hackney, and such horses never get heavy in hand. Loose loins, but well sprung back ribs, are often found in good chasers. The loose loin gives freedom and the suppleness necessary to surmount big obstacles, provided the quarters are strong and muscular, and the knees slightly arched forward to give springiness to the landing. Calf knees are rarely associated with first-class steeplechase form, though common enough in racehorses, especially of the sprinting sort. Nothing prejudices one more against a colt than to have to stoop down to discover his sex. It is usually a sign of want of constitution and stamina. Nor have I ever seen a first-class horse without a *deep brisket*; it denotes staying and weight-carrying power. When selecting youngsters at the sale ring, I cordially

agree with Mr. Egerton-Warburton that there is very much to be
gleaned from the walk. It is difficult to convey the idea to another,
but the colt that is going to race has the stride of a racehorse, and
turns his stifles well out, showing them to be muscular, and the
track of his hind foot should without any effort in a walking gait,
come quite a foot over the front hoof track. His hind quarters, from
top of coupling, should be distinctly higher than his withers for great
speed and ability to carry weight. Rounded muscular loins and short
back, leg high, and joints large, especially the knee-caps. Neither
the hocks nor knees should be far from the ground, though many
first-class racehorses are shaped to the contrary. The width of knee-
caps, looked at from behind, will give a better idea of the probable
size of the animal, at full growth, than perhaps any other point
about him. It is very conspicuous in the Melbourne family. Many
of our best stayers have been light-fleshed animals, showing little
muscle about the thighs. The first time I saw Australian Peer, after
the late William Gannon purchased him, was about a month before
the Randwick Meeting, at Sydney, where he astonished everyone by
easily defeating the hitherto invincible Trident at three miles w.f.a.
Mr. Gannon asked me to go out to the stables and have a look at
him. As a young three-year-old he had very lean thighs and
gaskins for an otherwise handsome horse in condition. I remarked:
"One thing I feel very sure of; you have got a high-class stayer,
both by breeding and shape. He has no lumber to carry, and ought
to be able to gallop all day." As it elicited no opinion from the
owner, I dropped the subject, but was quite prepared for the result
of the race, which was wired up country. But "they gallop in all
shapes," and Musket, in the front rank of stayers, was built with
dray-horse quarters, nor do I remember ever seeing a more bull-
necked stallion. Without being at all fat, his neck was almost a
deformity with muscle. A grand success at the stud, but, like most
horses that are bred away from Birdcatcher, and too much to
Touchstone, Melbourne, and Pantaloon, his stock, as a rule, had

wretched legs, and most of the breed, especially when allied with Fisherman, will not train on for this reason. Trenton is an exception, but he also had such a curby, suspicious hock, that I strongly advised Mr. Willie Cooper to refuse delivery of him until examined by a vet. Talking of training naturally brings one to the subject of riding. I was struck by a remark made in a late American paper by Taral, their crack jockey, who was interviewed recently on the subject. He is of opinion that a jockey should ride as much forward on his mount as he can possibly get. "Take a short hold, and get right on to his ears," or something to that effect, is his advice; and indeed most of the American boys ride with their legs in front of the flaps, sitting almost on top of the horse's shoulders. The happy medium appears to be the correct style. I wrote to Australia in 1882 that Archer pleased me more than any other jockey, because he seemed to ride entirely in the stirrups and forward, and rarely sat back in his saddle. I can see him now coming up the rise at the finish of the Middle Park Plate on Macheath, with a double turn of the reins round both hands firmly pressed on the colt's withers, and bearing most of his weight there, instead of over the back and loins. I have known one or two good amateurs in New South Wales ride in this fashion—notably the late P. W. Anderson, who could squeeze more out of the last few strides of a tired horse than any other amateur I ever saw. "The Chifney rush" (like the "*long*," low" style of racehorse) has gone for good, and that any jockey could be so successful lying back to finish on a horse's loins speaks volumes for the goodness of his mounts and the curious perversity of a fashion that was opposed to all scientific principles, unless, indeed, he were coming down a steep gradient. But a first-class horseman will instinctively adapt his riding to the style, stride, and general action of his mount, or the gradients of the course he happens to be riding over. A man riding to hounds knows instinctively that, if he takes the panel right in front of him (and twenty yards away), his horse will either have to take off too far from the obstacle, or else too close under it, so he makes up his mind in a moment to bear to the right or left to save his horse the trouble of thinking it out for himself (and some horses won't think). A good rider is always in sympathy with his mount, and this is, after all, the secret of a successful jockey. Much of the bad temper met with in racehorses is caused by this antagonism of the two natures. Another fruitful source of evil temper is delay at the starting post. To a high-spirited colt, in the pink of condition, and eager to get away, no more devilish device could be invented than to keep him fretting his heart out for half an hour at the post, or an hour and three-quarters, as I saw in Chicago in 1893, when Boundless won. Garrison, who rode the horse, was one of the greatest delinquents, as he refused to come up to the line until most of the field were tired to death. And so it will always be, more or less, until the " Starting Gate " is universally adopted. It is now being used with great success in Australia. I believe I was the first to work out the idea, and in a series of articles on " Turf Reform," which I wrote for *The Pastoralist* (Sydney) some years ago, had a model of the gate for publication, but was persuaded by the editor not to do so until I had patented it. The idea was given to an architect, and he in turn to a machinist to work out details, until it became common property. The pressing of a button (or the dropping of a weight) releases a wire netting (or cord netting) screen, which flies upwards, and leaves the course clear. Before we are much older we shall see a light electric railway and a comfortable car running on the inside of all circular courses. At present the stewards of a race meeting are mere dummies, who see little or nothing of the race until the finish, and have no opportunity of detecting any foul riding or pulling which goes on at every race meeting. The moral effect upon jockeys would be immense, if they knew that officials were running along with them, only twenty yards away, and noting all their movements.

GENERAL SUMMARY.

Firstly.- That out of about 100 original mares constituting the foundation of the English thoroughbred, only about fifty are represented to-day.

Secondly.—That out of the surviving families not more than about twenty play an important part in modern pedigrees, and only about nine or ten of the twenty appear to be indispensable in first-class pedigrees.

Thirdly.- That the progeny of three families have practically run a dead heat in the English classic winnings of Derby, Oaks, and Leger, viz., Nos. 1, 2, and 3 ; also that these three, with Nos. 4 and 5, represent the *running* element. *vital* force in pedigrees, but (with exception of 3) are not successful as sire lines, which are confined to Nos. 3, 8, 11, 12, and 14.

Fourthly.—That no horse has been a marked success as a sire unless descended directly from the 3, 8, 11, 12, or 14 families, or *inbred strongly to them.* That where there has been any exception to this rule, as in Blacklock's case, he has only succeeded by having the sire element strong in his mates.

Fifthly.—That no pedigree of any great horse of modern days can be found without some of the *running* and *sire* lines in the *three top removes.*

Sixthly.—That good males are bred by returning strongly the best strains of blood on *dam's* side of stallion's pedigree, and the reverse rule holds good if good females are desired.

Seventhly.—That the bulk of evidence is in favour of comparatively outbred stallions being superior to inbred ones, while the reverse holds good of mares, because in a state of nature the females of a herd must of necessity be more inbred than the male ; hence the natural law of compensation.

Eighthly.—That phenomenal horses mostly have some incestuous inbreeding at three or four removes on side of dam or sire, with a strain of similar blood on opposite side of pedigree to nick with same.

Ninthly.—That if the first mating of sire and dam produces a high-class racehorse, as in Isonomy's case, the mare at once should be bred to some other horse of an opposite strain of blood for a couple of seasons and then put back to original stallion. In like manner if the first result is promising in appearance, but not a high-class performer, the mating should be continued for three or four years as in Carbine's case. *i.e.*, provided other conditions as mentioned above are complied with.

.

AMOUNTS WON IN 1893 BY THE DESCENDANTS RESPECTIVELY OF THE DARLEY ARABIAN, THE BYERLY TURK, AND THE GODOLPHIN ARABIAN.

THE DARLEY ARABIAN.

ECLIPSE
Value, £394,197 5s.

THE GODOLPHIN ARABIAN.

MATCHEM
Value, £19,118.

THE BYERLY TURK.

HEROD
Value, £33,980.

INDEX.

PEDIGREES.